Growing *in* Holiness
through the Psalms

Growing *in* Holiness
through the Psalms

Insights from Charles Spurgeon's *Treasury of David*

DAVID J. MCKINLEY

Foreword by Geoffrey Chang

WIPF & STOCK · Eugene, Oregon

GROWING IN HOLINESS THROUGH THE PSALMS
Insights from Charles Spurgeon's *Treasury of David*

Copyright © 2023 David J. McKinley. All rights reserved. Except for brief quotations in critical publications or reviews, no part of this book may be reproduced in any manner without prior written permission from the publisher. Write: Permissions, Wipf and Stock Publishers, 199 W. 8th Ave., Suite 3, Eugene, OR 97401.

Wipf & Stock
An Imprint of Wipf and Stock Publishers
199 W. 8th Ave., Suite 3
Eugene, OR 97401

www.wipfandstock.com

PAPERBACK ISBN: 978-1-6667-6208-2
HARDCOVER ISBN: 978-1-6667-6212-9
EBOOK ISBN: 978-1-6667-6213-6

VERSION NUMBER 072523

Unless otherwise indicated, all Scripture quotations are taken from the Holy Bible, New International Version®, NIV®. Copyright © 1973, 1978, 1984, 2011 by Biblica, Inc.™ Used by permission of Zondervan. All rights reserved worldwide. www.zondervan.com. The "NIV" and "New International Version" are trademarks registered in the United States Patent and Trademark Office by Biblica, Inc.™

Scripture quotations marked (ESV) are from The ESV® Bible (The Holy Bible, English Standard Version®), copyright © 2001 by Crossway, a publishing ministry of Good News Publishers. Used by permission. All rights reserved.

Scriptures quotations marked (KJV) are taken from the KING JAMES VERSION (KJV): KING JAMES VERSION, public domain.

Scripture quotations marked (NASB) are taken from the New American Standard Bible®, Copyright © 1960, 1971, 1977, 1995, 2020 by The Lockman Foundation. Used by permission. All rights reserved. www.lockman.org.

Scripture quotations marked (NLT) are taken from the Holy Bible, New Living Translation®, copyright ©1996, 2004, 2015 by Tyndale House Foundation. Used by permission of Tyndale House Publishers, Carol Stream, Illinois 60188. All rights reserved.

To my wife, Laura
You are an inspiring example of holiness
with your loving obedience to the Lord
and your caring love for people.
Thank you for your constant encouragement during this project.

Good wives are also fruitful in kindness, thrift, helpfulness, and affection.... Truly blessed is the man whose wife is fruitful in those good works, which are suitable to her near and dear position.
—Charles H. Spurgeon

Contents

Foreword by Geoffrey Chang | ix
Preface and Acknowledgments | xi

Introduction: Recovering Holiness and the Psalms | 1

Part I: The Path of Growing in Holiness

Chapter 1
Discovering the Path of Growing in Holiness | 17

Chapter 2
The Nature of Growing in Holiness | 32

Chapter 3
Our Heart and Holiness | 45

Chapter 4
Our Emotions and Holiness | 63

Chapter 5
Our Conduct and Holiness | 80

Part II: The Path to Growing in Holiness

Chapter 6
God's Initiative in Holiness | 91

Chapter 7
Scripture and Holiness | 107

Chapter 8
Prayer and Holiness | 125

Chapter 9
Community and Holiness | 142

Chapter 10
Life's Trials and Holiness | 157

Chapter 11
Nature and Holiness | 173

Conclusion | 186

Appendix | 191

Bibliography | 199

Foreword

I REMEMBER ONCE LISTENING to a retired pastor preach on the danger of worldliness. As someone who was shaped by a previous generation, he talked about the need to keep the Sabbath, be sober and self-controlled, be pure in speech, and other concerns that I had not considered much. As one who was immersed in the culture of my day, I remember being struck by how foreign his concerns seemed to me. But this is how worldliness works. It so shapes our minds and hearts that we no longer notice its effect on our lives. Is it any surprise, then, that any teaching on holiness might seem strange or foreign to us?

Therefore, in any study of sanctification—of growing in holiness—we need help from Christian perspectives outside of our own culture. This can include Christians from other countries, but it can also include Christians from the past. In this book, David McKinley has provided us with one such faithful teacher to help us grow in our holiness. Charles Haddon Spurgeon pastored in London in the second half of the nineteenth century. Through his preaching, thousands came to know of the grace of God in the gospel. But Spurgeon was not content merely to have converts. Rather, as a pastor, he was concerned to see his converts be baptized and brought into the discipleship of the local church. Through the ministry of his church, thousands of Christians grew in holiness and were mobilized to take the gospel throughout London and around the world.

In this volume, McKinley draws from the treasury of Spurgeon's teaching on the Psalms to help us grow in the Christian life. So more than just relying on Spurgeon's wisdom, this book is meant to help us meditate on the word of God, "like a tree planted by streams of water" (Ps 1:2–3). By focusing on the Psalms, McKinley provides not only biblical and theological teaching on the Christian life, but practical pathways for growing as a Christian.

This would be a great book to read with young Christians, or any Christian for that matter. After all, rather than being the exception, spiritual growth should be the norm for any Christian indwelled by the Holy Spirit. The best outcome in reading this book would be a life-long commitment to meditating on the Psalms, and all of Scripture, allowing it to be a lamp to your feet and a light for your path (Ps 119:105).

Dr. Geoffrey Chang
Assistant Professor of Historical Theology,
Curator of the Spurgeon Library
Midwestern Baptist Theological Seminary
Kansas City, MO

Preface and Acknowledgments

CHARLES SPURGEON'S *TREASURY OF David* contains rich insights into the Psalms. I began mining this expositional quarry while I wrote my earlier book, *The Psalms for Everyday Living*, which provided meditations on the whole Psalter. The psalms' theological and experiential depth convinced me that these seasoned writers had much to teach us about holy living. Examining the entirety of the Psalter provided pertinent biblical themes related to sanctification so that we could grow in holiness. Thus, this collection of writings function as an invaluable guide on the pathway to spiritual maturity. Convinced of their role in our lives, I continue the daily reading of the Psalms which are shaping my mind and heart to follow Jesus with a greater commitment. I pray for God to use this volume to spur you on in your pursuit to become more like Jesus Christ, who is the ultimate standard of holiness.

    I am grateful to those who contributed to this book. Thank you to Dr. Geoff Chang who took the time out of his busy schedule to write the foreword. He, among others, is providing us with scholarly work on Charles Spurgeon. Drs. Mel Loucks and Michael Woodcock gave me invaluable input from their theological and Old Testament perspectives. Mary Walsten patiently and perseveringly corrected my grammatical errors. Matthew Wimer, the editorial production manager, and his team have been superb to work with for several months. Finally, my wife, Laura, encouraged me with her prayers and interest in this project.

Introduction
Recovering Holiness and the Psalms

A PIECE OF FURNITURE in front of the sanctuary of my home church in Winnipeg, Manitoba, intrigued me. A small table, not used for the Lord's Supper, had the words HOLINESS UNTO THE LORD carved into the front panel. As a teenager, I had no idea what these words meant, and it appeared others did not know because they couldn't give an answer to my genuine question. Yet, as the Sunday night services drew to a close, in response to the pastor's invitation, a few people would walk down the aisle, kneel at this table, and presumably confess their sins in private prayer to God. Sitting in the back pew, I wondered about their big sins that would prompt them to walk to the holiness table in front of the congregation. But, on the other hand, I was only too glad my sins were small enough that I did not have to confess my sins publicly. Remaining seated in my chair was good enough for me.

I assured myself that I did not need to go to the holiness table as a teenager! I was a member of good standing in my church, having covenanted to abstain from various "sinful" practices that would impair my personal holiness. Besides, I was actively involved in essential church activities. Now I know that, in light of blatant sin with strained and broken relationships and discord, it is a marvel that the holiness table wasn't crowded with people—including myself! Any pursuit of holiness based on somewhat faulty standards fails to address the real issues.

My childhood experience reminds me that a misunderstanding of holiness obscures the issue of sin in people's lives. Throughout the decades, various approaches to holiness, such as crisis experiences ("entire sanctification") or passively trusting God ("let go; let God"), have been adopted. However, these attempts have yet to reach the holiness expected in people's lives. This is largely so because the "deep and pervasive nature of sin in the life of a believer" is downplayed.[1] J. I. Packer reminds us that "we are all sick and damaged, diseased and deformed, scarred and sore, lame and lopsided, to a far, far greater extent than we realize."[2] Regrettably, we don't always grasp this reality about ourselves. As a result, we aren't only "invalids in God's hospital," but we are "all prone to damaging delusions" about ourselves and what is needed to grow in holiness.[3] It is no wonder that we may struggle in our spiritual growth!

Holiness may seem archaic in these modern times, which makes matters worse. We often prefer to speak about dysfunctionalities, addictions, and authenticity rather than encouraging people to pursue a holy life. Years ago, Packer expressed concern for the "sidelining of personal holiness which has been a general trend among Bible-centered Western Christians." He laments, "The shift of Christian interest away from the pursuit of holiness to focus on fun and fulfillment, ego-massage and techniques for present success, and public issues that carry no challenge to one's personal morals, is a fact. To my mind it is a sad and scandalous fact, and one that needs to be reversed."[4] To support his claim that holiness is not taken seriously by Christians, he gave three pieces of evidence. One, the topic of holiness is lacking in preaching and teaching. Two, holiness is not an essential criterion for church leaders. Three, holiness is not emphasized in evangelism.[5] Thus, his book *Rediscovering Holiness*, written in 1992, sought to correct the declining emphasis on holiness.

Twenty years after Packer expressed his grave concern about the disregard for holiness among Bible-believing Christians, Kevin DeYoung echoed the same grave concerns to a new generation. He believes many people view holiness as an option, leaving it to individuals to decide whether or not they want to pursue holiness. Out of a fear of appearing judgmental, legalistic, or giving up on the hard work of pursuing a godly life, holiness has become a non-issue for many who attend our churches. He unequivocally states,

> The hole in our holiness is that we don't really care much about it. Passionate exhortation to pursue gospel-driven holiness is barely heard in most of our churches . . . I'm talking about the failure of Christians, especially younger generations and especially those most disdainful of "religion" and "legalism," to take

---

1. Morden, *Communion with Christ*, 251.
2. Packer, *Rediscovering Holiness*, 40.
3. Packer, *Rediscovering Holiness*, 40, 42–43.
4. Packer, *Rediscovering Holiness*, 9.
5. Packer, *Rediscovering Holiness*, 33–34.

seriously one of the great aims of our redemption and one of the required evidences for eternal life—our holiness.[6]

DeYoung lays it on the line: "There is a gap between our love for the gospel and our love for godliness. This must change."[7]

More recently, John MacArthur expressed his concern regarding today's evangelical movement. While there is an emphasis on many of the major doctrines of the Christian faith, he laments, "Holiness does not appear to be one of them, let alone the main one."[8] He reiterates, "The truth of sanctification, together with words like holiness, godliness, and Christlikeness are all but gone from popular Christian discourse."[9] He explains the reason for this neglect: "My concern was—and still is—that the movement as a whole has stressed and overstated the principle of Christian liberty with the necessary balance. True Christian liberty means deliverance from sin's bondage and the law's condemnation, not freedom from the law's moral precepts."[10]

In stark contrast to this silence on holiness among today's churches, Scripture clearly calls us to a life of holiness. God expected the Israelites to be holy daily (Lev 19:2; 20:7, 26). The apostle Peter called the believers in the first-century church to a life of holiness (1 Pet 1:15–16; 2 Pet 3:11). They have been set apart for God and his purposes for their lives. This lifestyle is not optional for Jesus' followers. The writer of Hebrews urges his readers to pursue holiness (12:14) or a "practical holiness of life."[11] Since this type of life is not optional, we must "make every effort" to live this way. Being set apart for God entails rejecting sinful attitudes (such as bitterness) and activities (12:15–16).

How can we ever expect to grow in holiness? Can we expect to live holy lives in light of a holy God and our sinfulness? Perhaps this is too naïve. Nevertheless, we might conclude this if not for the assurance that we have God's empowering grace which enables us to grow in holiness (Heb 12:15; 2 Pet 1:3, 5). God has given us all the divine resources we need to grow in godliness. Our role is to use his resources so that we may grow spiritually.

The Psalms are one of the resources God has provided for the spiritual growth of his people. The Psalms have been consistently used for singing and prayer, from the days of the Levites leading the services in the Temple,

6. DeYoung, *Hole in Our Holiness*, 10, 18–19.
7. DeYoung, *Hole in Our Holiness*, 20.
8. MacArthur, *Sanctification*, 50.
9. MacArthur, *Sanctification*, 53.
10. MacArthur, *Sanctification*, 50.
11. Bruce, *Epistle to the Hebrews*, 364.

4   Growing in Holiness through the Psalms

to the time of Jesus, followed by the practice of the first-century church and beyond. With this rich tradition, the Psalter has served as a core element of church life for two millennia.[12] In light of this, we have to ask ourselves why the Psalms have had such a significant role and influence among God's people.

The Value of the Psalms

In the fourth century, Athanasius, bishop of the African church in Alexandria, wrote to his friend Marcellinus, who asked for guidance on how to read the Psalter. Athanasius told him that the Psalms "disclose the full range of the inner movements in the soul" which are the different "dispositions" or emotions such as anger, joy, and fear. These emotions indicate the condition of our soul or inner life. When we are willing to acknowledge what is occurring in the interior regions of our lives, then it is possible to begin "the healing and the correction needed for each movement."[13] The Psalms serve as a resource for a person to repent, confess, bear afflictions, pray, and praise the Lord.[14] In other words, "the words of this book can serve as a guide for every aspect of human life."[15]

In addition to the Psalms instructing us, they allow us to enter into the writers' experiences. To his same friend, Athanasius said that when individuals read the Psalms, "they recognize them as being their very own words. . . . They feel as though they are the ones speaking and they take to heart the words of the songs as if they were their own."[16] Using the Psalter for prayer and singing is an excellent approach to remembering and experiencing the Psalms in our minds and hearts. The Psalms contribute to our holiness working from the interior territory to the outer regions of our lives.

Jumping ahead to the Reformation, Martin Luther also recognized the Psalms' contribution to godliness. "We learn how we are to conduct ourselves with respect to God, to our friends, and to our foes, and how we are to act in all cases of danger and uncertainty."[17] In a similar vein to Athanasius's insights, he stated that we could discover the psalmists' inner thoughts:

---

12. Wenham summarizes church leaders, from the postapostolic age until the Reformation, who have expressed the Psalter's importance for congregational use (*Psalter Reclaimed*, 14–17).

13. Athanasius, *Letter to Marcellinus*, 20, 23, 32.

14. Athanasius, *Letter to Marcellinus*, 16.

15. Athanasius, *Letter to Marcellinus*, 35.

16. Athanasius, *Letter to Marcellinus*, 17.

17. Wolfmueller, "Martin Luther's Introduction," lines 16–17.

> We have not only laid open to us their words and their works, but their very hearts—the vital treasure of the soul—so that we can look into the ground and foundation of their words and works, that is into their hearts. . . . It is impossible for me to dive into the heart of a man whose works I alone see, and of whose reputation I only hear. As I should much more prefer hearing the language of a saint to seeing his actions, so I would rather look into his heart and inspect his soul than hear his language.[18]

The Psalter enables us to "look directly into the heart of God's saints."[19]

We cannot take the Psalms lightly for Luther considered them a "small Bible, or an epitome of Christianity and godly men, so that those who have not the means of reading the whole Bible may find the summary and sense condensed in a small volume."[20] Walter Brueggemann summarizes Luther's view of the Psalms which "articulate the whole gospel of God in a nutshell."[21] The Psalms portray the significant themes of the gospel. We see humanity's sinfulness, repentance, God's forgiveness for confessed sin, and love for his covenant people. We see his people wanting God to transform their lives so that they love him and act in ways that honor the Lord.

John Calvin also affirmed the importance of the Psalter. He wrote, "The Psalms are replete with all the precepts which serve to frame our life to every part of holiness, piety, and righteousness."[22] In addition to the Psalter's instructions, this collection of writings give us an "anatomy of all the parts of the soul for there is not an emotion of which anyone can be conscious that is not here represented as in a mirror." Calvin noted that the Psalms function like a mirror to

> call or rather draw, each of us to the examination of himself in particular, so that none of the many infirmities to which we are subject, and of the many vices with which we abound, may remain concealed. It is undoubtedly a rare and singular advantage when all lurking places are discovered, and the heart is brought into the light, purged from that most baneful infection, hypocrisy.[23]

---

18. Wolfmueller, "Martin Luther's Introduction," lines 55–65.
19. Leupold, *Exposition of the Psalms*, 27. The quote is attributed to Martin Luther.
20. Wolfmueller, "Martin Luther's Introduction," lines 25–27.
21. Brueggemann, *Message of the Psalms*, 17.
22. Calvin, *Commentary on the Psalms*, xxxix.
23. Calvin, *Commentary on the Psalms*, xxxvii. Athanasius stated that the Psalms function like a "mirror" because they allow the reader "to see himself and the inner movements of his own soul in them" (*Letter to Marcellinus*, 19).

From helping us to explore our inner life, the Psalms then lead us to pray, asking God to change us. "Whatever may serve to encourage us when we are about to pray to God, is taught us in this Book,"[24] summarized Calvin. When these "maladies" are exposed to the Psalms, then we can be confident that "the soul [can be] freed and disentangled from all these impediments."[25]

In the nineteenth century, Charles Spurgeon concurred with the Reformers' view on the Psalms' importance. While at the Metropolitan Tabernacle in London, he preached over four hundred sermons on the Psalms for nearly forty years. To aid in family worship during the week, he wrote *Morning by Morning* and *Evening by Evening*, which included many devotionals based on the Psalms. When he witnessed the eclipse of the Psalter's importance in the church's life, he lamented, "It is to be feared that the Psalms are by no means so prized as in earlier ages of the Church."[26] To address the decline of the Psalms' use in the churches, he embarked on a twenty-year writing project culminating in a seven-volume commentary known as the *Treasury of David*. Drawing from the rich insights from Augustine to the Reformers and the Puritans, the *Treasury of David* would be available for pastors and laypeople. Spurgeon, who represented the Calvinist tradition of holiness during England's Victorian era,[27] would influence countless numbers of people who wanted to grow in holiness.

Spurgeon clearly understood the Psalms' contribution to one's holiness. He counsels, "In these busy days, it would be greatly to the spiritual profit of Christian men and women if they were more familiar with the Book of Psalms, in which they would find a complete armoury for life's battles, and a perfect supply for life's needs. Here we have both delight and usefulness, consolation and instruction."[28] They instruct, Spurgeon notes, by informing us regarding what we may expect in our Christian lives. For example, the Psalter reveals that the "breadth of experience stretches from the jaws of hell to the gate of heaven."[29] The psalmists' experiences are strikingly similar to ours, whether it is worshiping the Lord, facing trials, or enjoying fellowship with God's people. They have gone ahead of us and provided a road map of their experiences for us who follow. They prepare us for our spiritual journey because they tell us what we can expect to encounter. Like them,

24. Calvin, *Commentary on the Psalms*, viii
25. Calvin, *Commentary on the Psalms*, xxxvii
26. Spurgeon, *Treasury of David*, 5:vi.
27. Bebbington examines four perspectives of holiness among England's churches in the nineteenth century. The High Church, Calvinist, Wesleyan, and Keswick traditions were influenced by the cultural setting of the day (*Holiness*, 92–93).
28. Spurgeon, *Treasury of David*, 6:vi.
29. Spurgeon, *Treasury of David*, 6:vi.

we will travel through valleys, dry times, and mountain-top moments. The psalmists' prayers and praises shape our hearts and feelings and enable us to grow spiritually.[30]

The Psalms were not only meant to inform but also to be experienced by us. For Spurgeon, he confesses that "the Psalms were a royal banquet to me, and feasting on its contents, I have seemed to eat angels' food."[31] With growing personal conviction, he believed each individual "must traverse the territory of the Psalms" and what they offer us not by study but by the Holy Spirit and experience.[32] Setting the Psalms to music was one means to make this experience possible. Spurgeon believed that singing the Psalms which are "sacred hymns" has the advantage of expressing "all modes of holy feeling"[33] which profoundly affects the human heart as well as the mind. Outside of the church services, he continued, the Psalms could be sung as "ballads" and "love songs" by individuals while working.[34]

In other words, Spurgeon believed the Psalter contributes to our personal holiness at whatever stage of life and situation we find ourselves. The Psalms, he comments, "are fit both for childhood and old age; they furnish maxims for the entrance of life, and serve as watchwords at the gates of death. The battle of life, the repose of the Sabbath . . . yea, even heaven itself may be entered with Psalms."[35] The Psalter is our guide for the pathway to holiness.

Since Spurgeon's day, others have underscored the importance of the Psalms for our personal growth. For example, Tremper Longman believes that the raw honesty of the psalmists enables us to identify with them. He succinctly states, "The reader becomes the 'I' of the psalm."[36] The Psalms help us "by putting its teaching chiefly in the form of the recital of experiences," in contrast to the didactic teaching of the New Testament, according to Martyn Lloyd-Jones.[37] The Psalms provide rich teaching because it is "the great soul book in the Bible," asserts Dallas Willard, because the Psalter "deals with life in its depths and with our fundamental relationship to the One who is the keeper of our soul."[38] He adds, "Still today the Old Testa-

---

30. Spurgeon, *Treasury of David*, 5:vi.
31. Spurgeon, *Treasury of David*, 5:vi.
32. Spurgeon, *Treasury of David*, 2:vi.
33. Spurgeon, *Treasury of David*, 5:vii.
34. Spurgeon, *Treasury of David*, 5:vii.
35. Spurgeon, *Treasury of David*, 5:vii.
36. Longman, *Psalms*, 10.
37. Lloyd-Jones, *Faith on Trial*, 12.
38. Willard, *Renovation of the Heart*, 207.

ment of Psalms gives great power for faith and life. This is simply because it preserves a conceptually rich language about God and our relationships to him. If you bury yourself in the Psalms, you emerge knowing God and understanding life."[39] As a result, God can radically change us. N. T. Wright asserts,

> The regular praying and singing of the Psalms is *transformative*. It changes the way we understand some of the deepest elements of who we are, or rather, who, where, when, and what we are . . . They do this in order that we may be changed, transformed, so that we look at the world, one another, and ourselves in a radically different way, which we believe to be God's way.[40]

The Psalms are an invaluable resource for growth in holiness.

The faithful use of the Psalter throughout the centuries bears testimony of its value for cultivating holy lives. The Psalms not only examine our conduct but also probe the interior regions of our lives (including our longings and emotions), often neglected in favor of learning how to behave godly. Also, the Psalms guide us in our appropriate responses to God. For example, the psalmists lead us in life's rhythms, including confession, repentance, life in solitude and community, and worship before God. Thirdly, the Psalter provides us with real-life experiences of individuals who wrestled with sin and struggled with people and their relationships with the Lord. Their story becomes our story in our pursuit of growing in holiness.

The Current Plight

Yet, the use of the Psalms in churches has significantly diminished, lessening the Psalters' influence among congregations. Willem VanGemeren emphatically states, "Though no OT [Old Testament] book has been more important in the history of the church than the Book of Psalms, we are in danger of losing it." He believes that one of the reasons for the eclipse of the Psalms is the lack of use among God's people.[41] As a result of this decline, there has been a clarion call to recover or regain the Psalms' use in congregational worship. Dietrich Bonhoeffer offers both a warning and hope: "Whenever the Psalter is abandoned, an incomparable treasure

---

39. Willard, *Divine Conspiracy*, 65.
40. Wright, *Case for the Psalms*, 6–7.
41. VanGemeren, *Psalms, Proverbs, Ecclesiastes, Song of Songs*, 5.

vanishes from the Christian church. With its recovery will come unsuspected power."[42]

Wright believes the minimal use of the Psalter in congregational worship contributes to a "great impoverishment" among the churches. The Psalms are "the Bible's own spiritual root system for the great tree we call Christianity." He comments, "I find it impossible, therefore, to imagine a growing and maturing church or individual Christian doing without the Psalms."[43] Thus, he believes that there is an "urgent task" to recover the use of the Psalter in congregational worship. He pleads, "All of us need to find ways of allowing the hymnbook God has given us to be the means of personal and communal transformation, renewal, and growth. . . . The Psalms, which Jesus himself sang and within which he was formed in his vocation, not only describe this transformation but are part of the God-given means of bringing it about."[44]

Gordon Wenham also expresses the same concerns. After stating the historical role of the Psalms in churches throughout the centuries, he bluntly asks, "Is it not time our churches recovered this practice?" He believes it is vital to do so because the Psalms "mold one's character and heightens one's love of God." The repeated use of the Psalms as they are intended in our lives, he says, "alters one's relationship [with God] in a way that mere listening does not."[45] By singing and praying the Psalter, he wants to see it become a more significant part of our lives.

I join the growing chorus of those who want to see greater integration of the Psalms into the Sunday corporate prayers and worship. Without abandoning the community of faith on Sundays, my appeal is to use the Psalter from Monday to Saturday as a critical means for one's spiritual growth. In one sense, this is not a novel suggestion. Billy Graham regularly read through the Psalms during his lifetime. Eugene Peterson, among many others, made it his practice to read one psalm daily and challenged his students to do the same.[46] This book encourages followers of Jesus Christ to grow in holiness by regularly reading the Psalms with its significant themes related to personal holiness. When the Psalms soak into our minds and hearts, we can expect personal transformation to occur, transcending self-improvement programs. The Psalms "all serve to glorify God . . . to lead us

---

42. Bonhoeffer, *Psalms*, 26.
43. Wright, *Case for the Psalms*, 164.
44. Wright, *Case for the Psalms*, 1–5, 168–69.
45. Wenham, *Psalter Reclaimed*, 55, 23, 34.
46. Taylor, *Open and Unafraid*, xvi, xx.

into the will and way of God."[47] Holiness honors God through a genuine change of character which leads to obedience.

We can grow in holiness when we carefully study, reflect, and apply the Psalms to our lives. Therefore, we will explore the Psalter by frequently mentioning Spurgeon's *Treasury of David* throughout the following chapters. There are a few reasons for adopting this approach.

First, his work on the Psalms incorporates holiness within the essential doctrines such as God, sin, salvation, sanctification, and the church. The Puritans, who integrated Christian theology and life, influenced Spurgeon and his writings. Packer states that their biblical knowledge "was no mere theoretical orthodoxy. . . . They yoked their consciences to his word, disciplining themselves to bring all activities under the scrutiny of Scripture, and to demand a theological . . . justification for everything they did." For their activities to honor God, an inner life transformation had to occur. Richard Lovelace comments, "Above all, Puritanism was a movement that sought for purity in the hearts and lives of parishioners." He says that Puritan spirituality focused on sanctification or growth in holiness.[48] Packer asserts, "Puritanism was at heart a spiritual movement, passionately concerned with God and godliness."[49] In other words, the Puritans focused on a comprehensive view of holiness, including a changed heart and behavior. In light of the Puritans' influence on his life and ministry, it is not surprising that Spurgeon provides us with a better understanding of holiness within the context of rich theological teaching embedded in the Psalms and the rest of Scripture.

Second, Spurgeon had a passion for being godly, as reflected in his writing on the Psalms. Commenting on Ps 17:15, he writes, "To behold God's face and to be changed by that vision into his image, so as to partake in his righteousness, this is my noble ambition; and in the prospect of this I cheerfully waive all my present enjoyments."[50] Growing in holiness was his life's ambition knowing that he would be perfectly holy one day when he saw Jesus face-to-face.

Spurgeon was not interested in any so-called piety if it did not influence the outward life. Neither was he impressed by moral living if one's heart was devoid of Christ's love. But, being the great preacher he was, he knew his commentary on the Psalms must apply to our lives. So, he urges us to avoid sin, challenges us to pursue and trust God, and be mindful of all God's provisions given to us to grow in holiness. This spiritual growth

---

47. Foster, *Prayer*, 110.
48. Lovelace, "Afterword," 300–301.
49. Packer, *Quest for Godliness*, 28.
50. Spurgeon, *Treasury of David*, 1:221.

transforms one's interior life, impacting daily speech and behavior.[51] He comments, "To love holiness, to have the motives and desires sanctified, to be in one's inmost nature obedient to the Lord—this is the surest method of making the whole run of our life efficient for its great ends."[52] In other words, he is concerned about "outward practical holiness" which would be evident in everyday living.[53] Holiness is a life-changing process that we must experience. So it shouldn't be surprising that Spurgeon and Puritan writers mention the word "holiness" six hundred times throughout the *Treasury of David*.

Third, as one reads through the *Treasury of David*, it is evident that Spurgeon experienced the vast array of situations and emotions described by the psalmists. He knew what it was like to be rejected by people, experience God's deliverance, enjoy intimacy with God, and feel abandoned by him. Spurgeon also experienced the physical and emotional suffering which so commonly afflicted the psalmists. As we read the exposition of the Psalms in the *Treasury of David*, Spurgeon enters into the psalmists' lives by expressing his reflections and life experiences, providing us with a rich insight into the Psalms. Since he loved the Psalms and was so intimately acquainted with them, he hoped he, as well as the psalmists, would be our "companion" through our journey of holiness in the Psalms.

Before we proceed further, a few comments about the meaning of holiness are in order. The term "holiness" may seem somewhat quaint to describe spiritual maturity today. However, holiness was a common theme among the Puritans who greatly influenced Spurgeon. For them, holiness was used "in a sense so broad as to include in it every aspect and dimension of the godly life."[54] Since Spurgeon is a "latter-day Puritan"[55] in his theology, it is not surprising that he frequently uses the term "holiness" in his preaching and writing.[56] Since Scripture calls us to a life of holiness (Lev 11:44, 19:2; 2 Cor 7:1; 2 Tim 1:9; 1 Pet 1:15–16; 2 Pet 3:11), "holiness" is not an anachronistic term. The Bible fundamentally views holiness as a separation from sin accompanied by an inner consecration to God expressed by ethical conduct aligned with God's holy character. In the following chapters,

---

51. I am indebted to Morden's fine treatment of Spurgeon's view of holiness in chapter 9. His work brought to my attention the theme of "holiness" in the *Treasury of David*, which is the focus of my book (*Communion with Christ*, 223–57).

52. Spurgeon, *Treasury of David*, 1:177–78.

53. Spurgeon, *Treasury of David*, 1:376; 5:211; Morden, *Communion with Christ*, 223–24.

54. Packer, *Quest for Godliness*, 39.

55. Packer, *Quest for Godliness*, 69.

56. Morden, *Communion with Christ*, 223–57.

holiness will refer to spiritual growth in both one's character and behavior ("practical holiness") or the transformation of the whole person (1 Thess 5:11). We are to become like Jesus Christ.

The term "godliness" will also be used throughout the book. Its meaning is closely associated with holiness, as the apostle Peter suggests (2 Pet 3:11). Godliness emphasizes one's conduct or piety which flows out of one's devotion to God. For clarity, "godliness" will refer to our exterior lives (actions and speech). Thus, godliness is treated synonymously with practical holiness which manifests the transformed interior life.

Overview of This Book

In the first section of this book ("The Path of Growing in Holiness"), we will explore the nature of growing in holiness. The Psalms provide a necessary perspective to grasp and appropriate for our lives. Chapter 1 reveals a discovery of two paths we can choose for our lives. One path will ultimately lead an individual away from God, eventually bringing disappointment and doom. The other path, the way of holiness, will draw a person closer to the Lord, leading one to flourish in life. Two descriptive perspectives elaborate this God-path. Brueggemann describes this path by identifying three distinct phases (orientation, disorientation, and new orientation) in the Psalms. The other descriptive analogy is the spiritual pilgrimage through life. Chapter 1 will elaborate on John Bunyan's *Pilgrim's Progress*, which has many metaphors related to the Psalms.

In chapters 2 to 5, we will examine the nature of growing in holiness from within the context of the Psalms. Chapter 2 provides a general overview on personal growth in holiness. Chapter 3 addresses the topic of the heart, a significant theme in the Psalms. Since the heart is the "mirror of the soul," this area of our life is strategic in spiritual growth. While we often overlook our emotions in studies on sanctification, chapter 4 touches on several emotions that need to be transformed to progress in our spiritual growth. While we may want to deny or suppress our feelings, the Psalms shed light on the relationship between emotions and personal holiness. When we address our interior life with its heart and emotional issues, the spiritual transformation will continue to work out to change our conduct positively. Chapter 5 surveys the Psalms in order to highlight various aspects of our behavior before God and with those around us.

The book's second section ("The Path to Growing in Holiness") probes several avenues the Psalms emphasize to cultivate our spiritual growth. In chapter 6, we will discover how God is actively involved in our holiness. As

Packer expresses it, "The study of holiness is a mapping of the life of God in the human soul."[57] Since Scripture and prayer are prominent in the Psalms, we will explore them in chapters 7 and 8. While these chapters focus on an individual's private time with the Lord, chapter 9 addresses the importance of community, which fosters and expresses our spiritual growth. Whether we are by ourselves or in a community with others, we will experience trials that God uses to deepen our walk with him further. Chapter 10 explores three important categories of trials in the Psalms we will encounter. While this world can bring difficulties and hardship to us, God's created world also brings us joy and delight. Finally, chapter 11 discusses how nature can contribute to our holiness. These chapters are instructive for us and show how God can use everything to accomplish his purposes in our lives.

Each of the chapters include brief incidents from Spurgeon's life. He not only eloquently wrote about holiness but passionately sought and lived it throughout his years. These vignettes illustrate how he lived a holy life and how we can do the same. If you are not well acquainted with Spurgeon, his life may entice you to learn more about him.

Finally, a comment on the way you should approach this book. The book intends to be primarily instructive and applicable. It is helpful to read contemplatively with the mind and heart, allowing the Holy Spirit to reveal growth points for further personal transformation. Read each chapter slowly so that the truths of the Psalms can percolate in our thoughts and permeate our hearts. Take time to read through the following chapters. You can use the reflection questions and formative exercises in the appendix for further review. Personal growth occurs when we reflect on Scripture, make decisions, and apply insights to daily life.

---

57. Packer, *Rediscovering Holiness*, 37.

PART I

The Path of Growing in Holiness

Chapter 1

Discovering the Path of Growing in Holiness

Charles was the firstborn child of godly parents, John and Eliza Spurgeon. John was a part-time pastor of a small church, and his mother was a woman of prayer. Charles had the beginning of a solid family upbringing. Due to financial hardship in the family, he was sent to live with his paternal grandparents at the age of fourteen months. The young boy would spend five years with them. It was there Charles came across John Bunyan's *Pilgrim's Progress* which captivated his imagination for the rest of his life. The story of Christian's journey to the Celestial City strongly influenced Charles years later in his preaching and writing. After living with his loving grandparents, Charles grieved when he had to return to his parents' home. In his early life, Charles experienced both stability and upheaval. But in these few years, his future life would be primarily shaped by the theme of spiritual pilgrimage.[1]

CHARLES SPURGEON'S FONDNESS FOR *Pilgrim's Progress* were reflected in his lectures where he confessed, "Next to the Bible, the book I value most is John Bunyan's 'Pilgrim's Progress.' I believe I have read it through at least a hundred times. It is a volume of which I never seem to tire; and the secret of

---

1. Dallimore, *Spurgeon*, 4–7; Morden, *C. H. Spurgeon*, 15–18.

its freshness is that it is so largely compiled from the Scriptures." Spurgeon went on to say that *Pilgrim's Progress* is an allegorical story that mirrors our life experiences. He commented, "The characters described by John Bunyan have their living representatives today, and his words have a message for many who are found in our congregations at the present time."[2]

The experiences of those who follow Jesus Christ in *Pilgrim's Progress* continue to be replicated in the following generations of believers. Thus, it is not surprising that Bunyan's classic book shaped Spurgeon's perspective of the Psalms and its application to our lives. Since it was a delight for him to travel through the Psalms, he wants to be our companion or fellow pilgrim as we join him in this spiritual journey. Pilgrimage provides us with another perspective to better understand the "map of experience" if we are to grow in holiness.

The Two Paths

For a long time, Ps 1 has been considered an introduction to the Psalter. Spurgeon describes the first psalm as a "preface" because it is "a notification of the contents of the entire Book . . . the text upon which the whole of the Psalms make up a divine sermon."[3] Going back to Basil and Jerome in the fourth century, others have also viewed Ps 1 in much the same way.[4] While introductions to books are often considered unimportant, Ps 1 is different. It provides a framework that shapes our understanding of the Psalter in general and holiness in particular.

Spurgeon tells us that the psalmist wants "to teach us the way to blessedness, and to warn us of the sure destruction of sinners."[5] The psalmist tells us that we can choose the righteous life (vv. 1–3) or the unrighteous life (vv. 4–5). More specifically, "There are two types of people, two types of life, and two conclusions."[6] Throughout the Psalms, the righteous are encouraged to continue following God's way of living. The Hebrew word for "way" (*derek*) sheds light on why it is so important to choose this particular path. It is reasonable because it is perfect (18:30).[7] His way may be frightening and overwhelming, but he is there with us (77:19). The only appropriate response is

---

2. Spurgeon, *Pictures from Pilgrim's Progress*, 7.
3. Spurgeon, *Treasury of David*, 1:1.
4. Longman, *Psalms*, 46; Kidner, *Psalms*, 63; Wenham, *Psalter Reclaimed*, 59.
5. Spurgeon, *Treasury of David*, 1:1.
6. Wenham, *Psalter Reclaimed*, 116.
7. When the abbreviation "Ps" is omitted throughout the book, the reader may assume the chapter and verse refers to the Psalms unless the context suggests otherwise.

to ask God to help us follow his ways (25:4, 27:11). In contrast, the course of the wicked (1:1) is a wandering "in a trackless waste" without God (107:40). They may prosper on this path for a while (37:7), but believers know that God will guard and keep us on his way (91:11). If we follow his way, we have God's promise that "blessed are all who fear the Lord" (128:1).

In light of the importance of the placement of Ps 1 as an introduction to the Psalter, it is worthwhile to explore the two pathways described in this psalm. By considering the blessings of holiness and then the dire consequences of ungodly living, we are invited and encouraged to energetically pursue a life of growing in holiness.

Living Rightly

The godly intentionally avoid "thinking, behaving, and belonging" along the lines of those opposed to God's ways (v. 1).[8] Distancing themselves from those who resist God, the godly prioritize studying and meditating on God's revealed will, living vibrantly, and belonging to God (vv. 2–3). As a result, they are righteous in their character (v. 2) and conduct (vv. 2, 5–6). Consequently, they will flourish (v. 3). Living rightly requires developing an exemplary character shaped by cultivating a personal relationship with God and knowing and obeying his ways. Godly conduct is the outflow of a holy character.

The one who is committed to following the path of God is "blessed" (v. 1; 119:1, 3).[9] There are two ways a person is blessed. First, Spurgeon points out that "blessed" in Hebrew is plural, and therefore, one who is devoted to the Lord will receive a "multiplicity of the blessings" or favors of God.[10] It is also possible to interpret "blessed" as a state of "happiness."[11] Spurgeon, among others, refers to the Sermon on the Mount where Jesus uses the word "blessed" nine times (Matt 5:3–11). This latter view is preferred because the Hebrew word for blessed/happiness (*ashre*) is used consistently (twenty-four times) with the other beatitudes commonly mentioned throughout the Psalter. While "happiness" might appear to trivialize a blessed life, such is not the case. The same Hebrew word was used by the queen of Sheba, who told Solomon, "How happy your men must be!" (1 Kgs 10:8). Their happiness was not based on selfish gain or a euphoric experience. Instead, they

---

8. Kidner, *Psalms*, 64.

9. Kidner states that "blessed" is mentioned twenty-six times in the Psalms (*Psalms*, 64).

10. Spurgeon, *Treasury of David*, 1:1.

11. Kidner, *Psalms*, 64.

were happy because they can listen to Solomon's wisdom which came from God (3:11–12). True happiness flows out of the right relationship with the Lord.

In other words, as we grow in holiness, true happiness is experienced. Spurgeon affirms that "there is no greater happiness than to be perfectly holy,"[12] which is not perfection but the desire not to sin against God. Spurgeon urges us to settle this matter in our hearts and live by one primary axiom: "holiness is happiness."[13] A truly happy life involves following the righteous path, even with all of life's challenges, because we desire to live with God's pleasure. When we can say, "It is well with my soul," which is a sense of well-being, then we are genuinely happy. In Ps 1, the writer is speaking of a blessed life in ideal terms with no qualifications. Elsewhere, the psalmists remind us that they do experience pain and suffering. "Even when the righteous do not feel happy, they are still considered 'blessed' from God's perspective. He bestows this gift on them. Neither negative feelings nor adverse conditions can take his blessing away."[14] Jesus affirmed this paradox by telling them they can experience true happiness while they mourn and are persecuted (Matt 5:4, 10). This happiness is possible by following the way of God revealed through his word (Ps 1:2; Luke 11:28).

If Ps 1 provides a framework for the Psalter, the opening of Ps 119 reinforces this framework with the same themes of blessing and following God's pathway. Spurgeon recognizes this likeness.[15] While the one who follows God's path will be blessed, Spurgeon recognized that there is a condition for this blessing. If we are on this "holy way" but allow sin to dominate our lives, then we "miss a great measure of the blessedness which is in him [Jesus Christ] as our way."[16] Conversely, "the more complete our sanctification the more intense our blessedness."[17] The more we grow in holiness, the more we will experience God's blessing on our lives. This blessing is his promise to us.

Living Wrongly

Those who don't choose to live rightly are the ungodly or the "wicked" (1:4). Not surprisingly, their life is very different compared to the righteous (v.

---

12. Spurgeon, *Treasury of David*, 5:139.
13. Spurgeon, *Treasury of David*, 5:140.
14. VanGemeren, *Psalms, Proverbs, Ecclesiastes, Song of Songs*, 53.
15. Spurgeon, *Treasury of David*, 5:140.
16. Spurgeon, *Treasury of David*, 5:140.
17. Spurgeon, *Treasury of David*, 5:140.

1). They have no interest in God and his laws, preferring instead to spend time with those who are like them. Their actions reveal how they distance themselves from God and conform to the world by "accepting its advice, being party to its ways, and adopting the most fatal of its attitudes."[18] As a result of the choices they make, they experience the consequences of their decisions. Like chaff, they have no spiritual substance and are easily carried away (v. 4). In terms of their thinking and behavior, their lives are in sharp contrast to the godly.

They consequently face God's judgment (v. 5). They "shall not stand their ground; they shall flee away; they shall not stand in their own defense."[19] Neither will they have any place among God's people whom they mocked (v. 1). The mockers receive what they chose. Instead of flourishing, they "perish" (vv. 3, 6), which is understandable because it is the "way" that also perishes and is left in ruins. Psalm 2 paints a detailed picture of those who rebel against God (vv. 1–6). They are encouraged to give up their foolishness and be wise (2:10). They would be wise if they lived rightly before God, as described in Ps 1.

Psalm 1 describes two contrasting ways to live (v. 6). First, a person can choose to be committed to God and his truth (v. 6a). This allegiance to him is expressed by shaping the inner life, including the thoughts, according to the Bible and by associating with others who love the Lord. This person flourishes in life (v. 3, 92:12–14) because God is watching and caring for her (v. 6a). Second, one lives apart from God and experiences the destructive consequences (v. 6b). These two varying lifestyles are descriptive of two opposing paths in life—the way of God and the way of humankind.

This perspective of two disparate pathways is not unique to the Psalms. Solomon tells us that there are the "ways of wicked men" and the "ways of good men" or those who are righteous (Prov 2:12–15, 20). Isaiah told people about the "Way of Holiness" exclusively reserved for the redeemed "who walk in that Way." Those who practice wickedness "will not journey on it" (Isa 35:8–9). Centuries later, Jesus tells us that he is the way (John 14:6); therefore, we must choose what path to follow for our lives (Matt 7:13–14). The holy path leads to heaven and informs us on the way to live on earth where we can also experience his favor and be truly happy as we follow in his ways. Years later, the apostle John spoke of only two paths we can choose. We can walk in the light, which is following the way of Jesus (1 John 1:7, 2:6). Or, we can walk in the darkness, which is opposed to God's ways

---

18. Kidner, *Psalms*, 64.
19. Spurgeon, *Treasury of David*, 1:5.

(1:6; 2:9, 11). Scripture does not allow us to buy into our culture's repudiation of two mutually exclusive paths.

The Psalms remind us that there are only two paths from which we can choose in this life. "So, the two ways, and there is no third, part forever."[20] The psalmist and the rest of the Psalter are instructing us that there is only one pathway to holiness. Those who know Jesus are on the "highway of holiness" which is a "pathway we can walk" by obedience because God's grace enables us.[21]

Two Perspectives on the Path of Holiness

An Orientation-Stage Perspective

Brueggemann has provided a framework by which we can identify with the psalmists' diverse experiences in their writings.[22] With his perspective, we can see ourselves in their "seasons of life."[23] As we experience nature's transition from winter to spring and summer to autumn, we also move from one season of life to another in our personal lives. These transitions can be challenging; they may be burdensome and overwhelming. It's not surprising if we resist the change by wanting to return to the former and more familiar circumstances. However, God is sovereign behind the seasons and their transitions, accomplishing his purposes throughout the dynamic changes. One of his divine purposes is the transformation of our lives. Therefore, we can grow in holiness as we relate our seasons of life to the psalmists' experiences.

In the first season, the psalmists' times of "well-being" characterizes orientation. The writers know that "life makes sense."[24] Since God is sovereign, the psalmists "affirm that the world is a well-ordered, reliable, and life-giving system because God has ordained it that way and continues to preside effectively over the process."[25] In light of this, the psalmists trust God and experience joy and delight in God and his world.[26] The songs of creation (8, 33, 104, 145), the Torah (1, 15, 24, 119), wisdom (14, 37), and

---

20. Kidner, *Psalms*, 66.
21. Bloesch, *Holy Spirit*, 319.
22. Brueggemann discusses his framework in his books, *The Message of the Psalms: A Theological Commentary* and *Praying the Psalms*.
23. Brueggemann, *Message of the Psalms*, 19.
24. Brueggemann, *Praying the Psalms*, 3.
25. Brueggemann, *Message of the Psalms*, 25.
26. Brueggemann, *Message of the Psalms*, 19.

relationships (131, 133) reflect a well-ordered life and God's goodness. Even the "songs of retribution" (such as 112) belong in this season of "well-being" because "the world is ruled by God with moral symmetry. . . . The world works so that persons receive the consequences of their actions." The world is governed by a "righteous God. Everything is all right."[27] We can identify with the psalmists' experiences when we enjoy those times of "well-being." Life is good—stable, productive, enjoyable, and filled with praise to God and all he has given us.

However, life is not static, but ever-changing. The psalmists remind us that life shifts all too quickly. Difficult and painful circumstances move us from a well-ordered life to the second season, termed *disorientation*. The well-ordered world we knew comes undone, and we are confronted by "the loss of control of our lives."[28] It may be broken relationships, financial loss, life-threatening disease, or the unexpected destruction of property. In this chaos, we are flooded by "a rush of negativities, including rage, resentment, guilt, shame, isolation, despair, hatred, and hostility." Since we live in a world impacted by sin, "much of the Psalms [are] in the form of complaint and lament."[29]

The Psalter expresses two kinds of lament that we share in our lives. The *external* outcries reflect the psalmists' personal, painful experiences of God's abandonment (13) and the arrogant enemies' attacks (35 and 86). The external laments include laments by God's people who are attacked by their enemies (74 and 79) and are deported as refugees to Babylon (137). Life has become disorienting for the psalmists, and their laments assume "that the trouble has happened because Yahweh has not guaranteed a stable life... Even when disorientation is caused by an enemy, the appeal is still to Yahweh. . . . Sometimes, Yahweh is blamed, and sometimes not."[30] In addition to the external laments, the psalmists express laments due to what they are *internally* experiencing—namely, guilt. In these psalms, the loss of intimacy with God is very disorienting, and sin must be confessed before God to restore the relationship (32, 51, 143, 130).

We are only too glad when we realize the storms in our lives have moved away and the dark days are replaced with more pleasant ones. We have moved from disorientation to a *new orientation*. We are "surprised by a new gift from God" who sovereignly replaces the darkness and despair with

---

27. Brueggemann, *Message of the Psalms*, 28–47.
28. Brueggemann, *Message of the Psalms*, 11.
29. Brueggemann, *Message of the Psalms*, 20.
30. Brueggemann, *Message of the Psalms*, 88–89.

light and joy.[31] In his goodness, he gives his people renewed hope in him and a new lease on life itself. Brueggemann comments, "Israel sings songs of new orientation because the God of Israel is the one who hears and answers expressions of disorientation and resolves experiences of disorientation."[32] The writers of the Psalter echo this new orientation. The "Psalms regularly bear witness to the surprising gift of new life experiences just when none had been expected."[33] A sampling of these Psalms includes personal songs of thanksgiving (30, 34, 40:1–10, 96:10, 97:1, 99:1, 103, 138), community songs of thanksgiving (65, 66, 124), and hymns of praise (117, 135, 103, 113, 146–150).

We may assume that these psalms of new orientation are a return to the "old status quo" or a "return to the old form, a return to normalcy as though nothing had happened."[34] However, these particular psalms "are not about the 'natural' outcome of trouble, but about the *decisive transformation* made possible by this God who causes new life where none seems possible"(italics his).[35] With this new life, Bruce Demarest states that "brokenness gives way to wholeness, weakness to strength, and bondage to freedom."[36] Because God has stepped in and revealed himself in a more profound way to his people, these psalms communicate "experiencing spiritual renewal, a deepened relationship with God and joy supplanting despair."[37] Now, the "reoriented heart longs for holiness—a life set apart for and empowered by God. . . . Radically reoriented souls . . . possess a burning passion for holiness in thought, word, and deed."[38] To reiterate the thesis of this book, the Psalms are a guide to growing in holiness—in our character and conduct.

A few observations are in order here. First, this orientation framework "provides us a way to think about the Psalms concerning our common human experience, for each of God's children is in transit along the flow of orientation, disorientation, and reorientation."[39] This perspective is understood and felt by the psalmists and today's followers of Jesus. Second, each of these three orientation states is important and interrelated. While we may want to paint a rosy view of life, this model reminds us that we can't gloss

---

31. Brueggemann, *Message of the Psalms*, 20.
32. Brueggemann, *Message of the Psalms*, 125.
33. Brueggemann, *Message of the Psalms*, 123–24.
34. Brueggemann, *Praying the Psalms*, 11.
35. Brueggemann, *Message of the Psalms*, 125.
36. Demarest, *Seasons of the Soul*, 130.
37. Demarest, *Seasons of the Soul*, 15.
38. Demarest, *Seasons of the Soul*, 130–31.
39. Brueggmann, *Praying the Psalms*, 3.

over the harsh realities of life (disorientation) portrayed in the Psalms and our lives. Brueggemann believes the church has failed to give proper attention to the psalms of disorientation in favor of the more enjoyable psalms of praise and thanksgiving. However, these more painful psalms "lead us into dangerous acknowledgment of how life really is." He says that a robust faith in God allows us to embrace "experiences of disorder."[40] Third, this framework reveals a sovereign God actively involved in each of these dynamic stages of our lives to accomplish his purposes. We enjoy his blessings through the experiences of a well-ordered life (orientation), the trials he sends our way (disorientation), and a deepened life of intimacy and love with God and others (new orientation). Through each of these phases, we can bear the fruit of growing in holiness.

The Pilgrimage Perspective

The Psalms view the Christian life as a pilgrimage. The writer of Ps 119 recognizes that he is a "stranger on earth" (v. 19) living in exile in this "foreign land."[41] David states that he is "an alien, a stranger" and his people are "passing pilgrims" in this world (39:12).[42] Their identity as pilgrims prepared them to face the dangers they would face in this "alien world."[43]

The goal of this spiritual journey is to enjoy the fullness of God's presence both in the present and in the world to come. Those who have "set their hearts on pilgrimage" (84:5) seek a profound spiritual experience centered on the Lord. To do so, one must follow God's way. He provides a pathway that guides us to righteous living (1:6). Scripture is the most reliable guide because it functions as a light for us along this pathway (119:105). To enjoy God's presence, the pilgrim must say, "I consider all your precepts right, I hate every wrong path" (119:128). Spurgeon elaborated, "Those who love the ways of God are blessed. When we have God's ways in our hearts, and our heart in his ways, we are what and where we should be, and hence we shall enjoy the divine approval.[44]

While the word "pilgrimage" is mentioned once in the Psalms (84:5), the Songs of Ascent (120–134) certainly reinforce the pilgrimage motif. Spurgeon calls this collection of psalms the "Pilgrim Songs" because

---

40. Brueggmann, *Message of the Psalms*, 52.

41. Spurgeon, *Treasury of David*, 5:172. Psalm 39:12 also mentions David stating he is "an alien, a stranger" and we are "passing pilgrims" in this world.

42. Spurgeon, *Treasury of David*, 2:219.

43. Kidner, *Psalms*, 458.

44. Spurgeon, *Treasury of David*, 3:434.

individuals and groups sang them on their way to Jerusalem for the feasts.[45] In addition to a literal movement within a geographical setting, Spurgeon notes that there is also a spiritual progression (an "ascent") in these songs. The pilgrim begins in a distant land living among wicked people. He does not relish these people and realizes he has lived among them too long (120:5–7). He is homesick for a better place to enjoy God's presence. With this longing, the pilgrim commences his journey (121) and arrives in Jerusalem (122) to celebrate the feasts and worship God. Psalm 123 reminds us that our spiritual journey is not just about reaching a place but also about enjoying God himself. Spurgeon remarks, "Here we look to the Lord himself, and this is the highest ascent of all by many degrees. The eyes are now looking above the hills, and above Jehovah's footstool on earth, to his throne in the heavens."[46] One might assume this is the end of the spiritual journey, but it is not.

Our spiritual pilgrimage is not like moving in a straight line from points A to B. Rather, we move forward cyclically, much like a bicycle wheel in motion.[47] That is, we will experience a cycle that includes times of intimacy in God's presence and trials that greatly challenge our faith. In this cycle, our lives are purified, our walk with the Lord is strengthened, and we progress in holiness. Psalm 125 views adversities not as a setback in our spiritual journey, but Spurgeon affirms that this song represents another step "in the ascent, another station in the pilgrimage is reached." He says the pilgrim has a deepened trust in the Lord for present and future adversities.[48] Spurgeon viewed Ps 126 as a further progression in our pilgrimage. We shouldn't only enjoy abiding with God (125), but we must bear fruit. "Here the truster becomes a sower," Spurgeon comments, "faith works by love, obtains a present bliss, and secures a harvest of delight."[49] Spurgeon reminds us whatever may come our way in life, "observe how in each of these songs the heart is fixed upon Jehovah only."[50] Of course, our spiritual pilgrimage extends beyond enjoying time alone with God. Growth in holiness also occurs in the context of relationships in society and family, as shown in Pss 127, 128, and 133. These three psalms will be further discussed in chapter 9 ("Community and Holiness").

---

45. Spurgeon, *Treasury of David*, 6:5.

46. Spurgeon, *Treasury of David*, 6:39.

47. I am indebted to Dr. Mel Loucks, who compared spiritual pilgrimage as cyclically in a phone conversation.

48. Spurgeon, *Treasury of David*, 6:58.

49. Spurgeon, *Treasury of David*, 6:68.

50. Spurgeon, *Treasury of David*, 6:83.

Once again, family love is tested, which is a further opportunity to grow spiritually. Spurgeon offers this insight on Ps 129: "Inasmuch as patience is a higher, or at least more difficult, grace than domestic love, the ascent or progress may perhaps be seen in that direction."[51] Our patience will be even further tried and matured as we wait on the Lord during the "sharper sorrows" which are described in Ps 130.[52] When we learn patience, our spiritual growth continues. Referring to Ps 131, Spurgeon remarks, "Lowliness and humility are here seen in connection with a sanctified heart, a will subdued to the mind of God, and a hope looking to the Lord alone."[53] Our faithfulness to the Lord in afflictions shapes our character, and the Lord rewards us (132:18) with his benediction of blessing on our lives (134).

Having read *Pilgrim's Progress* numerous times throughout his life, Spurgeon reflects Bunyan's language and thinking in his own *Treasury of David*, which is his multi-volume exposition of the Psalms.[54] For example, over eighty times, he uses "pilgrim" or "pilgrimage" to describe the psalmists' experiences and what we may expect to face in today's world. Spurgeon does this intentionally. Pilgrimage is a significant motif that represents Spurgeon's theology of progressive holiness. Growing in holiness is a lifelong pursuit, enabled by God's grace, marked by times of joy and experiences of adversity. Spurgeon states that we are on a "life journey" characterized as "steady progress" and a "quiet advance." At the same time, the journey will be "rough," "stern," and "hard."[55] This perspective of pilgrimage illustrates Spurgeon's practice of borrowing names of persons and places from *Pilgrim's Progress*.

As a pilgrim-stranger in this world, the place one dwells is "the house of my pilgrimage" (119:54 KJV). Even if he lived in a palace, it was "the inn at which he rested, the station at which he halted for a little while." Whatever he possessed was only temporary because he "knew that he was not at home in this world, but a pilgrim through it, seeking a better country."[56] Spurgeon's words are reminiscent of Gaius' inn in *Pilgrim's Progress*. This inn was for the exclusive use of weary pilgrims passing through, so Christian's wife, Christiana, and her children rested before moving on to the Celestial City.[57]

51. Spurgeon, *Treasury of David*, 6:108.
52. Spurgeon, *Treasury of David*, 6:118.
53. Spurgeon, *Treasury of David*, 6:136.
54. Morden states how Bunyan's writings influenced Spurgeon's experiences, sermons, and spirituality. In particular, Bunyan's emphasis on pilgrimage gave Spurgeon a framework to understand the Christian life (*Communion with Christ*, 26–30).
55. Spurgeon, *Treasury of David*, 5:141.
56. Spurgeon, *Treasury of David*, 5:241.
57. Bunyan, *Pilgrim's Progress*, 293.

The ultimate destination of our spiritual journey is the Celestial City or heaven.[58] For the Israelites, their pilgrimage ended when they reached Jerusalem or Zion (84:7; 42:4). To arrive at the "holy mountain" where God dwells (43:3) is, in Spurgeon's words, the "celestial palace above" or heaven for today's believers.[59] Commenting on Ps 121, a "pilgrim song," Spurgeon remarks, "Happy are the pilgrims to whom this Psalm is a safe conduct; they may journey all the way to the celestial city without fear."[60] As previously mentioned, the primary focus is not on a place but a person. The desire is to be in and enjoy God's presence.

The Psalms' pilgrim motif should both inform and shape our life experiences. We tend to forget our proper relationship to this world, but the Psalms remind us of our transitory stay on planet earth. We are pilgrims journeying through this life, pursuing God while holding loosely to our material possessions. We are foolish to crave for what will all-too-soon pass away and neglect our pursuit of loving God. Pilgrimage puts our lives in perspective and shapes our priorities. An intentional focus on the biblical theme of pilgrimage contributes to the growth of personal holiness.

Our pilgrimage will involve a spiritual battle until we reach the Celestial City. Even though Ephesians 6 frequently mentions this warfare, Spurgeon draws our attention to the Psalter. "In these busy days, it would be greatly to the spiritual profit of Christian men and women if they were more familiar with the Book of Psalms, in which they would find a complete armoury for life's battles, and a perfect supply for life's needs."[61] The Christian life as a spiritual battle.[62] Throughout the Psalms, Spurgeon underscores this reality in our spiritual journey through the "map of experience."

Our spiritual battle involves our sinful nature. For example, using imagery from *Pilgrim's Progress*, the young child, Passion, demands immediate gratification. For such people, their "reward is in this life" (17:14). Commenting on Psalm 45:10 ("Forget your people and your father's house") Spurgeon informs us that renouncing sin is a battle because our sinful nature was built in the "City of Destruction." In *Pilgrim's Progress*, Christian lived in the City of Destruction, which he had to escape if he wanted to find eternal life.[63] Our sinful human nature strongly influences our life experiences.

58. Bunyan, *Pilgrim's Progress*, 181–90.
59. Spurgeon, *Treasury of David*, 2:293.
60. Spurgeon, *Treasury of David*, 6:15.
61. Spurgeon, *Treasury of David*, 6:vi.
62. Bloesch states, "The idea of the Christian engaged in spiritual warfare was pervasive among the Puritans, but it is also found in the mainstream of the Reformation, even in the mystical tradition of the Christian faith" (*Holy Spirit*, 321).
63. Bunyan, *Pilgrim's Progress*, 5–6; Spurgeon, *Treasury of David*, 2:319.

Our spiritual battle also involves external temptations which shape our daily responses. For example, on the way to the Celestial City, Christian had to pass through the town of Vanity, which had a fair where "all sorts of vanity could be sold." Items for sale included merchandise, status, and pleasures, in addition to cheap entertainment and free offers for sinful activities.[64] We, too, travel through Vanity Fair.[65] As a result, our vanity tempts us to get whatever we can so that people judge us by our appearance and all we have. Commenting on Psalm 62:9, Spurgeon gives a somber reminder that none are immune, for "even God's own children are too apt to be bitten with this madness."[66]

Ultimately, our battle is against Satan and his demonic forces. The psalmist mentions "the ways of the violent" (17:4). Spurgeon reminds us that there are only two roads to take in this life—heaven or hell. The latter option spells destruction in this life and beyond death. Satan, who is Apollyon, confronts Christian in *Pilgrim's Progress*.[67] Spurgeon remarks, "The paths of the destroyer have often tempted us; we have been prompted to become destroyers too, when we have been sorely provoked, and resentment has grown warm."[68] Fortunately, God provides us with the spiritual weapons, such as a shield (18:30), we need in this battle. He gives us his resources so that "we might be unconquered in battle and unwearied in pilgrimage."[69]

Pilgrimage involves a spectrum of life experiences. Like Christian in *Pilgrim's Progress* and the psalmist who found himself in "the depths" (30:1), we will, in our pilgrimage experience, find ourselves in the "Slough of Despond" or the muck which includes the "fears, doubts, and discouraging apprehensions about oneself that arise" in one's soul.[70] We may also have times of terror and fear (48:5–6) and find ourselves, like Christian and his friends, "in Giant Despair's grip . . . there they quivered with dismay . . . fear took hold of them."[71] We may even pass through the "shadow of death" (23:4), which Christian had to go through on his way to the Celestial City.[72] On the other hand, we will know the joys along our spiritual pilgrimage with

---

64. Bunyan, *Pilgrim's Progress*, 103–7.
65. Spurgeon, *Pictures from Pilgrim's Progress*, 92.
66. Spurgeon, *Treasury of David*, 3:52.
67. Bunyan, *Pilgrim's Progress*, 65–71.
68. Spurgeon, *Treasury of David*, 1:217.
69. Spurgeon, *Treasury of David*, 1:245.
70. Bunyan, *Pilgrim's Progress*, 11.
71. Spurgeon, *Treasury of David*, 2:361. Bunyan, *Pilgrim's Progress*, 319–22.
72. Bunyan, *Pilgrim's Progress*, 71.

Jesus. In Ps 84:6, the pilgrims experienced the blessing of God's refreshing provisions. Spurgeon comments, "The happy pilgrims found refreshment even in the dreariest part of the road.... There are joys of pilgrimage which men forget in the discomforts of the road."[73] Like Christian who enjoyed the Delectable Mountains, we can experience God's many delights which encourage us along our pilgrimage.[74]

The pilgrimage includes the experience of companionship. Throughout *Pilgrim's Progress*, Christian and his wife, Christiana, met many people (such as Help, Hopeful, Faithful, Interpreter, and Mercy) who encouraged them along their way to the Celestial City. Spurgeon mentions some of these names when he writes about our spiritual pilgrimage. For example, when the psalmist describes being in the "slimy pit" and the "mud and mire" (40:2), Spurgeon mentions Help and Great-heart, who guided "the pilgrims along the heavenward road."[75] It is a great experience to have friends who accompany us through our pilgrimage.

To sum up, the pilgrimage perspective provides another beneficial description of the Psalms, which correlates with the path of holiness. This pilgrimage motif is clearly rooted in the Psalter and is extensively incorporated into Spurgeon's writing on the Psalms. Our discussion on the ways the Psalter contributes to personal holiness may be understood through the pilgrimage analogy. The pursuit of holiness occurs over a lifetime until the day we reach heaven. Growth in holiness does not come easily because we are engaged in a spiritual battle. As the New Testament reminds us, we are aliens in this world which we are passing through (Heb 11:13; 1 Pet 1:1, 2:11). The Psalms remind us that God has given us all the resources we need to defeat sin and become more like Jesus.

Conclusion

Both perspectives—orientation-stage and pilgrimage—give us great insight to the Psalter's path of holiness traveled by both the psalmists and generations of Jesus-followers. Both views provide us with the diverse experiences of those who have gone before us. Though the imagery of the orientation-stage and pilgrimage is different, both clearly and accurately describe the path to personal holiness. The way of holiness includes seasons whereby we are enjoying our relationship with God and his people. At other times, we

---

73. Spurgeon, *Treasury of David*, 3:434.
74. Bunyan, *Pilgrim's Progress*, 141.
75. Spurgeon, *Pictures from Pilgrim's Progress*, 19.

undergo trials, spiritual dryness, and other setbacks which come our way. On this note, DeYoung encourages us,

> When it comes to sanctification, it's more important where you're going than where you are. Direction matters more than position. Your future progress speaks louder than your present placement. So cheer up: if you aren't as holy as you want to be now, God may still be pleased with you because you are heading in the right direction."
>
> The psalmists' wide range of experiences supply us with a pathway which we can use with confidence in our pursuit of holiness.[76]

Having established that the psalmists have provided us with a pathway to pursue holiness, in the next chapter, we will turn to explore the relationship between the nature of holiness and our interior life.

---

76. DeYoung, *Hole in Our Holiness*, 138.

Chapter 2

The Nature of Growing in Holiness

At one point during his sermon, Charles Spurgeon declared,

> We feel that we have within us a tendency to sin, and that tendency is our misery: from this tendency we must be emancipated, or we are no more free than the captive who has had the manacles removed from one wrist but feels the iron eating into the other arm.... Since our new birth there remains no rest for us short of being perfectly like our God in righteousness and true holiness.... We may now be called "The Irreconcilables," for we can never be at peace with evil. We cannot tolerate sin. The thought of it pains us; and when we fall into a sinful act we are cut to the quick. We thirst to be pure, we pant to be holy, and we shall never be satisfied until we are perfectly so.[1]

Spurgeon understood sin's influence and the necessity to resist sin to grow in holiness. To combat the pernicious nature of sin, he warned people to avoid any places which appealed to their human nature. He alerted them about the dangers of live theater and papers which would entice young men. It was essential not to pay attention to others who "ridicule our holy fear of sin."[2] Spurgeon also instructed his congregation on the ways they could exemplify holy living. He encouraged parents to practice family worship with their children. He urged individuals to avoid spiritual

---

1. Spurgeon, "Sin Subdued," lines 9–20.
2. Nettles, *Living by Revealed Truth*, 256.

decline by reading the Bible, praying and communing with the Lord, and attending Sunday church services. People had to nourish their lives with spiritual means to grow in holiness.[3]

SPURGEON NOT ONLY SPOKE about holiness, but he lived such a life. As a pastor, he knew that ungodly character would undermine the established trust with the congregation.[4] He practiced financial integrity, was lovingly committed to his wife and two sons, and demonstrated a genuine love for others.[5] It is not surprising his life impressed others. A newspaper editor admiringly spoke of Spurgeon's life: "This spirituality is so rare in men of great powers that it is invariably the way to influence."[6] Spurgeon's character and actions are accurate markers of holiness in his life.

Images of ascetics who live in harsh and solitary settings may shape our perception of a holy life. Or, we are influenced by those who voice interminable prayers or quote Bible verses in nearly every conversation. For others, godliness means sharing the plan of salvation with the one sitting next to her on a flight. We assume that this matter of holiness must be relegated to professional religious people. Consequently, many of us feel that our pursuit of becoming godly is beyond our reach. Sadly, extreme or exaggerated distortions which reflect very little of a biblical perspective on godliness shape our view of holiness.

We need Scripture, such as the Psalms, to shape our understanding of holiness and its application in our daily lives. The psalmists function as our spiritual guides, and Spurgeon's *Treasury of David* supplies us with his further insights on holiness.

The Big Picture of Holiness

We want to explore the general nature of personal holiness before examining the specific expressions of godliness. On the need for purity in our lives ("How can a young person stay pure?" Ps 119:9, NLT), Spurgeon states,

> Let him not, however, shrink from the glorious enterprise of living a pure and gracious life; rather let him enquire the way

---

3. Nettles, *Living by Revealed Truth*, 257.
4. Chang, *Spurgeon the Pastor*, 151.
5. Morden, *C. H. Spurgeon*, 94–98.
6. Morden, *C. H. Spurgeon*, 98.

by which all obstacles may be overcome. Let him not think that he knows the road to easy victory, nor dream that he can keep himself by his own wisdom; he will do well to follow the Psalmist, and become an earnest enquirer asking how he may cleanse his way. Let him become a practical disciple of the holy God.[7]

His comments reflect the fundamental nature of personal holiness. First, the source of holiness originates in the very nature of God. Second, we reflect God's nature by growing in holiness in our character and conduct. A "pure" or holy life is expressed in "practical" ways in everyday living.[8] To be a follower of Jesus is to "become a practical disciple of the holy God."[9] Third, growth in personal holiness is not a "road to easy victory" but a challenging process with "obstacles" along the way. Fourth, when Spurgeon speaks of a "gracious life," he indicates that a holy life is only possible by God's grace. Sheer willpower and effort will lead to dismal failure apart from God's power working in our lives. We can cultivate holiness in our lives by listening to the psalmists and practicing what they say.

Holiness Is Rooted in the Nature of God

The holiness of God is a dominant theme throughout the Psalms. The words "holy" and "holiness" are mentioned forty-two times throughout the NIV translation of the Psalter. The Psalms commonly describe God as "holy" (16:10, 22:3, 71:22, 78:41, 89:18). Psalm 99 mentions "holy" four times, prompting Spurgeon to suggest that this psalm "may be called The *Santus* or the Holy, Holy, Holy Psalm."[10] God is holy (vv. 3, 5, 9), and this is expressed in various ways. His "name" or character is holy (v. 3). Therefore, God has "no flaw or fault, excess or deficiency, error or iniquity. He is wholly excellent, and is therefore called holy." Based on his nature, God reveals his holiness through his actions in our world (v. 4). "In his words, thoughts, acts, and revelations," God reveals holy nature to us.[11]

What is related to God is also considered holy. His "name" is holy (30:4, 33:21, 97:12, 103:1, 105:3, 106:47, 111:9, 145:21) as are his Spirit (51:11), "ways" (77:13), promises (105:42) and "heaven" (20:6). Objects associated

---

7. Spurgeon, *Treasury of David*, 5:157.

8. The concept of practical holiness is not unique to Spurgeon. For example, J. C. Ryle uses the term "practical holiness" to describe how holiness is expressed in ten different ways in our lives (*Holiness*, 79–86).

9. Spurgeon, *Treasury of David*, 5:157.

10. Spurgeon, *Treasury of David*, 4:222.

11. Spurgeon, *Treasury of David*, 4:222.

The Nature of Growing in Holiness 35

with God's presence such as the hill or mountain of Zion (2:6, 3:4, 15:1, 43:3, 46:4, 48:1, 87:1), the temple situated on it (5:7, 11:4, 28:2, 65:4, 68:5, 79:1, 138:2) and the angels (89:5, 7) are all described as holy. Not surprisingly, the Psalms describe those associated with God as holy. The priests are expected to be "consecrated" before God (106:16), and the worshipers of God (106:16) are expected to live as "saints" (16:3, 34:9). Both words—consecrated and saints—use the same Hebrew word (*kadosh*) to convey the idea of avoiding whatever displeases God and therefore, living free from impurity. God's people dedicated to him are expected to live morally pure lives.[12]

Therefore, our personal holiness is deeply rooted in God. Given who he is and our sinful nature, we need to consider two dimensions of holiness. First, God declares that we are righteous through the atonement of Christ (Rom 3:21–26, 8:33–34). This righteousness refers to justification which delivers us from condemnation. Second, justification also provides the foundation for us to grow in holiness, which is called sanctification or progressive holiness[13] ("being made holy," Heb 10:14). By our position in Christ, he offers us all the necessary resources to be made righteous throughout our lifetime. The Psalms primarily address the latter aspect of holiness. God, who moves into our lives, can begin to purify us so that we can gradually become examples of holy living. We will further explore his vital and foundational role in our growth in holiness in chapter 6.

The New Testament echoes the Psalms' emphasis on sanctification or growing in holiness and its relationship to God's character. Jesus told his listeners, "Be perfect, therefore, as your heavenly Father is perfect" (Matt 5:48). D. A. Carson points out that the form of this verse is identical to Lev 19:2, which uses "holy" instead of "perfect."[14] R. T. France points out that "perfect" (*teleios*) refers to completeness or wholeness. Jesus is speaking about a life that is "totally integrated to the will of God, and thus reflecting his character. . . . The conformity to the character of God, to which Israel was called in their role as God's special people . . . is now affirmed as the goal of the disciples of Jesus."[15]

In much the same manner, the apostle Paul urges his readers, "Be imitators of God" (Eph 5:1). God expects us to "mimic" or copy him. Imitating God requires a change of character. Paul tells us that we are "created to be like God in true righteousness and holiness" (Eph 4:24). God wants us to go through a renewal process which enables us to increasingly reflect his image

12. Brown, *New Brown-Driver-Briggs-Gesinius*, 872.
13. Hoekema, "Reformed View," 75.
14. Carson, *Matthew*, 160–61.
15. France. *Matthew*, 129–30.

(Col 3:10). In the same letter to the Colossian believers, Paul tells them that God's image is seen in Jesus Christ (1:15). Thus, holiness is understood as fulfilling God's purpose for our lives by becoming more like Jesus Christ in his character and conduct. Spurgeon notes, "Holy living is a choice evidence of salvation."[16] Peterson once journaled what he expressed throughout his life, "I guess what I am most interested in these days is holiness. I am on the watch for saints . . . I want to be a saint."[17] His longing should be our longing.

Holiness Involves Our Whole Being

There are two dimensions of our growth in personal holiness: the inner life (character) and the outer life (conduct). Holiness provides us with a pathway that integrates both of these.

The formation of a godly character is fundamental to everyday living. Yet, the thought of becoming holy seems preposterous and rather daunting if we pursue it. When the psalmist asks, "Who may ascend the hill of the LORD?" (Ps 24:3), our immediate response might be, "No one!" However, the psalmist claims that it is possible to have a pure heart and "stand in his holy place" (v. 4a). A pure heart requires not loving idols (v. 4b) and instead choosing to be devoted to God. For us, this devotion involves loving God through a relationship with Jesus. Loving God is our motivation to pursue holiness in good and challenging times. "This inner love . . . must be the mainspring of Christian integrity in our public walk. The fountain must be filled with love to [sic] holiness, and then the streams which issue from it will be pure and gracious."[18] Thus, we can see why there is an "imperative need of purity within."[19] Acts of piety without a love for God were all too common among the religious leaders of Jesus' day. And it continues today, masquerading as godliness, but in reality, it is only moralism.

In contrast, holiness involves growing purity in our attitudes, motives, thoughts, emotions, and longings. In short, our soul needs to become pure. Spurgeon sums it up this way, "To love holiness, to have the motives and desires sanctified, to be in one's inmost nature obedient to the Lord—this is the surest method of making the whole run of our life efficient for its great ends."[20] Our inner life, which shapes character, is the starting point for holiness. But it's only one side of the coin.

16. Spurgeon, *Treasury of David*, 2:390.
17. Collier, *Burning in my Bones*, 91.
18. Spurgeon, *Treasury of David*, 1:242–43.
19. Spurgeon, *Treasury of David*, 1:371.
20. Spurgeon, *Treasury of David*, 2:177–78.

True holiness, which begins in the heart with its desires and motives, influences our character and, consequently, our actions and speech. David tells us that we must also have "clean hands" combined with truthful words (v. 4). "There must be a work of grace in the core of the heart as well as in the palm of the hand, or our religion is a delusion."[21] The mark of God's power at work in our lives will be an "outward, practical holiness."[22] With genuine holiness, the inner and outer spheres of our lives are integrated. Our conduct and speech must reflect Jesus' life regardless of where we live. Growing in holiness is measured by greater integrity between our unseen world and what is visible to those around us.[23]

Thorough-going holiness, which affects the totality of our lives, is emphasized again by David in Ps 15. He informs us that "blameless" (holy) people can come into God's presence (vv. 1–2). Fortunately, he is not referring to one who is perfect but to one's "character."[24] Spurgeon comments, "In perfection this holiness is found only in the Man of Sorrows, but in a measure it is wrought in all his people."[25] Our character reflects a much lesser degree Jesus' character. Even though our holiness pales in comparison to Jesus' perfect holiness, we can't underestimate the priority of the transformation of our character in relation to holiness. This healthy posture protects us from falling into the trap of living a virtuous life without loving God. Besides, God is not impressed! As Spurgeon notes, "God desires not merely outward virtue, but inward purity.... He cares not for the pretense of purity, he looks to the mind, heart, and soul. Always has the Holy One of Israel estimated men by their inner nature, and not by their outward professions; to him the inward is as visible as the outward, and he rightly judges that the essential character of an action lies in the motive of him who works it."[26] However, if we limit holiness to inward purity, we have a distorted view of holiness.

21. Spurgeon, *Treasury of David*, 1:371.
22. Spurgeon, *Treasury of David*, 1:371.
23. Packer writes, "Personal holiness is personal wholeness—the ongoing reintegration of our disintegrated and disordered personhood as we pursue our goal of single-minded Jesus-likeness" (*Rediscovering Holiness*, 93).
24. Spurgeon, *Treasury of David*, 1:177. Ryle comments, "I do not say for a moment that holiness shuts out the presence of indwelling sin.... But it is the excellence of a holy man that he is not at peace with indwelling sin, as others are" (*Holiness*, 87).
25. Spurgeon, *Treasury of David*, 1:177.
26. Spurgeon, *Treasury of David*, 2:403; Packer, *Rediscovering Holiness*, 98–106. He addresses the interior life with its desires. "Holiness is viewed first and foremost as the detaching of desire from created things in order to attach it through Christ to the Creator." He then proceeds to discuss the need to cultivate the virtues of character (such as faith, hope, and love) in our lives and our motivations.

Psalm 15 also informs us that genuine holiness moves from our interior life (the "heart") to our outer life, which is a "description of outward character."[27] Holiness is expressed in doing what is right (vv. 2–3, 5) and rejecting what is patently wrong (v. 4, 26:10–11). The one who opposes evil loves godliness. As Spurgeon reminds us, "True religion is always practical, for it does not permit us to delight ourselves in a perfect rule without exciting in us a longing to be conformed to it in our daily lives."[28]

A biblical perspective of growing in holiness involves becoming increasingly like Jesus Christ. In the apostle Paul's language, God wants us to be "conformed to the likeness of his Son" (Rom 8:29). Thus, Spurgeon states, "We should keep the image of God so constantly before us that we become in our measure conformed unto it."[29] Being conformed to Jesus involves a change in our desires, thoughts, and attitudes (Eph 4:22–24). Becoming more like Jesus necessitates changes in our emotions, speech, and how we relate to others (Col 3:8–9, 12–17). In other words, every area of our lives must be transformed (Rom 12:2). This transformation ("metamorphosis") is akin to the caterpillar which becomes a larva and eventually a butterfly. Our whole being must radically change to become more like Jesus.

Holiness Involves Gradual Growth

Holiness can feel overwhelming when we talk about becoming like Jesus and being blameless. In response to the psalmist who asked how we can be pure (119:9), Spurgeon acknowledges that there are no "greater difficulties" than this calling to be holy. Pursuing holiness "is the work; this is the difficulty"[30] which lies before us. Rather than being daunted by pursuing holiness and giving up, we need encouragement. The Psalms give us the hope we need.

The long-term perspective is essential to our growth in holiness. Because the pervasive polluting influence of sin mars us, we will never be perfectly holy in this life. Since we cannot expect perfection here on earth, we must look to life beyond the grave. Psalm 17:15 reminds us that those who know God will see him one day after we die and awake in his presence. When we come into God's presence and see his face, Ps 73:24 declares that we will see his glory ("afterward you will take me into glory"). Heaven is the place where "we shall be like him, for we shall see him as he is" (1 John 3:2).

---

27. Spurgeon, *Treasury of David*, 1:177.
28. Spurgeon, *Treasury of David*, 5:139.
29. Spurgeon, *Treasury of David*, 1:242.
30. Spurgeon, *Treasury of David*, 5:157.

No longer will sin taint us and holiness will be perfected. The present challenges in our growth in holiness are worth it when we look to eternity. "We can cheerfully put up with the present," Spurgeon encourages us, "when we foresee the future. What is around us just now is of small consequence, compared with afterward."[31] For now, we can experience a "foretaste of heaven" to the degree we live in holiness.[32]

Therefore, we must be honest about our personal growth in holiness. This growth, known as "positional sanctification," begins at conversion (Acts 20:32, 26:18; 1 Cor 1:2, 6:11). Spurgeon acknowledges, "We fear that no man can claim to be absolutely without sin," and then he reminds us that we are not to "designedly, willfully, knowingly, and continuously do anything that is wicked, ungodly, or unjust."[33] The Psalms are not naïve regarding the reality of our sin and its influence in our lives (51, 139:24), so we must be wise in the expectations of our Christian growth. Each of us will be at various stages of holiness in our spiritual pilgrimage. Some are "faulty in many ways" while others "walk in the light more fully, and maintain closer communion with God."[34] Wherever we are in our spiritual journey, the way of holiness "is not learned in a day" and therefore, "we must not think to obtain it without earnest effort."[35] Growing in holiness must be a "habitual" practice requiring personal discipline.[36] Reminiscent of *Pilgrim's Progress*, personal holiness is a spiritual battle here on earth.

The New Testament bears testimony to the messages of the Psalter. With sin lurking in our lives, holiness will not be perfected in our character and conduct while we are on earth. Holiness is an ongoing active renewal process (Rom 12:2; Col 3:10) throughout our lives. We shouldn't be alarmed when we fall short of godliness.

Holiness Involves God's Grace

Recognizing that this pursuit of holiness requires intentional effort, one might assume this ambition is nothing more than a moralistic self-improvement program requiring everything we can muster up within ourselves. Unfortunately, this is a distorted view of holiness. While we have our responsibility, we can't grow in holiness by self-management. In light of God's

31. Spurgeon, *Treasury of David*, 3:252–53.
32. Spurgeon, *Treasury of David*, 5:140.
33. Spurgeon, *Treasury of David*, 5:143.
34. Spurgeon, *Treasury of David*, 5:140.
35. Spurgeon, *Treasury of David*, 5:141.
36. Spurgeon, *Treasury of David*, 5:141.

holy character, our natural propensity to sin, and the temptations swirling around us, we desperately need to depend on his divine power if we want to reflect godliness or the life of Jesus. We are incapable of achieving personal holiness by self-effort, but Spurgeon assures that "through grace [we] are conformed to his image."[37]

Psalm 45:2 mentions God's grace in one's speech ("your lips have been anointed with grace"). This grace is God's power given in "superabundance" which positively affects the way we speak to others, according to Spurgeon.[38] While "grace" is only mentioned once in the Psalter, this does not preclude God from revealing his empowering grace to his people. We see God's gracious actions expressed throughout the Psalter. In general terms, God deals bountifully with us so that we may live and obey his truth (119:17). Spurgeon points out that the psalmist recognizes he needs God's "great provision" for his "great needs" which include living obediently before the Lord. The "spiritual life" requires "the Lord's bounty, for it is the noblest work of divine grace, and in it the bounty of God is gloriously displayed. The Lord's servants cannot serve him in their own strength, for they cannot even live unless his grace abounds towards them." Thus, the psalmist "must throw himself upon God's grace, and look for the great things he needed from the great goodness of the Lord."[39] The psalmist recognizes that God's grace sets the heart free to obey the Lord (119:32). Spurgeon states, "God must work in us first, and then we shall will and do according to his good pleasure."[40] This verse anticipates Phil 2:13: "It is God who works in you to will and to act according to his good purpose."

God's empowering grace is also evident in how he relates to us. He is our shepherd who gives us divine strength and carries us through life (28:8–9). He is the one who teaches and guides in the pathway of holiness (25:4, 8–9). These expressions of God's grace are given to us to "bring sinners into the way of holiness and conform them to his own image . . . he will renew transgressors' hearts and guide them into the way of holiness."[41] God shows his grace to forgive and "take away all [our] sins" (25:18) when we confess our brokenness to God. Chapter 6 will discuss the grace God gives us so that we have his resources to grow in godliness.

If we want to avoid falling prey to the seduction of the world's values and remain devotedly loyal to God, we need God's empowering grace to

---

37. Spurgeon, *Treasury of David*, 1:176.
38. Spurgeon, *Treasury of David*, 2:316.
39. Spurgeon, *Treasury of David*, 5:171.
40. Spurgeon, *Treasury of David*, 5:193.
41. Spurgeon, *Treasury of David*, 1:394.

resist sin and stay humble (Jas 4:4–6). Paul gives full credit to this divine power, enabling us to see our lives changed. He tells the Corinthian believers that they "are being transformed" into the likeness of Jesus (2 Cor 3:18). Lest they take any credit for this, Paul informs them that God's Spirit makes possible growth in holiness. His grace or divine power enables them to become like Jesus Christ in character and conduct. Peter reiterates Paul's words when he urges his readers to grow in grace (2 Pet 3:11, 18). It is God's power that makes it possible for us to be transformed both in our character (holiness) and conduct (godliness).

The Blessing of Holiness

Does it matter if we grow in godliness? If we can't achieve the perfect image of Jesus during this lifetime, maybe a lackadaisical attitude is acceptable. While there are many reasons not to assume such a posture in life, we must consider one supreme reason. A life of holiness gives us the privilege of experiencing God's blessing on our lives. "Holy living ensures a blessing as its reward from the thrice Holy God, but it is itself a blessing of the New Covenant and a delightful fruit of the Spirit," promises Spurgeon.[42] Those who pursue God and his ways experience God's favor or blessing. The Psalter commonly mentions that they are "blessed." In addition to a blessed life in Ps 1 discussed in chapter 1, Ps 32:1–2 shouts a "blessed" pronouncement to those who are forgiven for their sins. This is possible for today's reader when we accept God's provision of atonement through Jesus Christ's death on the cross. We live with joyful awareness because God has pardoned us from the guilt of sin. Spurgeon connects the blessing of Ps 32 with the blessing of Ps 1. That is, Ps 32 announces God's forgiveness which is the basis for the blessing of a fruitful life in Ps 1.[43] In theological terms, Ps 32 expresses the blessing of justification (a right standing with God through the forgiveness of sins), which provides the foundation for us to experience the benefit of sanctification or growing in holiness mentioned in Ps 1. As Spurgeon notes, "He who is pardoned, has in every case been taught to deal honestly with himself, his sin, and his God. . . . Free from guilt, free from guile. Those who are justified from fault are sanctified from falsehood."[44] When we know we have God's favor on us with his acceptance and divine help to live for him, we are truly blessed.

---

42. Spurgeon, *Treasury of David*, 1:376. Leslie C. Allen mentions that "blessing" refers to the areas of creation, worship, and everyday life (*Psalms*, 75–86).

43. Spurgeon, *Treasury of David*, 2:81.

44. Spurgeon, *Treasury of David*, 2:82.

Two other psalms also mention how those who seek godliness may be "blessed." Psalm 112:1 declares God's favor rests on those who deeply revere God. This attitude toward God indicates one's interior life of devotion for God. As we have repeatedly seen, one's conduct reflects the inner life. In this case, reverence for God leads one to find "great delight in his commands" (v. 1). We may assume the psalmist thinks only of an intellectual enjoyment of Scripture. However, Spurgeon astutely notes the response to his commands. The one who seeks to grow in godliness will "observe them with delight."[45] Those who revere God do so with a delightful attitude and obedience to his commandments. In turn, God will delight in pouring his blessings on such people.

Identical to Pss 1, 32, and 112, Ps 119 commences with a double proclamation of God's blessing on those who pursue personal holiness (vv. 1–2). Once again, we see the two sides of the holiness coin. Purity in our interior life is the catalyst for obedience to God's truth. One who walks in godliness is not perfect ("blameless") but seeks God and obeys him. This pursuit of God is the mark of godliness. Spurgeon summarizes the reasons why one experiences God's blessings: "They [the blessed] are preserved from defilement (v. 1), because they are made practically holy (vv. 2–3), and are led to follow after God sincerely and intensely (v. 2)."[46] More pointedly, Spurgeon says, "Purity in our way and walk is the truest blessedness."[47] In other words, growing in holiness is the pathway to enjoying God's blessing on our lives. "Doubtless, the more complete our sanctification the more intense our blessedness."[48]

The Psalter is unequivocal in its claim: those who pursue holiness can expect and enjoy God's blessing. But what does this blessing precisely mean? In a word, it centers on happiness. Unfortunately, both in Spurgeon's day and our day, the label "holy" has a negative connotation. The Christian life is commonly perceived as an adherence to a "not-to-do" list which removes enjoyable activities. Who wants to be known as a killjoy and a fuddy-duddy among friends? Spurgeon refuted this perspective by objecting, "True religion is not cold and dry!"[49] He would have nothing to do with such a dismal view of personal holiness.

Contrary to his critics who believed holiness had very little to do with a joyful life, Spurgeon argued holiness has everything to do with happiness—a

---

45. Spurgeon, *Treasury of David*, 5:15.
46. Spurgeon, *Treasury of David*, 5:139.
47. Spurgeon, *Treasury of David*, 5:139.
48. Spurgeon, *Treasury of David*, 5:140.
49. Spurgeon, *Treasury of David*, 5:139.

term he frequently applied to holiness.[50] God's blessing is a person's richest source of happiness. When sin is forgiven (32:2), the person bubbles with joy! Since "blessed" is plural in Hebrew, Spurgeon exclaims, "Oh, the blessednesses! The double joys, the bundles of happiness, the mountains of delight!"[51] A forgiven person who lives in gratitude to God discovers that "holiness is his happiness."[52] We also experience true happiness when we are in awe of our holy God and delightfully obey him (112:1). "It is a blessed thing to delight in holiness, and surely he who gave us this delight will work in us the yet higher joy of possessing and practicing it," Spurgeon assures us.[53] Rather than a holy life being a dreary experience, we discover that there is "no greater happiness than to be perfectly holy."[54]

Following Jesus and pursuing holiness will be challenging at times. But since we are made for God's purposes and designed to become like Jesus Christ, we need to "settle it in our hearts as a first postulate . . . that holiness is happiness."[55] Then, with a humble resolve to grow in holiness, we can join with Spurgeon who vowed to "set it [holiness] before me as my life's ambition."[56] If we want to be truly happy, we would do well to follow in his footsteps.

Conclusion

We have explored the nature of personal holiness and have discovered that God intends us to grow in holiness in every sphere of our soul. Holiness must shape our interior life, including the desires of our heart, the will to choose to obey, and the emotions filled with true happiness. Our interior life needs to be transformed to move us from our sinful nature to increasing conformity to Jesus Christ. Growth in holiness will impact our speech and actions. No part of our being is to remain untouched in the pursuit of holiness. With the knowledge that holiness is God's plan for our lives, we can

50. The *Treasury* mentions various authors who equate "happiness" with "blessedness" (Spurgeon, *Treasury of David*, 1:4, 19).

51. Spurgeon, *Treasury of David*, 2:82.

52. Spurgeon, *Treasury of David*, 5:15. Ryle encourages us to "follow after eminent holiness ourselves, and recommend it boldly to others. This is the only way to be really happy. . . . Let us feel convinced, whatever others may say, that holiness is happiness" (*Holiness*, 75). Packer remarks that holiness is "essentially a happy business" *Rediscovering Holiness*, 87).

53. Spurgeon, *Treasury of David*, 5:209.

54. Spurgeon, *Treasury of David*, 5:139.

55. Spurgeon, *Treasury of David*, 5:140.

56. Spurgeon, *Treasury of David*, 5:140.

throw ourselves into this pursuit of holiness. Spurgeon encourages us not to "shrink from the glorious enterprise of living a pure and gracious life."[57]

Since a biblical view of holiness must permeate every part of the "anatomy of the soul," we must explore one of its essential areas—the unseen heart. In the Psalms, the heart is central to one's growth in holiness. We will explore this area of our lives in the next chapter.

---

57. Spurgeon, *Treasury of David*, 5:157.

Chapter 3

Our Heart and Holiness

Charles Spurgeon disdained moralism. To live a good, ethical life apart from the supernatural work of the Holy Spirit was unthinkable for him. Moralism ran contrary to the true nature of holiness. Yet, in his day, churches were filled with people who lived good moral lives without a personal relationship to Jesus Christ. However, trying to adopt this approach to the Christian life, Spurgeon said, was like trying "to teach a tiger the virtues of vegetarianism."[1] Attempting to change behavior without a fundamental change in one's nature will be a dismal failure in the long run. It's not surprising that Spurgeon warned his theological students that they should not moralize in their preaching. Their task was not to "whiten tombs, but to open them."[2]

For Spurgeon, the spiritual heart was at the core of holiness. This priority shaped the way he lived his life. For example, he disliked written prayers and liturgy which contributed to formalism and ruled out the heart. Prayers had to come from deep within a person. So, his prayers were fervent and heartfelt. At one time, Spurgeon remarked, "Prayer with the heart is the heart of prayer."[3] Even if a person stumbled in public prayer, this was acceptable to Spurgeon as long as the prayer came from

---

1. Reeves, *Spurgeon on the Christian Life*, 95.
2. Reeves, *Spurgeon on the Christian Life*, 67.
3. Morden, *Communion with Christ*, 137–38.

the heart. Likewise, when Spurgeon preached, he did not want to give intellectual sermons which ignored the individual's heart. Addressing the importance of the heart, he commented, "The object of all true preaching is the heart: we aim at divorcing the heart from sin, and wedding it to Christ."[4] As Michael Reeves states, Spurgeon's goal was to see both unbelievers and followers of Jesus to be "transformed at the very deepest level, their affections and desires turning away from their naturally cherished sins to Christ."[5] Spurgeon's preaching aimed at the heart in order to see his people grow in holiness.

Spurgeon's dislike for moralism, and his priority on the heart in prayer and preaching are expressions of his own heart for Jesus Christ. At his church, the Metropolitan Tabernacle, he fervently prayed, "Oh to love the Saviour with a passion that can never cool. . . . Oh to delight in God with a holy overflowing rejoicing that can never be stopped, so that we might live to glorify God at the highest bent of our powers, living with enthusiasm, burning, blazing, being consumed with the indwelling God who worketh all things in us according to his will."[6]

To sum up, "Spurgeon's heart desire was to increasingly delight in God. He wanted to know Him more, to love Him more, to enjoy closer and closer fellowship with Him . . . he wanted to 'live to glorify God' with energy and 'enthusiasm.'"[7]

For those who are interested in godly living, it is not uncommon to give particular attention to their conduct whether it be in the home, the workplace, or in church. This focus often leads them to conform to certain expectations formed and enforced by others. They may appear godly by outward appearances, but if one could peer into the inner chamber of the individual's life, the person might be shocked and disillusioned by what is discovered below the surface. Resentment may be brewing toward others who have imposed apparently unfair standards on the person. Anger and bitterness is aimed at God, who is seemingly responsible for the miserable failures to live a victorious and joyful Christian life. Failure to pay attention

---

4. Reeves, *Spurgeon on the Christian Life*, 66.
5. Reeves, *Spurgeon on the Christian Life*, 66.
6. Morden, *C. H. Spurgeon*, 88–89.
7. Morden, *C. H. Spurgeon*, 88–89.

to the interior life actually hinders true holiness occurring within the follower of Jesus.

Approaches to godliness which give exclusive focus to the intellect or to the emotions lack the needed balance. James Houston reminds us that if we are "too rational or too emotional," it will hinder the goal to "develop an authentic faith in God."[8] Rationalism and sentimentalism are extremes, and thereby inadequate by themselves to pave the way to holiness. These approaches must be avoided because they lack an integrative center for our lives. This does not mean that we ignore or dismiss the intellect or the emotions. Both of these are elements of authentic holiness.

In order to become more like Jesus, we have to pay attention to the human heart. Qoheleth, the wise writer of Proverbs, instructs us, "Above all else, guard your heart for it is the wellspring of life" (Prov 4:23). He knew the importance of the heart and we would do well to heed his advice. Contrary to the popular opinion that the heart is synonymous with emotions, the biblical understanding of the heart is more comprehensive than this limited view of the heart. The extensive biblical use of the word "heart" (over eight hundred fifty times in the Old Testament) is an indication of the importance of the heart in our lives and growth in holiness. The Hebrew word for "heart" (*lev*) is mentioned nearly a hundred times in the Psalms. This word is used synonymously with the "soul."[9]

Spurgeon understood the importance of the heart, which he says "is the rudder of the soul, and till the Lord take it in hand we steer in a false and foul way."[10] Elsewhere, he comments that the heart is the "region which is so vital as to be the very source of life."[11] Therefore, holiness entails a spiritual progression in "our hearts and lives."[12]

Spurgeon wasn't alone in stressing the importance of the heart in human existence. According to Packer, the heart is the "central core of the personal self." Out of the heart flows "the thoughts, desires, motivations, emotions, dreams, attitudes, plans, hopes, [and] reactions."[13] Houston states that the heart is the core of a person's life. The emotions, will, and intellect "are all united in the heart. Clearly, it also focuses on the innermost part of the human personality, the meeting place between people and God."[14]

---

8. Houston, *Heart's Desire*, 17–18.
9. Sorg, "Heart," 180–84.
10. Spurgeon, *Treasury of David*, 2:405.
11. Spurgeon, *Treasury of David*, 2:407.
12. Bebbington quotes Spurgeon who preached on sanctification (*Holiness*, 45).
13. Packer and Nystrom, *Praying*, 191.
14. Houston, *Heart's Desire*, 18–19.

It is the heart which "unites the mind, will and emotion in an integrated way of living, allowing us to think, desire, and feel as a whole person."[15] Willard also views the heart as the "center or core to which every other component of the self owes its proper functioning." He goes on to say, "The heart is where decisions and choices are made for the whole person. That is its function."[16]

The heart is not only the integrative center of our lives, but it is essential for personal growth in holiness. Since Spurgeon believed that the "heart is the master" in our lives, it is God who "must change the heart, unite the heart, encourage the heart, strengthen the heart, and enlarge the heart, and then the course of [one's] life will be gracious, sincere, happy, and earnest."[17] Only the Lord can "circumcise" the human heart, making it possible for his people to wholeheartedly love him (Deut 30:6). The one who has a spiritually circumcised heart is enabled to love and obey God (Deut 10:12–16).

In the New Testament, the inner work of God transforming our "circumcised" hearts (Rom 2:29) will be reflected in changing our character and our conduct (Gal 5:22–23; 2 Pet 1:3–8). By paying proper attention to the heart, we discover new insights about the nature of holiness, the distorted desires and longings which hinder holiness, and the essential path to growing in holiness. Spurgeon's thoughts are in alignment with the Puritans who would say, "The heart of holiness is holiness in the heart."[18] Commenting on the necessity of "clean hands and a pure heart" (24:4), Spurgeon remarked,

> True religion is heart-work. . . . We may lose our hands and yet live, but we could not lose our heart and still live; the very life of our being lies in the inner nature, and hence the imperative need of purity within. There must be a work of grace in the core of the heart as well as in the palm of the hand, or our religion is a delusion. May God grant that our inward powers may be cleansed by the sanctifying Spirit, so that we may love holiness and abhor all sin.[19]

Packer identifies the heart as a critical area in order to transform one's conduct. He writes that "holiness begins with the heart. Holiness starts inside a person, with a right purpose that seeks to express itself in a right performance."[20] Also describing holiness in practical terms, Willard states,

---

15. Houston, *Heart's Desire*, 16.
16. Willard, *Renovation of the Heart*, 29–30.
17. Spurgeon, *Treasury of David*, 5:193.
18. Packer, *Rediscovering Holiness*, 77.
19. Spurgeon, *Treasury of David*, 1:376.
20. Packer, *Rediscovering Holiness*, 22.

"Those with a well-kept heart are persons who are prepared for and capable of responding to the situations of life in ways that are good and right."[21] In other words, if we desire to please God by the way we live out our faith, then we must give serious attention to the heart so we can be "actively responsive to God."[22]

Yet, in our moments of honesty, we have to admit that our hearts don't always long for holiness. We are painfully aware that we live with a "dividedness that infects the Christian heart." At times we want to flee from God and other times we want to cling to him. This longing and craving for God reminds us that we experience a "homesickness for holiness."[23] This chapter explores the heart that is at home with God, the ways which alienate us from feeling at home with God, and the ways our hearts can increasingly be at home with the Lord.

The Heart of Holiness

In this section, we will survey the Psalms to discover various characteristics of the human heart which longs to grow in holy character and conduct.

A Trusting Heart

David exclaims, "My heart trusts in him, and I am helped" (28:7). This "heart trust" does not occur automatically in our lives because it requires "heart work."[24] Like cardio exercises, our faith has to be exercised and stretched in life's daily challenges and by doing so, our trust will be strengthened over a period of time. Our trusting hearts are ultimately shaped not by our efforts, but by our confidence in the living and powerful God. David testifies, "I trust in the Lord" (31:6) rather than the "worthless idols" (v. 6) which compete for one's heart. This trust in God and rejection of competing gods contribute to David's life of holiness. That is, we are better positioned to face whatever comes our way, which leads us to the next characteristic of a holy heart.

---

21. Willard, *Renovation of the Heart*, 29.
22. Packer, *Rediscovering Holiness*, 22.
23. Williams, *Singleness of Heart*, 2.
24. Spurgeon, *Treasury of David*, 2:22.

A Steadfast Heart

When our trust in the Lord grows, our hearts are steady and ready to face what is ahead of us. David testifies, "My heart is steadfast, O God, my heart is steadfast" (57:7). Considering that David was confronted by his enemies (v. 6), Spurgeon remarks, "One would have thought he would have said, 'my heart is fluttered' but no, he is calm, firm, happy, resolute, established."[25] In a similar fashion, Ps 108 speaks of the same steadfast heart. Here, David begins with praise with a steadfast heart (vv. 1–5). Spurgeon understands a steadfast heart to mean that "I am settled in one mind and cannot be driven from it. My heart has taken hold and abides in one resolve."[26] David's words in the opening verses of this psalm "express the continued resolve and praise of a man who has already weathered many a campaign, has overcome all home conflicts and is looking forward to conquests far and wide."[27] Trust in the Lord and his past deliverance foster a steady heart prepared to face life. This heart attitude of trust enables him to move on to prayer "in a remarkably confident manner" (vv. 6–12).[28]

A Pure Heart

David indicates that the path to a steadfast heart is a "pure" heart (51:10). Given the reality of sin in our lives, is it an unrealistic expectation to have a pure heart? Asaph, a leader in David's Levitical choirs, would respond with a resounding "no." He declares, "Surely God is good to Israel, to those who are pure in heart" (v. 1). The psalmists provide us with two aspects of a pure heart.

First, this heart is undivided. In Ps 86:11, David, a man after God's heart, asks God to give him an undivided heart so that he may fear or revere the Lord. His full allegiance is to God. However, a holy heart committed to God still has struggles. As Spurgeon puts it, "Give me one heart to walk therein, for too often I feel a heart and a heart, two natures contending, two principles struggling for sovereignty."[29] When we surrender to sin's influence, our hearts are affected and Spurgeon notes, "A man of divided heart is weak."[30] Therefore, "the heart must not be divided with many objects if the

---

25. Spurgeon, *Treasury of David*, 2:477.
26. Spurgeon, *Treasury of David*, 4:426.
27. Spurgeon, *Treasury of David*, 4:425.
28. Spurgeon, *Treasury of David*, 4:425.
29. Spurgeon, *Treasury of David*, 3:466–67.
30. Spurgeon, *Treasury of David*, 3:467.

Lord is to be sought by us."³¹ We need an undivided heart (v. 11b), which makes purity a real possibility in our lives. We obey and worship the Lord (vv. 11–12) with all of our heart (119:2), which has been purified of divided loyalties.

Second, a pure heart involves cleaning up the impurities in our hearts. When David speaks of the importance of a pure heart (24:4) we are reminded that can't fool ourselves about the condition of our spiritual hearts. Spurgeon warns us, "False motives may at times sway us, and we may fall into mistaken notions of our own spiritual condition before God. . . . No true heart can rest in a false view of itself."³² A correct view of the human heart includes both the pervasiveness of sin and the reality that our hearts can become increasingly pure. Cleaning up our hearts requires God's work in our daily activities. "There must be a work of grace in the core of the heart as well as in the palm of the hand, or our religion is a delusion."³³ As our hearts become more purified, we will have a greater longing for God.

A Longing Heart

Holiness is also characterized by a longing for God (42:1–2). While the psalmist employs the term "soul" rather than "heart," these two words are used interchangeably. The psalmist describes longing for God with our whole hearts (119:2) and our soul (119:20). Spurgeon describes the psalmist's longing for God as "heartsick" and "his very self, his deepest life, was insatiable for a sense of the divine presence."³⁴ The psalmist has a continual longing for God. Spurgeon writes, "Thirst is a perpetual appetite, and should not be forgotten, and even thus continual is the heart's longing after God. When it is natural for us to long for as for an animal to thirst, it is well with our souls, however painful our feelings."³⁵ A longing for a stronger personal relationship with the Lord and to be more like him contributes to our personal holiness.

The longing of our hearts for God includes our desires. Commenting on the soul longing for God (119:20), Spurgeon states, "True godliness lies very much in desires. As we are not what we shall be, so also we are not what we would be. The desires of gracious men after holiness are intense. . . .

---

31. Spurgeon, *Treasury of David*, 5:142.
32. Spurgeon, *Treasury of David*, 5:191.
33. Spurgeon, *Treasury of David*, 1:376.
34. Spurgeon, *Treasury of David*, 2:270–71.
35. Spurgeon, *Treasury of David*, 2:271.

What a blessing it is when all our desires are after the things of God. We may well long for such longings."[36]

This same heart longing is expressed in Ps 63:1 ("my soul thirsts for you, my body longs for you"). Spurgeon challenges us: "Only after God, therefore, let us pant. Let all desires be gathered into one. Seeking first the kingdom of God" is the expression of a longing heart.[37] We are wise to long for God, for "only God himself can satisfy the craving of the soul." Then, we are deeply contented, regardless of our circumstances. We share the psalmist's experience that, as Spurgeon says, "There was no desert in his heart, though there was a desert around him."[38]

A half-hearted pursuit shouldn't characterize our longing for God. The psalmist uses three terms in Ps 84:1 to describe his passion for God. He "yearns," "faints," and will "cry out" to the LORD. This longing is "holy love-sickness" which is "deep and insatiable."[39] This longing wasn't for deliverance or a quick fix from God. "It was God himself that he pined for, the only living and true God. His whole nature entered into his longing," Spurgeon emphasizes.[40] Holiness is reflected in one's joy, aroused by Jesus' love.

What does it actually mean for our hearts to long for God? Spurgeon elaborates, "Seeking after God signifies a desire to commune with him more closely, to follow him more fully, to enter into more perfect union with his mind and will, to promote his glory, and to realize completely all that he is to holy hearts."[41] Our longing to enjoy fellowship with the Lord, as well as obey and live for his purposes, are reflections of a holy life. Of course, our longing for God is not something we can muster up within ourselves. Seeking after God is a "mark of grace" which gives us the power to grow in holiness.[42] With our longing for God satisfied, we are able to rest more fully in his presence.

A Restful Heart

When we are caught up in the hassles and frustrations of the day, we can respond in ways that are far less than pleasing to God. David experienced cruel opposition (62:3–4, 116:3). However, at the same time, he found "rest"

36. Spurgeon, *Treasury of David*, 5:73.
37. Spurgeon, *Treasury of David*, 3:66.
38. Spurgeon, *Treasury of David*, 3:65.
39. Spurgeon, *Treasury of David*, 3:433.
40. Spurgeon, *Treasury of David*, 3:433.
41. Spurgeon, *Treasury of David*, 5:142.
42. Spurgeon, *Treasury of David*, 2:271.

in who God is (62:1–2, 116:5–7). Spurgeon comments, "The presence of God alone could awe his heart into quietude, submission, rest, and acquiescence; but when that was felt, not a rebellious word or thought broke the peaceful silence."[43] A restful heart can become a restless heart and so David reminds himself of the importance of not forgetting to find rest in God (62:5). This suggests that there must be some intentionality on our part. As Spurgeon puts it, "The soul is apt to be dragged away from its anchorage . . . we must, therefore, stir ourselves up to maintain the holy position which we were at first able to assume."[44] By God's grace, we have to habitually cultivate a heart which finds rest in the character of God. With a heart focused on God, we are enabled to obey him.

An Obedient Heart

The willingness to obey God is the outflow of a heart which has grown in trust, steadfastness, purity, a longing for God, and resting in him. In Ps 27:7–14, the psalmist declares he hears God's voice calling him to come and talk to his LORD (v. 8). In response, he says, "LORD, I am coming" (v. 8 NLT). He is obeying God! Spurgeon comments, "If we would have the Lord hear our voice, we must be careful to respond to his voice. The true heart should echo the will of God." This is possible when we have a "cheerful obedience of heart."[45] The holy heart is sensitive to God's voice and responds in obedience to it. Here we see the beautiful connection between growth in holy character and willing obedience by godly conduct.

Heart Issues Hindering Holiness

Often, we excuse our negative reactions by placing the blame on challenging life experiences. However, Ps 80:1–7 steers us away from a focus on externals. The psalmist cries out to God to restore us (vv.3–7). Spurgeon notes that the best turn of events is not "that of circumstances but of character."[46] We need to call out to God to restore or renovate our needy hearts which must be aligned with God's heart. In this section, we will examine the psalmists who refer to the conditions of the heart which hinder holiness.

---

43. Spurgeon, *Treasury of David*, 3:48.
44. Spurgeon, *Treasury of David*, 3:50.
45. Spurgeon, *Treasury of David*, 2:4.
46. Spurgeon, *Treasury of David*, 3:388.

A Fickle Heart

Psalm 78 gives us the sad account of the Israelites who were disloyal to God even though he was faithful to them. Twice, Asaph writes their "hearts were not loyal" to God (vv. 8, 37). They had fickle hearts. As a result, they disobeyed and forgot God's goodness (vv. 10–11). Their spiritual dementia led them to rebel against God (vv. 17–19, 40–41). Spurgeon comments that "they were fickle as a weathercock, every wind turned them, their minds was not settled on God." As he painfully reminds us, we can be "hot today for holiness, but cold towards it tomorrow. . . . Surely the heart is a chameleon."[47]

As an expression of rebellion against God, the Israelites' fickle hearts led them into the unholy practice of idolatry (vv. 56–58). Our idols may be material objects and possessions which we devote ourselves to with excessive attention and time (115:4). There are also the intangibles which we adore such as status and success. This idolatry is a matter of the heart for it "is not consistent with true grace in the heart," declares Spurgeon.[48] Idols ensnare our hearts (106:36), which leads to a destructive lifestyle (vv. 37–39). False idols consume our lives, leaving us like them—living, but dead (115:8) rather than enjoying God's presence. We have to acknowledge that we, who confess love for Jesus, are prone to be fickle people!

An Envious Heart

Asaph mentions that God is good to those who are pure in heart (73:1). In contrast, he honestly admits he had an envious heart (v. 3) because he notices the many ways the wicked have prospered—physically (v. 4), with ease of life (v. 5), with power (vv. 6–11), and economically (v. 12). His envious heart affected his actions (v. 2). To keep a pure heart seemed to be an exercise of futility (v. 13), which is a wrong assumption based on verse 1.

We may also envy those who are godly and successful. The Israelites envied Moses and Aaron (106:16). "It is the mark of bad men that they are envious of the good, and spiteful against their best benefactors."[49] Spurgeon observes that the Israelites had crossed the Red Sea or the "sea of weeds" but "far worse seeds grew in their hearts."[50]

---

47. Spurgeon, *Treasury of David*, 3:339.
48. Spurgeon, *Treasury of David*, 3:344.
49. Spurgeon, *Treasury of David*, 4:368.
50. Spurgeon, *Treasury of David*, 4:366.

Our consumeristic society incessantly appeals to our human nature with ways we can have more and presumably be happier. The psalmist admits to the personal draw toward "selfish gain" (119:36). He had, Spurgeon says, a "wandering desire, an inordinate leaning of his soul to worldly gain." In such cases, he comments, "The only way to cure a wrong leaning is to have the soul bent in the opposite direction. Holiness of heart is the cure for covetousness. What a blessing it is that we may ask the Lord even for an inclination. Our wills are free, and yet without violating their liberty, grace can incline us in the right direction."[51] The pursuit of holiness redirects the heart's longing for God rather than for fleeting temporal possessions.

Therefore, we need to be cautious about an envious heart controlling our lives. Spurgeon warns that "errors of heart and head soon affect the conduct. There is an intimate connection between the heart and the feet.... How ought we to watch the inner being, since it has so forcible an effect upon the outward character."[52] Since envy affects our character and conduct, growing in holiness enables us to resist an envious heart.

A Stubborn Heart

Although the word "stubborn" is used only twice in the Psalter (78:8, 81:12) to describe God's people, the reality of stubbornness is seen throughout the pages of Scripture. In Ps 81:12, we are told that God "gave them [the Israelites] over to their stubborn hearts." Spurgeon sadly notes, "No punishment is more just or more severe than this . . . they are let alone to work out their own destruction." Their stubborn hearts led to following their own ways which are "at all times in direct opposition to God's way."[53] Stubborn hearts foster unholy living before God and others.

The Psalms paint a clear picture of our hearts plagued by sin, which hinders our pursuit of holiness. When you and I don't trust in God's character and his word, we chase other gods to give us what we want. With fickle hearts marked by rebellion and envy, we pursue those idols believing they will help us. We will hold stubbornly to this belief until such time as God is able to break into our lives. Then, he is able to begin to do a new and good work in our lives.

---

51. Spurgeon, *Treasury of David*, 5:210.
52. Spurgeon, *Treasury of David*, 3:247.
53. Spurgeon, *Treasury of David*, 3:402.

Renewing the Heart toward Holiness

In order to move from our lives being dominated by sin, our hearts require radical renewal. As Willard notes, "The greatest need you and I have—the greatest need of collective humanity—is *renovation of our heart*. That spiritual place within us from which outlook, choices, and actions come has been formed by a world away from God. Now it must be transformed" (italics his).[54] How does this heart renewal occur in the lives of those who know Jesus Christ as Savior?

A Broken Heart

Songs, novels, and personal stories tell us that each of us aren't immune from suffering a broken heart. When our hearts are broken, it is one of life's most painful experiences which can keep us from entering into a closer relationship with others. Yet, God can use our broken hearts to cultivate growth in holiness in our lives. With insight, Spurgeon remarks, "No heart is so whole in its seekings after God as a heart which is broken . . . it may be broken and be whole, and it can never be whole until it is broken."[55] Brokenness is a paradoxical path to holiness or wholeness.

King David experienced insults, rejection and the accompanying scorn, disgrace, and shame. As a result, he lived with a broken heart (69:19–21). God, in his mercy, sees our broken hearts and when we call out to him; he hears our needy cries for divine help (v. 32). In our brokenness, the need for God shapes our humbled heart to be dependent on him. Humility is an essential mark of holiness.

Sometimes our hearts are broken by our own foolish actions. In Ps 38:1–9, David is in physical (vv. 3, 7) and spiritual agony (vv. 4, 8) due to the guilt of his sin. He describes his heart as "badly crushed" and experiences "agitation" (NASB) in his heart (v. 8). Spurgeon believes this psalm stands out because of its description of sin. "The fact is, it is a spiritual leprosy; it is an inward disease which is here described." Once again, we see David calling out to the Lord for help. It is a hopeful sign when a believer does reach out to God and Spurgeon comforts us by reminding us that it is God who "reads the longings of our heart. . . . The good Physician understands the symptoms of our disease and sees the hidden evil which they reveal, hence

---

54. Willard, *Renovation of the Heart*, 14.
55. Spurgeon, *Treasury of David*, 5:142.

our case is safe in his hands."[56] Spiritual healing can begin when we yield our hearts to the one who best knows our "anatomy of the soul."

In Ps 51:17, David refers to his "broken spirit, a broken and contrite heart." Spurgeon explains that a broken heart involves "deep sorrow" and a "mourning for sin."[57] This response to God places him in the right position before God. "A heart crushed is a fragrant heart . . . contrite hearts he seeks after."[58] This is the only verse in the Psalms that refers to contrition as synonym for brokenness. One thinks of Peter who denied Jesus three times. We are told that he "broke down and wept" (Mark 14:72). While tears may be shed, it is the condition of the heart which is most critical here.

Psalm 73:21-24 further describes a broken heart. The psalmist has wrestled with envy (vv. 1-12), has questioned his own holiness (v. 13), and has felt pain in his heart (vv. 16). Now he is filled with bitterness and anguish (v. 21). Spurgeon comments, "His pain had been intense. . . . It was a deep seated sorrow, and one which penetrated his inmost being."[59] The psalmist is a pain-filled, broken man. However, this is the starting point for spiritual recovery! He has a transformative experience of God's presence in the sanctuary where he worshiped God (v. 17). He realizes that the so-called "good life" is not so great and now he affirms God is still actively involved in his life (vv. 23-24). Rather than focusing his thoughts on the prosperity of the wicked, his attention is riveted on the Lord (v. 25). As Spurgeon says, "Our former mistakes are a blessing, when they drive us to this. The end of our own wisdom is the beginning of our being wise."[60] In recognition of our brokenness, we realize that only Jesus can heal us by his many means of grace extended to us.

We also need to be broken about the unconscious sins in our hearts. After David honestly admitted his hatred of his enemies (139:22), he asks God to search his interior life in order to expose any unconscious sin in his life (vv. 23-24). We need the Holy Spirit to probe and surface to our conscience any wrongful thoughts, attitudes or desires. As Spurgeon puts it when we pray, "Read not alone the desires of my heart, but the fugitive thoughts of my head. . . . [God] is graciously inclined towards us, and is willing to bend his omniscience to serve the end of our sanctification."[61]

---

56. Spurgeon, *Treasury of David*, 2:200.
57. Spurgeon, *Treasury of David*, 2:407.
58. Spurgeon, *Treasury of David*, 2:407.
59. Spurgeon, *Treasury of David*, 3:252.
60. Spurgeon, *Treasury of David*, 3:252.
61. Spurgeon, *Treasury of David*, 6:266.

We need to be broken of those sins we are very aware of and those that are revealed to us by God.

Confession of Sin

It is a fallacy to believe we can truly heal our broken lives apart from God's help. Our self-management techniques will short-circuit the full recovery and healing we need. We may want to suppress our sin by arguing we don't need to confess since God is omniscient and knows our wrongfulness anyhow. In Ps 32:2, David warns us of the negative consequence when we don't acknowledge our wrongdoing. He was convicted of sin but he remained silent (v. 3). By not confessing his sins, he was affected physically and emotionally. While his physical strength was sapped, he groaned incessantly (v. 4). David also suffered spiritually because he realized that God's "hand was heavy upon me" (v. 4, 51:8). Spurgeon observes, "He was silent as to confession, but not as to sorrow."[62] Unconfessed sin drains our hearts of joy and robs us of the healing of our brokenness.

David recognized he had to turn to God who would rebuild his life (51:1). The wise course of action is to confess our sin against others before God (vv. 2–5) because, ultimately, we have sinned against him (v. 4). Spurgeon wisely notes, "To injure our fellow men is sin, mainly because in so doing we violate the law of God."[63] Growth in holiness demands a right response to God and to others. The vertical and horizontal dimensions of holiness are inseparable.

Confession also includes those sins which aren't initially so obvious to us. David knew that God desires "truth in the inner parts" or the inner recesses of his soul (51:6). It is for this reason David asks God to search his heart to make himself aware of those less glaring sins (139:23–24). Holiness, without going deep into our hearts, is shallow. Spurgeon notes,

> Reality, sincerity, true holiness, heart fidelity, these are the demands of God. He cares not for the pretense of purity, he looks to the mind, heart, and soul. Always has the Holy One of Israel estimated men by their inner nature, and not by their outward professions; to him the inward is as visible as the outward, and he rightly judges that the essential character of an action lies in the motive of him who works it.[64]

---

62. Spurgeon, *Treasury of David*, 2:82.
63. Spurgeon, *Treasury of David*, 2:403.
64. Spurgeon, *Treasury of David*, 3:403.

Since confession plays an important part in our holiness, Spurgeon says we should wisely ask God to "unveil the secrets of the soul" in order to "bring out our sins."[65] This is not easy for us because it includes acknowledging the embarrassing sins which we have deeply buried by our denials and rationalizations. Holiness does require radical heart surgery.

Honest confession before God benefits our growth in holiness in two ways. First, confession keeps our hearts tender before God. Spurgeon notes, "It is useless to conceal [sin], for it is well known to God; it is beneficial to us to own it, for a full confession softens and humbles the heart."[66] Second, confession facilitates a clean heart which influences the rest of our lives (51:10). Spurgeon comments that "the affections must be rectified first, or all our nature will go amiss. The heart is the rudder of the soul, and till the Lord take it in hand we steer in a false and foul way."[67] The inclination of our hearts' desires shape the direction of our lives. Holiness originates within the heart and its desires and emanates to our actions and speech.

Therefore, confession is good for the soul because it contributes to our holiness. When we willingly open our hearts to God, he is able to expose sin in the dark recesses and begin the process of bringing about much-needed healing. However, an awareness and confession of sin is insufficient to cultivate holiness because it is only one step in the process of sanctification. We also need a changed heart.

A Renewed Heart

The Psalms express the desire for a renewed heart. For example, David asks the Lord to give him a pure heart and a steadfast spirit (51:10). This can't be done by sheer effort on our part, so Spurgeon explains that God's intervention in our lives is very much needed. In verse 10, David uses two words ("create" and "renew") to highlight our need for God's grace. The Hebrew word for "create" (*bara*) is only used in the Old Testament with God as the subject. God can only create (*bara*) the world (Gen 1:1). Likewise, he has to create "what is not there at all" in our hearts and renew "that which is there but in a sadly feeble state."[68] Following our confession of sin, the renewal of our spiritual hearts rests with God's active working in our lives. With his power, God is able to give people a new heart (Ezek 36:26; Jer 24:7).

---

65. Spurgeon, *Treasury of David*, 2:83.
66. Spurgeon, *Treasury of David*, 2:83.
67. Spurgeon, *Treasury of David*, 2:405.
68. Spurgeon, *Treasury of David*, 2:405.

Throughout Ps 119, the psalmist expresses seven times the desire for renewal (vv. 25, 37, 40, 107, 149, 154, 156). What is the nature of this renewal? In the language of his day, Spurgeon states the psalmist is asking for a "quickening" which is a revival of his spirit. "In reviving the life," Spurgeon notes, "the whole man is renewed." He is suggesting that we need revival when we are "depressed in spirit, weak, and bent toward the ground."[69] This is particularly true when we are going through afflictions and suffering (119:107). Spiritual renewal is also needed to enable us to resist yielding to the influence of sin by being conformed to God's will (119:40). To see this become a reality, Spurgeon declares, we need the "Holy Spirit who can pour new life into us." Spurgeon is not referring to the new birth, but to the need to grow in holiness. As he says, "Let the life we already possess show itself by longing for more."[70] God desires to renew our lives by a greater dependence on him for spiritual strength to resist the influence of sin. Whatever the specific need, the psalmist's plea to "renew my life" (119:156) captures the full range of spiritual renewal. This transformation includes "more love, more grace, more faith, more courage, more strength," which enables us to enjoy God and face life's challenges.[71] The renewal of the heart is a dynamic process ultimately involving God's working in our lives. His activity in us allows us to experience a holy life.

The evidence of a renewed heart is marked with consecration or dedication to God. For example, David exhorts God's people to "turn from evil and do good; seek peace and pursue it" (34:14). This is genuine consecration which is evidence of holiness. Spurgeon clarifies that "Positive virtue ['do good'] promotes negative virtue ['turn from evil']; he who does good is sure to avoid evil."[72]

In Ps 73:25–28, Asaph contrasts himself with those who desert and abandon God (v. 27). He testifies that "God is the strength of my heart" (v. 26). Consequently, comments Spurgeon, "He turns away from the glitter which fascinated him to the true gold which was his real treasure. He felt that his God was better to him than all the wealth, health, honor, and peace, which he had so much envied."[73] With a renewed heart, he is passionate about God. "His heart would be kept up by divine love," Spurgeon continues, "and filled eternally with divine glory. . . . There is nothing desirable save God; let us, then, desire only him. All other things must pass away; let

---

69. Spurgeon, *Treasury of David*, 5:189.
70. Spurgeon, *Treasury of David*, 5:212.
71. Spurgeon, *Treasury of David*, 5:414.
72. Spurgeon, *Treasury of David*, 2:125.
73. Spurgeon, *Treasury of David*, 3:253.

our hearts abide in him, who alone abides forever."[74] It is not surprising that Spurgeon emphasized a consecrated life because it was "fundamental to true holiness."[75]

The relationship between consecration and holiness is clearly seen in Ps 37:27, 31. David dedicates his life to God (v. 27) because his interior life is in order (v. 31). Spurgeon comments on this relationship: "To love holiness, to have the motives and desires sanctified, to be in one's inmost nature obedient to the Lord—this is the surest method of making the whole run of our life efficient for its great ends."[76] Holiness is possible by a renewed heart which wants to lovingly obey God.

A Life of Repentance

With a heart that is being renewed by God, we will turn away from anything that is displeasing to God. Repentance isn't only necessary the first time we enter into a relationship with Jesus Christ, but it is an ongoing necessity to cultivate our loving relationship with him. Even though the word "repentance" or its cognates don't appear in the Psalms, the Psalter addresses the nature of repentance and its relationship to holiness.

Two basic types of repentance are portrayed by the psalmists. Shallow repentance is described in Ps 78:32–37. The Israelites are in the desert where God punished them for their disobedience. They eagerly turn to God by saying all the right things to him (vv. 24, 36). However, they lied because their hearts were not right before God (vv. 36–37). This superficial repentance occurs when serious heart work is not thoroughly done and minds are not really set on the Lord. Spurgeon notes, "There was no depth in their repentance; it was not heart work."[77] As a result, this kind of repentance only reflects a fickle heart which hinders true holiness.

A genuinely repentant heart is revealed by a real change in one's actions. In Ps 51:13–15, David genuinely repents of his sin. After turning away from sin (vv. 1–12), David mentions that he will teach others God's ways so that "sinners will turn back to you" (v. 13). With the repentance of his sin, he wants God to use his own past actions for, as Spurgeon says, the "recovery of many who . . . have turned aside unto crooked ways."[78] Finally, David's repentance is reflected by a right heart attitude, which prompts him

---

74. Spurgeon, *Treasury of David*, 3:253.
75. Morden, *Communion with Christ*, 228.
76. Spurgeon, *Treasury of David*, 2:177–78.
77. Spurgeon, *Treasury of David*, 3:339.
78. Spurgeon, *Treasury of David*, 2:406.

to worship God (vv. 15, 17). The pursuit of holiness requires ongoing repentance of our wrongdoing. This would be arduous if it were not for our hearts being renewed by God's Spirit. When our heart is rightly postured before God, then we desire to repent so that we can progress along our journey in holiness.

A Life of Integrity

When our hearts have been broken and sin has been acknowledged, God renews our hearts with a new desire to love and obey him. Now it is possible to live with integrity because the interior life is integrated with the exterior life. Integrity shouldn't be equated with a sinless life, otherwise integrity would be out of the reach for everyone. In fact, David—like us—was imperfect, and he was still known as a person of integrity (78:72). How could this be? Spurgeon explains that "whatever faults he had, he was unfeignedly sincere in his allegiance to Israel's superior king [Jehovah]; he shepherded for God with honest heart."[79] He had been a broken man who experienced divine mercy and renewal in his life. In gratitude to God, David's heart was fully committed to the Lord and he lived out the Lord's purposes by leading the nation of Israel. With a right heart he sought to live with integrity.

We frequently hear about individuals who appear to live with a strict code of morality. When troubling reports surface about the person's private life, we are dismayed at the lack of integrity. Their exterior and interior lives are clearly divided. In contrast, a person with integrity does not have a significant disconnect between these two areas. There is an integration between the interior life and the exterior conduct. Holiness is the integration of our inner and outer lives which is made possible when our hearts are renewed. A broken life followed by spiritual renewal illustrates that one can move from the stage of "disorientation" to a "new orientation" of holiness. This necessary focus on the heart contributes to growth in personal holiness with its impact on every area of our lives—including our emotions. In the next chapter, we will turn our attention to a wide range of emotions expressed by the psalmists.

---

79. Spurgeon, *Treasury of David*, 3:347.

Chapter 4

Our Emotions and Holiness

Early in his pastoral ministry in London, Charles Spurgeon experienced a horrible tragedy. At the very first service on a Sunday evening at the Surrey Gardens Music Hall, the auditorium was packed with people eager to hear the twenty-two-year-old preacher. Shortly after the service began, someone shouted words that created panic and a stampede of people trying to get out of the building. When it was all over, seven people were killed, with many more injured. Knowing that Spurgeon was a very sensitive man, the deacons took him to his home to avoid the painful scene. Nevertheless, he experienced profound grief.

In response to newspaper articles that ridiculed and attacked Spurgeon and his preaching, he once commented, "I am down in the valley partly because of two desperate attacks upon me."[1] Two years later, when people slandered him, Spurgeon wrote that his "heart was broken in agony."[2] Praise from others also made Spurgeon sad. He confessed, "It always makes me feel so sad—so sad that I could cry—if ever I see anything praising me; it breaks my heart; I feel that I do not deserve it."[3] His biographers describe him as a man who was "very tender and was easily moved to tears . . . he felt things deeply."[4] Another writes, "He was

1. Fullerton, *Charles Spurgeon*, 61.
2. Fullerton, *Charles Spurgeon*, 61.
3. Fullerton, *Charles Spurgeon*, 61–62.
4. Dallimore, *Spurgeon*, 186.

extremely sensitive, as he himself admitted, an emotional man for whom feelings were always very important."[5] He was a man who wore his feelings on his sleeve.

While he could easily cry, Spurgeon also enjoyed a good laugh. A friend of Spurgeon spoke of his laughter: "He had the most fascinating gift of laughter . . . and he had also the greatest ability for making all who heard him laugh with him."[6] On one occasion, while walking with a friend, Spurgeon stopped and said, "Come, Theodore, let us thank God for laughter."[7] He was also known to laugh when he preached. When asked about using humor in the pulpit, Spurgeon told of his friend who was surprised by how many times his pastor would restrain himself from telling more humorous stories. He once told his students, "I do believe in my heart that there may be as much holiness in a laugh as in a cry; and that, sometimes to laugh is the better thing of the two."[8] He was a joyful man!

For many of us, emotions have an awkward relationship with holiness. As a result, some choose to deny or repress their feelings to their detriment. Peter Scazzero states that ignoring our emotions is one of the primary symptoms of an emotionally unhealthy spirituality. He comments, "To the degree that we are unable to express our emotions, we remain impaired in our ability to love God, others, and ourselves well."[9] Others distrust their emotions by relegating them to a minor role in daily life. Others depend on feelings by allowing them to control decisions, attitudes, and actions. When emotions become an addictive force, individuals are "governed by feelings."[10]

We need to view our emotions as an integral part of our growth in holiness. Since this process involves becoming conformed to the image of Jesus Christ, we should expect joy and delight, grief and anger to be reflected in our lives. Holiness includes moving from sinful emotions, such as jealousy and fits of rage, to the fruit of the Spirit (Gal 5:19–23). When we

---

5. Morden, *Communion with Christ*, 289.
6. Dallimore, *Spurgeon*, 188.
7. Fullerton, *Charles Spurgeon*, 135.
8. Rhodes, *Yours, till Heaven*, 127.
9. Scazzero, *Emotionally Healthy Spirituality*, 26.
10. Willard, *Renovation of the Heart*, 125–27.

experience damaging emotions within us, they remind us of the need for further growth in godliness.

Our emotions are an integral part of what it means to be human. Spurgeon understood the role emotions have in our lives. He states, "The emotions of the soul are as important as the acts of life, for they are the fountain and spring from which the actions proceed."[11] Although feelings are an essential aspect of our lives, Spurgeon believed emotions must still be subject to and governed by God's will.[12] When John Calvin wrote about the "anatomy of all the parts of the soul" he referred to our emotions.[13] Since our emotions are an integral facet of our humanness, then growth in holiness must extend beyond our actions and words. When we focus on doing and saying the right things and relegate our emotions to the dustbin, we have short-circuited the process of holiness in our lives. Since the emotions "pervade" and "creep over into other areas of life," they must be aligned with God's will.[14] Willard states that since our emotions are "central for spiritual formation in the Christian tradition . . . feelings too must be renovated."[15] Our emotions function like a barometer revealing how we respond to daily life's pressures.

The Psalter is uniquely suited to address our emotional life so that we may grow holiness. The Psalms *identify* our emotions. David, the "sweet psalmist of Israel" (2 Sam 23:1 ESV), has precisely described our feelings because he went through "the school of heartfelt, personal experience."[16] Regarding the Psalms, Calvin remarked, "There is not an emotion of which anyone can be conscious that is not here represented." He continues to comment that it is the Holy Spirit who has drawn together in the Psalms "all the griefs, sorrows, fears, doubts, hopes, cares, perplexities, in short, all the distracting emotions" which we are accustomed to in our lives.[17]

God also uses the Psalms to *transform* our emotions. Athanasius wrote that the one who "engages the Psalter . . . bring[s] all the members of his body and his emotions into submission."[18] This change is possible because

11. Spurgeon, *Treasury of David*, 5:355.
12. Bebbington states that Spurgeon resisted the "romantic sentiment," which gave a higher priority to feelings rather than belief. He states, "The pendulum was swinging away from precise doctrine and toward accommodating sensibility, even among Evangelicals" (*Holiness*, 47–48).
13. Calvin, *Commentary on the Psalms*, xxxvii.
14. Willard, *Renovation of the Heart*, 124.
15. Willard, *Renovation of the Heart*, 117.
16. Spurgeon, *Morning and Evening*.
17. Calvin, *Commentary on the Psalms*, xxxvii.
18. Athanasius, *Letter to Marcellinus*, 33.

of the "elevated style" of the Psalms, which enables us to feel and to take to heart the psalmists' words as our own words.[19] The writers' words influence our interior lives when we absorb the Psalms into our minds and hearts. As Paul Griffiths states, "A memorized work . . . has entered into the fabric of its possessor's intellectual and emotional life in a way that makes deep claims upon that life."[20] Genuinely reading, singing, and praying the Psalms "mold one's character and heighten one's love of God."[21] The Psalter shapes our emotional life, enabling us to grow in holiness. We discover we can acknowledge and own some emotions we assumed we must deny. We become aware of those emotions which don't reflect the life of Jesus, and we are challenged to see them changed by God's grace.

We now turn to specific emotions experienced by the writers of the Psalms. The list of the following emotions is not exhaustive but is representative of those which are commonly expressed in our personal lives.

Sadness and Grief

We are well aware that we aren't immune to sadness and grief. However, we may not associate sorrow as a reflection of holiness. When we are told to always rejoice (Phil 4:4), we may feel we fall far short of godliness when we aren't very joyful. It is helpful to consider that sadness and grief are emotions of a holy God. The LORD grieved when he saw humanity's sinfulness in the days of Noah (Gen 6:6). Isaiah describes the Messiah-servant as "a man of sorrows, familiar with suffering" (Isa 53:3). When Jesus lived on earth, he expressed sorrow when his good friend Lazarus died (John 11:35). His grief reached a climatic point on the cross where he bore the guilt of sin and entered into the kind of experience of "God-forsakenness" that Psalm 22 expresses (Mark 15:34). The Holy Spirit is grieved by sin (Isa 63:10; Eph 4:30). Therefore, it is quite evident that sorrow is an emotion firmly rooted in God's nature. One caveat: our grief is not godly when caused by our foolish actions and selfish interests (2 Cor 7:10). The cause of our sadness helps us determine whether or not our feelings reflect godliness.

It shouldn't surprise us that the psalmists express varying degrees of sadness, including grief. We will discover that we may share common ground with the psalmists who pursued God amid their pain. David experienced intense sorrow when he underwent God's discipline due to his sin (6:1–3, 6–7). For example, he wept over his sick child borne to Bathsheba

---

19. Athanasius, *Letter to Marcellinus*, 15, 17.
20. Griffiths, *Religious Reading*. He is quoted by Wenham, *Psalter Reclaimed*, 22–23.
21. Wenham, *Psalter Reclaimed*, 23.

due to his illicit relationship with her (2 Sam 12:21–22). People who are pursuing holiness take their sins seriously. To his readers, David does not downplay his emotions; he admits them freely and honestly.

David also experiences sorrow and grief due to broken relationships (31:9). Those who were his friends have now become his enemies (vv. 11, 13, 15). David loved his son Absalom who eventually rebelled against his father's reign as king. When Absalom died, David grieved over his son who hated him (2 Sam 18:33–19:1, 6). As Spurgeon puts it, "Those who are nearest can stab the sharpest. We feel the slights of those who should have shown us mercy."[22]

David wasn't the only psalmist who felt profoundly sad about the loss of friends. One of Korah's sons became repulsive to his closest friends, companions, and loved ones. The loss of deep relationships deeply grieved him (88:8–9, 18). Spurgeon insightfully comments, "It is a piercing pain which arises from the desertion of dear associates; it is a wound which festers and refuses to be healed.... When God shuts friends out, and shuts us in to pine away alone, it is no wonder if we water our couch with tears."[23] Spurgeon reminds us of Jesus, who experienced the rejection of his closest friends, the disciples, who had been with him for three years. Jesus, the perfect Son of God, understands our grief since he experienced the same with his inner circle.

David also grieves over those who repaid his goodness with evil (35:12–14). Again, we think of Saul, who sought to murder him more than once. Yet, when Saul died, David lamented his death and encouraged his nation to remember his adversary (2 Sam 1:17, 23–24).

Sometimes, our grief stems from our lack of understanding of God's ways. For example, Asaph admits he was puzzled and frustrated by God, who allowed the wicked to prosper (73:12–14). God's lack of action was an enigma because Asaph maintained a godly life, but from Asaph's perspective, it didn't seem to matter to God (vv. 13–14). As a result, Asaph grieved and became embittered (v. 21). This was, Spurgeon says, "deep-seated sorrow ... which penetrated his inmost being."[24] Full of pain, he responded foolishly (v. 22), which can hurt others (v. 15). When we allow our grief to turn into bitterness, our actions will bring unnecessary suffering to others. Therefore, we must carefully guard our grief lest it leads others into sin.

It is essential to note the close relationship between sadness and holiness. When people disobeyed God's commandments, the psalmist

---

22. Spurgeon, *Treasury of David*, 2:61.
23. Spurgeon, *Treasury of David*, 4:4.
24. Spurgeon, *Treasury of David*, 3:252.

confesses, "Streams of tears flow from my eyes" (119:136). When we grieve over the things that break God's heart, we know our sorrow reflects a degree of personal holiness. How can we practice "holy sorrow" so that bitterness does not control us? The Psalms offer numerous ways to help us here.

First, we can learn to grieve as the psalmists do. Expressing sadness and grief is a holy act before God. Psalm 88 reminds us that we may experience prolonged sorrow and grief, leaving us feeling hopeless.

Second, God knows our sadness. He sees our grief (10:14) and knows the "anguish of my soul" (31:7). Since he knows, we can acknowledge our feelings of sadness. Spurgeon offers us insight here:

> He thinks not the worse of them for their rags and tatters. He does not misjudge them and cast them off when their faces are lean with sickness or their hearts heavy with despondency. Moreover, the Lord Jesus knows us in our pangs in a peculiar sense by having a deep sympathy towards us in them all; when no others can enter into our griefs, from want of understanding them experimentally, Jesus dives into the lowest depths with us, comprehending the direst of our woes, because he has felt the same. Jesus is a physician who knows every case; nothing is new to him. When we are so bewildered as not to know our own state, he knows us altogether.[25]

Third, the Psalms teach us to rest in God, who loves us no matter what may happen to us (6:2, 4, 9; 31:7, 9, 16, 19, 21). Referring to Ps 6, Spurgeon points out that David describes God as Lord five times. "Is not this a proof that the glorious name is full of consolation to the tempted saint? Eternity, Infinity, Immutability, Self-existence, are all in the name Jehovah, and all are full of comfort."[26] He is our source of consolation.

Fourth, we can learn to trust in God's sovereignty. When the psalmists are filled with sorrow, they repeatedly remind us to trust the Lord, who is in control (31:14; 35:4–8, 10).

Fifth, we are instructed that grief is an opportunity to grow in our intimacy with God. As we lean into him, he is willing to take us by the hand and hold us even in death when we enter his presence (73:23–26). He is our most treasured possession—even in times of profound sadness.

And sixth, the Psalms teach us to grieve with others who are going through painful times (35:13–14). We share the grief of others, including those who may not consider us their friends. Grieving is an opportunity to grow in love and holiness when we see others suffering.

---

25. Spurgeon, *Treasury of David*, 2:60.
26. Spurgeon, *Treasury of David*, 1:57.

The psalmists remind us by their own experiences that our feelings of sadness and grief are opportunities to reflect the likeness of Jesus and to grow in personal holiness.

Anger

Anger is one of those emotions we may be embarrassed to admit to ourselves and others. In part, our reticence may be due to our awareness of those Bible verses which tell us to get rid of anger and rage (Eph 4:31; Col 3:8). It's not surprising that we may find it difficult to associate the emotion of anger with personal holiness. However, this emotion does not originate with our sinful nature but with God. Throughout the pages of Scripture, anger is identified with God's nature. He was angry with Moses, who balked at God's call on his life (Exod 4:14). When the Israelites disobeyed, God was frequently angry with them throughout the centuries (Judg 2:12; 2 Chr 24:18). In his anger, he drove his people out of their ransacked land and brought them under the captivity of others (Jer 4:26; Ezek 21:31). Jesus, the son of God, also showed anger at those who were religious but had stubborn hearts (Mark 3:5). One day in the future, God will unleash his anger on the nations and those who have opposed him (Rev 6:16–17, 19:15).

Do the Psalms instruct us how our anger can be a reflection of holiness? The apostle Paul's words, "in your anger do not sin" (Eph 4:26), are commonly mentioned to indicate we can be both angry and godly. For example, the psalmist expresses indignation at those who have rejected God's revealed word and live wickedly (119:53). However, we often forget that Paul quotes from the Psalter (4:4). Several psalms explore anger, which is mentioned more often than we may realize. Many of these writings are traditionally called the "imprecatory psalms." We may be shocked by these psalms until we understand that the psalmists are expressing God's anger. Their psalms provide a rich resource on how we should address holy anger. Due to space, the following discussion covers a limited number of representative psalms on this topic.

In no mistakable terms, anger can contribute to sinful conduct such as verbal abuse (55:3) and destructive behavior (124:3). Clearly, actions like these can't be a part of our lives because they are contrary to a life of holiness. How can we "refrain from anger and turn from wrath" when we see people perpetuate evil (37:1, 8)? Is the psalmist referring to conduct or feelings of anger? The clue to the psalmist's exhortation (v. 8) is discovered in the word "fret" mentioned three times (vv. 1, 7, 8). When we see wickedness, Spurgeon states that we can "fume" and "become vexed" (v. 1). When we feel this way, we impatiently take matters into our own hands, which leads to evil (vv. 7–8). It is no wonder that he warns us, "Fretfulness lies upon the verge of great sin."[27] Our fretful actions fundamentally reflect anger both with God who has not responded to the evil and with the evil ones who have prospered (v. 8). David is telling us anger begins with our impatience with God, which then turns into personal reactions which are contrary to the ways God would act. Since this angry fretting is not constructive and is sinful, it must not be a part of holy living.

The corrective for fretting and angrily taking matters into our own hands is in learning to "be still" before God (37:7). This requires us to "hush the spirit [and] to be silent before the Lord," according to Spurgeon. Practicing holy patience means waiting for God to act rather than ourselves reacting out of anger. To wait for God to respond is an expression of personal holiness.[28] For this reason, we benefit by paying attention to the psalmists who frequently saw injustice and then appropriately cried out to God to act justly.

Therefore, it is possible to be angry without sinning (4:4). The psalmist instructs us to be still before God. Rather than stewing throughout the night over people's hurtful comments and angrily reacting the following morning, the psalmist suggests that we discipline ourselves to "search our hearts and be silent" before God. While Spurgeon applies this verse to unbelievers, those who know Christ need to allow God's Spirit to search our hearts (139:21–22). The Spirit will expose our unholy reactions as we review and meditate on the day and our schemes for the next day. If we respond in obedience, we can feel anger without sinning. Then, Spurgeon says, we can "sleep in peace" because a "quiet conscience is a good bedfellow."[29] Personal holiness includes refining our anger to extract impure motives and preempt hurtful actions. We can experience anger with a clear conscience while living at peace with ourselves and God.

What should be our response to the psalmists who angrily denounce their opponents? We may be shocked by their cries for their enemies to be banished (5:10), to be disgraced (6:10, 25:6, 35:4), and killed (35:8, 52:6, 54:5). It is important to note that the psalmists to don't take matters into their own hands. Instead, they call out to God, asking him to respond to these enemies with his anger (69:22–25). Consequently, the Psalter contains many references to God directing his anger to those who oppose him,

---

27. Spurgeon, *Treasury of David*, 2:173; W. David O. Taylor says that we are "undone" by our anger (*Open and Unafraid*, 83).

28. Spurgeon, *Treasury of David*, 2:170, 172–73.

29. Spurgeon, *Treasury of David*, 1:35, 37.

including his own people (2:5, 7:6, 56:7, 69:24, 78:49, 85:5, 90:7, 106:29). Indeed, Spurgeon warns that "God's indignation is no trifle; the anger of a holy, just, omnipotent, and infinite Being, is above all things to be dreaded."[30] The psalmists give us helpful insight here. In contrast to our anger, which often stems from a wounded ego or blocked desires, their anger is directed at sin, which has offended God. Spurgeon points out that Jesus, who prayed for his enemies, also spoke words that reflected the psalmists' anger (compare Matt 23:38 to Ps 69:25).

Growth in holiness allows us to be angry at what God is angry at in our world. If we are not offended by sin, then this may be an indication of our spiritual health. Also, the psalmists don't retaliate against their enemies, but leave the situation to God, who will deal with them. Unfortunately, we often retaliate with hurtful words or destructive actions. When we handle our anger as the psalmists did, we can continue to grow in godliness.

Guilt

It is not unusual for believers to experience false guilt. Due to others' comments and expectations, we might feel guilty when no wrongdoing has occurred. In addition, shame and embarrassment aren't uncommonly used to make a person feel unfairly guilty. Therefore, it's not surprising that we may not associate the emotion of guilt with holiness. However, feeling guilty about our sins is a healthy indicator that we are sensitive to those things that displease God. Guilt is "contrite remorse" which leads to repentance.[31] When David crept up to Saul with the opportunity to kill him, he cut off some of Saul's robe. Afterward, he was conscience-stricken and told his men, "God forbid that I should do such a thing to my master, the LORD's anointed, or lift my hand against him for he is the anointed of the LORD" (1 Sam 24:1–7).

The Psalter addresses the feelings of guilt in many of its repentance psalms (6, 32, 38, 102, 130, 143). Bonhoeffer informs us that they make us aware of "the total depth of the recognition of sin before God. They lead us to the confession of guilt and direct our complete confidence in the forgiving grace of God."[32] The guilt we feel is an integral aspect of our growing in holiness.

The psalmists, particularly David, aren't shy to describe the depths of guilt they experience. David, a man after God's heart, tells us, "My guilt has

30. Spurgeon, *Treasury of David*, 3:183.
31. Packer, *Rediscovering Holiness*, 124.
32. Bonhoeffer, *Psalms*, 51.

overwhelmed me like a burden too heavy to bear" (38:4). He goes on to admit that he groans in his heart (38:8; see also 6:3, 32:3) and outwardly weeps (6:6–7). The intense physical suffering he experiences (38:3, 5–7) shouldn't overshadow his profound sense of his guilt. Instead, the physical pain reflects his emotional guilt in the depths of his being. Here is an individual with an uneasy conscience causing him to be troubled about his sin.

The guilt feelings due to David's sin greatly troubles and affects him (38:3, 18). If we aren't alarmed at our sin, his experience rebukes us when we don't feel guilt for our sin before God. Spurgeon notes that "a sense of sin creates in the conscience a horrible unrest." Then he mentions, "It is well when sin is an intolerable load, and when the remembrance of our sins burdens us beyond endurance."[33] Too often, we lightly treat our sin rather than being disturbed by our sin.

David's feeling of guilt leads him to acknowledge the fact of his responsibility before God. The best response is to confess his sin (32:5, 38:18). We may admit we did something wrong, but by rationalizing our actions, we reject any guilt. However, a profound sense of our guilt is essential to holiness. For this reason, Spurgeon encourages us, "We must confess the guilt as well as the sin. It is useless to conceal it, for it is well known to God; it is beneficial to us to own it, for a full confession softens and humbles the heart."[34]

With acknowledgment of guilt and sin, David experiences God's blessing of joy in his life (32:1–2). He enjoys the forgiveness of sin (v. 1) and the joy of a pure heart. He is, as Spurgeon notes, "free from guilt, free from guile." The writer of Hebrews picks up the same theme by connecting a "sincere heart" with a "guilty conscience" which God cleanses (Heb 10: 21). Spurgeon exclaims that this is "the only and sure way to happiness."[35] Our sense of guilt due to sin is a sure and specific pathway to growing in holiness.

Joy

In our spiritual growth, we should expect to experience sadness, grief, anger, and guilt for our sins. But if we stayed here, we would miss out on the beautiful quality of joy. Willard describes this emotion as a "pervasive sense . . . of well-being: of overall and ultimate well-being." In contrast to pleasure

---

33. Spurgeon, *Treasury of David*, 2:199.

34. Spurgeon, *Treasury of David*, 2:83.

35. Spurgeon, *Treasury of David*, 2:81. Kidner states that "Happy [is] a more exuberant word than *Blessed*" (*Psalms*, 151).

in particular activities or objects, when we have joy, "*all* is well, even in the midst of specific suffering and loss" (italics his). We will discover this description aptly applies to the psalmists. Then, Willard makes a remarkable statement in light of our discussion on holiness: "Joy is the basic element of inner transformation into Christlikeness and of the outer life that flows from it."[36]

This joy is rooted in the Godhead. Jesus leaped for joy even in Mary's womb (Luke 1:44) and, he was "full of joy through the Holy Spirit" (Luke 10:21). To his heavenly Father, Jesus spoke of his joy within his disciples (John 17:13). If holiness involves becoming more like Jesus in character and conduct, it is not an exaggeration to suggest that joy is a chief quality of Christlikeness. It's not surprising, then, that joy dominated the early church's life. Since the fruit of the Spirit includes joy (Gal 5:22), we commonly see believers filled with this quality in their lives (Acts 13:52, 16:34; Rom 16:19). The apostles Paul, James, Peter, and John all wrote about joy as an integral aspect of the Christian life. They would affirm Ezra's words, "The joy of the LORD is my strength" (Neh 8:10). Therefore, it should not surprise us that the Psalms frequently mention joy. Thus, the Psalter is called *Tehillim*, or the "Book of Praises."[37] While we can say much about joy, the following comments are limited to people's expressions of this emotion and its relationship to holiness in the Psalms.

God is the source of joy in our lives. In Ps 4, David declares that it is God who has "filled my heart with greater joy" than anything else (v. 7). One way we discover his joy is by being in his presence (16:11, 21:6, 43:4). Spurgeon reminds us that "to draw near to God, who is such a joy to us, may well be the object of our hungering and thirsting."[38] Spending time with the Lord in quiet solitude provides a rich opportunity for God's joy to fill our lives.

We also know this supernatural joy when God's goodness fills us with gratitude. Psalm 126 is a song of praise celebrating the Israelites' release from Babylon and return to their homeland (126:3). After much grief because of their lengthy captivity, they are "filled with joy" (v. 3) which erupts with "songs of joy" (v. 5). Joy does not deny grief. Still, neither does our grief have to mark our lives permanently. Experiencing joy flows out of a life of gratitude for all that God has done for us (107:22). On these occasions, people are filled with "songs of joy" (20:5, 51:8).

---

36. Willard, *Renovation of the Heart*, 132–33.

37. Taylor, *Open and Unafraid*, 96. I am indebted to his work on "joy" in chapter 8 of his book.

38. Spurgeon, *Treasury of David*, 2:293.

We can also discover a profound feeling of joy in tough situations. In Ps 86, David describes himself as "poor and needy" (v. 1) because his enemies are trying to murder him (v. 14). Amid this tumultuous time, David asks God to bring him joy (v. 4). He knows that he can be filled with joy not by escaping from a dire situation, but by seeking God's face (27: 4–6). When anxiety overwhelms us, the Lord replaces it with abundant joy (94:19). Many years later, Paul and Silas are flogged and thrown in jail, where they praise God (Acts 16:25). These trying times are opportunities to draw close to the Lord. Spurgeon testifies, "I know that the nearer I am to thee [God] the greater is my joy."[39] Joy is God's gift of grace to us during overwhelming challenges.

Joy is an indication of growth in personal holiness. This incredible quality is the by-product of developing a closer relationship with God and being in communion with him. When Jesus speaks to his disciples, he tells them (and us) that we should abide by or remain in an intimate relationship with him (John 15:4, 5, 7). When we are, we will experience his joy in us (v. 11). Jesus' words are an echo of David, who expressed to the Lord, "You will fill me with joy in your presence" (16:11). David Taylor captures this thought: "To be full of God, in short, is to be full of joy."[40]

Closely associated with joy is the feeling of delight.[41] The psalmist connects these two emotions in Ps 43:4 with the phrase "joy and delight." Delight is not found exclusively among godly people because some revel in lies and war (62:4, 68:30). However, we can delight in God (37:4, 43:4) because he delights in us (149:4). We can specifically delight in God by relishing and savoring his word to us (112:1; 119:16, 24, 35, 47, 70, 77, 92, 143, 174). We delight in his revealed will because we "desire or ask for nothing but what will please the Lord."[42] Simply put, delighting in God and his will is a mark of personal holiness.

Love

Early in the life of the Jewish community, the people learned the Shema: "Love the LORD your God with all your heart and with all your soul and with all your strength" (Deut 6:5). This injunction expresses not only the central theme of Deuteronomy, but the central focus of the covenant relationship between God and his people. As he committed himself to loving

---

39. Spurgeon, *Treasury of David*, 3:464.
40. Taylor, *Open and Unafraid*, 102.
41. Willard, *Renovation of the Heart*, 132–33.
42. Spurgeon, *Treasury of David*, 2:171.

them without reservation, God wanted them to express their commitment by loving him with their whole being. Then, they could extend their love to others (vv. 6–9). Spurgeon notes that this "all-encompassing" love is expressed in a "willing and joyful obedience" to Jehovah God.[43]

The command to love the Lord and others would be hopeless unless they experience God's unfailing love. Throughout the Psalms, we are reminded of God's covenant love for his people throughout the generations (47:4, 78:68). His love has moral boundaries because he loves both justice (11:7, 99:4) and righteousness (33:5), and he equally hates injustice and wickedness. Therefore, he loves those who are just (37:28) and practice righteousness (146:8). God's love accurately reflects his holiness. As our love for God and others deepens, we grow in holiness.

Of course, our sinful nature has corrupted love. We can choose to love evil, rather than what is good (52:3). We can decide to love violence (11:5), pronounce curses on people (109:17), and love our illusionary false gods (4:3). We have the wrong priorities in what we love. We may even love noble things, but their importance in our lives is misplaced because we must love God above everything else. The Psalms serve as a corrective to our corrupted and disordered loves.

The Hebrew language has one word to broadly describe human and divine love (*ahab*). Therefore, the Old Testament does not distinguish the types of love which are articulated in the New Testament. We are called on to love God and everything associated with him for several reasons. One, we are to love God for who he is. Psalm 5:11 mentions loving God's name, which represents his nature or character.[44] This respectful attitude toward God shapes our hearts which is the main reason for worshiping him. David tells us that those "who love your name may rejoice in you" with gladness and joy (v. 11). "We love God, and therefore we delight in him."[45]

We also love God for what he has already done for us (31:23). David tells his people, "Love the LORD, all his saints!" *after* he has told them how God had shown his love to him by preserving his life (vv. 21–22). Having experienced God's protective care, David shows "clearly the deep love of the writer to his God," notes Spurgeon.[46] Psalm 116 gives us another account of the psalmist loving God who heard his prayer (v. 1). Spurgeon comments that God's gracious response to the psalmist's cry deepened his love for

---

43. Craigie, *Book of Deuteronomy*, 170.
44. Spurgeon, *Treasury of David*, 6:382.
45. Spurgeon, *Treasury of David*, 1:49.
46. Spurgeon, *Treasury of David*, 2:64.

God.[47] In other words, we don't have blind love for God. Our love for him is based on specific reasons. Spurgeon writes,

> The Psalmist not only knows that he loves God, but he knows why he does so. When love can justify itself with a reason, it is deep, strong, and abiding . . . when we love God our affection has its eyes open and can sustain itself with the most rigid logic. We have reason, superabundant reason, for loving the Lord; and so because in this case . . . reason and emotion go together, they make up an admirable state of mind.[48]

He goes on to say that David "loved God with all his heart . . . When a man's prayers are answered, love is the natural result."[49]

Finally, Ps 119 informs us that we love God because he has revealed his will to us. The writer exclaims, "Oh, how I love your law!" (v. 97). Spurgeon warns us that we "may know, read, hear, speak" and even preach God's word and "not love it." Along with the apostle Paul's reminder regarding the priority of love (1 Cor 13), Spurgeon says, "Love is the principal affection of all other . . . all the rest depend on it."[50] When our love for God and his revealed will becomes our priority in life, our affections will be appropriately ordered so that we don't have a greater love for gold and material possessions (v. 127). The psalmist's love for God gives him great delight in God's commandments (v. 47). "Where our love is, there is our delight."[51] This love for God brings us back to the previous comments regarding delight and joy. Jesus once told the parable of an individual delightfully discovering a great treasure (the kingdom of God). Then, after burying the treasure in a field, he joyfully sold his possessions to purchase this treasured discovery (Matt 13:44).

This passionate love for God's revealed will is expressed in various ways. One, we are motivated to obey God (119:167) and to love our friends and companions (38:11, 88:18). Equally, our love for God increases our hatred of evil, including those who oppose God with their sinful practices and beliefs (34:12; 97:10; 119:113, 163). As Spurgeon aptly puts it, "[David's] love was as ardent as his hate. True men love truth, and hate lying."[52]

The Psalter's unmistakable emphasis on love informs us that love is the primary mark of personal holiness. Likewise, the apostle Paul mentions love as the first characteristic of the fruit of the Holy Spirit (Gal 5:22) because

---

47. Spurgeon, *Treasury of David*, 5:66.
48. Spurgeon, *Treasury of David*, 5:67.
49. Spurgeon, *Treasury of David*, 5:67.
50. Spurgeon, *Treasury of David*, 5:333.
51. Spurgeon, *Treasury of David*, 5:229.
52. Spurgeon, *Treasury of David*, 5:424.

love is the greatest virtue in one's life (1 Cor 13:13). Growing in love is a mark of maturing holiness. Packer succinctly puts it this way: "Outwardly, holiness is obedience; inwardly, holiness is love in action. The love for God that prompts the obedience that expresses love for fellow human beings is holiness' true heart and heartbeat . . . it is love for God that makes the holy person tick, care, and serve."[53]

Fear

The emotion of fear grips many people in today's world, which is filled with violence, financial uncertainties, and political turbulence, in addition to our concerns. Thus, it is surprising that the psalmists don't express fear. This is remarkable when we consider the precarious situations in which David and the others found themselves. Numerous accounts of pursuits by enemies who sought to kill are reason enough to be fearful. Yet, there are scant references to the psalmists experiencing fear. We have to explore why this is the case.

Psalm 55:5 is one of the few times David admits his fear. This feeling was so great it made him tremble. His fear is genuine and understandable, with his enemies wanting to kill him (vv. 3–4). He only considered a miraculous escape as an option. But, it was unrealistic since he couldn't fly away like a bird (vv. 6–8). As David was, we too will be plagued by fear when we try to devise ways of addressing this emotion.

The psalmists often shout, "I will not fear!" (3:6; 23:4; 27:1, 3; 46:2; 49:5; 56:4, 11; 91:5; 112:7–8). They were not denying their emotions and putting up stoic faces. How could they not be afraid? Breathing exercises or chanting a religious mantra was not their "cure" for fear. Instead, they confront the reality of their fear with a fear of God. We don't generally like to speak of the fear of God, preferring to talk of being on friendly terms with God. We might even expect the psalmists to use a different Hebrew word to distinguish the fear of people from a fear of God. However, the same Hebrew word (*yare*) is used to describe the fear of people (55:5) and the fear of God. We can choose to fear people and circumstances or to fear God. We exchange our fear of danger and threats with a healthy fear of the LORD Almighty.

Rather than fearing people, David looks to the LORD (3:6, 27:1). "The powers of darkness are not to be feared" because he trusted in "the real power of the omnipotent I AM," says Spurgeon.[54] The sons of Korah adopt this same

---

53. Packer, *Rediscovering Holiness*, 178.
54. Spurgeon, *Treasury of David*, 2:1.

discipline in their lives. They choose not to fear their circumstances because God is their refuge and strength (46:1–2). As Spurgeon reminds us, "With God on our side, how irrational would fear be!"[55] In Ps 49:5, the sons of Korah again ask why one should fear. It is futile to place hope in one's wealth as a coping strategy (vv. 6–14). The only sane option is to trust in God (v. 15). Trusting in him involves an attitude of dependence on God who is worthy of reverence (40:3b). We can affirm with the psalmists, "When I am afraid, I will trust in you . . . in God I trust; I will not be afraid" (56:3–4, 11; see also 23:4; 112:7–8). Spurgeon does not idealize David when he makes this comment. "He does not claim never to be afraid, and he was no brutish Stoic free from fear . . . [he] was afraid." Then Spurgeon says that David's fear "did not fill the whole area of his mind" because he also feared or trusted God.[56] As we fear and trust the Lord, we will experience his love (103:17), fulfilling our deepest desires (145:19), and will lack nothing (23:1, 34:9).

Moving from fear which paralyzes us, to a fear of the Lord whom we revere, is the right direction for growing in holiness. Spurgeon realistically believes that we can never rid ourselves of fears. He states that "we are feeble" [and]. . . . It is possible, then, for fear and faith to occupy the mind at the same moment." But our fear can drive us to trust in the Lord.[57] Our holiness is not measured by the lack of fear but by deepening confidence in God whom we revere.

Conclusion

We know that there are several reasons why we should explore our emotional life. First, healthy relationships require relatively high "emotional intelligence" or a realistic awareness of one's emotions. By identifying with the psalmists' emotions, which are a mirror into our souls, Longman remarks that we can discover how we are "doing on the inside . . . we come to understand our thoughts and feelings better."[58] Second, by identifying what is going on internally, we can ask ourselves how we are doing in our growth in holiness: "Are we moving towards God or away from him?"[59] What we discover is rooted in a commitment to grow in holiness, which involves becoming increasingly like Jesus Christ. As his followers, Spurgeon teaches that "the call of discipleship includes experiencing our feelings, reflecting

---

55. Spurgeon, *Treasury of David*, 2:340.
56. Spurgeon, *Treasury of David*, 2:465.
57. Spurgeon, *Treasury of David*, 2:465.
58. Longman, *Psalms*, 56.
59. Longman, *Psalms*, 51.

on our feelings, and then thoughtfully responding to our feelings under the lordship of Jesus."[60] When we experience a broad spectrum of emotions, we can reflect on those feelings which need to become more like Jesus and ask God to transform them. So again, the Psalms contribute to growth in holiness.

---

60. Scazzero, *Emotionally Healthy Spirituality*, 71.

Chapter 5

Our Conduct and Holiness

Charles Spurgeon did not only preach and teach about godliness but also lived it in the ebb and flow of daily life. We see his godly life when we look at his conduct with society's neglected people. He knew that the wealthy oppressed so many of its oppressed citizens. Pitiful wages left many impoverished in the city. Widows and their children were usually destitute, struggling to survive. As they roamed the city streets, numerous homeless children begged and committed petty crimes. In addition, thousands of people received no formal schooling. Prostitution provided money for those who were desperate and destitute. Spurgeon bewailed the miserable conditions he witnessed,

> The objects of our care are not far to seek. They are at our gates; widows worn down with labour, often pale, emaciated, delicate, and even consumptive [tuberculous]; children half-famished, growing up neglected, surrounded with temptation. Can you look at them without pity? We cannot.[1]

These aren't the only ones who suffered. Those engaged in Christian ministry also had difficulty coping with the limited salaries they received.

In response to these groups of people who struggled to survive in society, Spurgeon acted with Jesus' love. He built and supported almshouses for needy widows and their children. Spurgeon had seventeen

---

1. Morden, *C. H. Spurgeon*, 141.

new houses constructed for them, and later, he added a school for four hundred orphans. In addition, he spearheaded the building of fourteen houses for five hundred boys and girls. This Stockwell Orphanage also included a dining hall, a laundry room, a gymnasium, a private hospital, a covered playground, and a swimming pool. Spurgeon loved these children! He often visited the orphanage and would give pennies to the children, much to their delight. In addition, Charles and his wife, Susannah, annually visited these orphans on Christmas Day and provided a special meal for them.

For those in pastoral ministry who received a minimal income, Charles and Susannah appealed for funds and volunteers to prepare and ship parcels of clothing and blankets to the poor pastors. This pastoral couple was concerned for these poor pastors who had retired but had limited funds to live.

Spurgeon promoted just causes, raised funds, and generously shared his resources with needy people. For example, when he received a significant gift of money to honor his twenty-five years of ministry at the church, he gave it all to his charitable works, and half of it went to the almshouses. His exemplary conduct contrasted with those who took advantage of so many in London.

In addition to these social issues which plagued his own country, Spurgeon spoke out against social injustices, such as slavery in the United States. Speaking against slavery came at a tremendous personal cost to him. His sermons in the United States, which had sold well, virtually ended during 1860–65. In addition, several places in the South burned his books at public ceremonies.[2]

God blessed the way Spurgeon conducted his life with his congregation and many other groups in society. By acting rightly with people, his work endured long past his lifetime. As a result of his godly conduct, he not only flourished but so did innumerable others who benefitted from how he treated them.

---

2. Nettles, *Living by Revealed Truth*, 345, 373, 504–5; Dallimore, *Spurgeon*, xv–xvi, 125–30.

In chapter 1, we discussed the Psalter's two distinct life paths which we can choose—namely, the path of righteousness and the path of wickedness (1:6). Embracing and living on God's pathway requires his transforming grace to change our lives, including our hearts and emotions. As Spurgeon put it, "The feet soon run when the heart is free and energetic."[3] When we experience inner transformation, we can begin to live a pleasing life to God. A holy life begins by transforming one's character, and then godly conduct follows. Spurgeon described this behavior as "practical holiness" (mentioned in chapter 2 regarding the nature of holiness), which is godliness. He disagreed with those who thought an inward experience with God was sufficient for personal holiness. "It is vain to prate of inward experience unless the daily life is free from impurity, dishonesty, violence, and oppression."[4] He refuted those who twisted the doctrine of justification and rejected godly conduct since they were saved and going to heaven.[5] He believed that our status before God, who declares us just and holy, must be lived out in our daily conduct. As Spurgeon expresses it, "True religion is always practical."[6]

We now want to explore how a righteous life can be evident in daily behavior. Again, the Psalter is an excellent resource for us. Anthony Hoekema states that the Psalms "describe the holiness of God's people primarily in ethical terms—involving doing righteousness, speaking the truth, loving mercy, and walking humbly with God."[7] Recognizing this, Luther assigned each psalm to one of the Ten Commandments, which outline God's ethical demands for his people. Luther connected nearly all the psalms to the first three commandments (related to the Lord) and the rest at a secondary level.[8] Our conduct is governed by a proper vertical relationship with God, which provides a moral compass for our relationships with others.

Years later, Wenham observed that minimal emphasis had been placed on the Psalter and its influence on ethics. So, he explored the Decalogue—or Ten Commandments—with its relationship to the Psalter.[9] God expected his law, which provided the standard for living rightly, to govern the conduct of his people. The Decalogue is explicitly and implicitly stated in the Psalms (1, 19, 119), which shapes our understanding of how we should conduct

---

3. Spurgeon, *Treasury of David*, 5:193.
4. Spurgeon, *Treasury of David*, 1:376.
5. Spurgeon, *Treasury of David*, 1:376.
6. Spurgeon, *Treasury of David*, 5:139.
7. Hoekema, "Reformed Perspective," 62–63.
8. Luther, *Reading the Psalms with Luther*, 9–10.
9. Wenham, *Psalter Reclaimed*, 105–7. I am indebted to his work in this area.

ourselves as God's holy people. By obeying the law, a person is considered righteous before God.

It is helpful to place the Decalogue in its context. God, who gave the Ten Commandments, entered into a covenantal relationship with his people. The Hebrew word *hesed* describes this covenant love throughout the Psalter, and the following chapter will examine this love more comprehensively. God's people can reciprocate by expressing the same *hesed* love through following his laws, and if they do, they are living holy lives. God expects this kind of life from his people (Lev 11:44; 1 Pet 1:16). Spurgeon notes that "righteousness in the Old Testament is not a matter of actions conforming to a given set of absolute standards, but of behavior which is in keeping with the two-way relationship between God and man."[10] Since we are committed to following God's path to holiness (chapter 1), we will practice the same covenant love (*hesed*) with God and others. By doing so, we are living consistently with our identity as the godly ones who show love to God and others. In reality, we reflect God's *hesed* love through our daily conduct. We see this in Ps 18:25: "To the faithful you show yourself faithful, to the blameless you show yourself blameless." Now we want to turn our attention to a few ways our conduct can express his *hesed* love by obeying God's commands.

Our Conduct with God

The first two commandments forbid worshiping any other gods except Yahweh. Therefore, idolatry is forbidden (Exod 20:3-4). Furthermore, the Psalms warn us not to worship other gods (81:9) and practice idolatry (115:2-8, 135:15-18). Therefore, it is foolish to worship idols because they are nothing compared to living God.

The third commandment forbids us to take God's name in vain (Exod 20:7). There is no explicit reference in the Psalter to this command. However, the Psalms include numerous references to the "name" of God. Since the word "name" represents one's character, we discover God is majestic (8:1, 9) and holy (97:12, 103:1, 105:3). Consequently, we should revere his character (5:11) and respond accordingly with praise (7:17, 9:2, 30:4, 61:8, 135:1, 149:3). Reverence for God governs our conduct before him.

God expects from us obedience, which is the fundamental expression of holiness. The psalmist declares that he is committed to obeying God's will ("To do your will, O my God, is my desire," 40:8). Genuine obedience (not hypocritical actions) flows from his inner "desire," which God's word

---

10. Seebass, "Righteousness," 3:355.

in his heart shapes. Psalm 119:2–3 mentions both obedience and the heart. Commenting on these verses, Spurgeon suggests that "Lovers of God's holy words . . . are made practically holy" by obeying the Lord.[11] While we may believe that escaping the solitude of the desert might help us avoid sinning, God calls us to walk in his way in society.[12] Obeying God's laws reflects the holiness of our hearts. Obedience is practical holiness or godliness.

However, obedience devoid of love falls short of true godliness. For this reason, conduct that includes worshiping God is associated with a holy life. His people reciprocate God's covenant love (*hesed*) by worshiping him. In the Psalter, the godly ones (*hasidim*) are most commonly associated with others worshiping God (30:4; 52:9; 132:9, 16; 145:10; 148:14; 149:1, 5). Genuine worship, motivated by our love for God in private (59:16) or public (149:1), is a mark of holiness.

Our Conduct with Others

The Ten Commandments and the rest of the Torah also contributed to governing conduct between individuals. Those whose behavior conformed to the Torah would be considered righteous by God. We have mentioned that the first three commandments address our relationship with God; the remainder primarily addresses our conduct with others. Since there is no explicit reference to the fourth commandment to keep the Sabbath day holy (Exod 20:8), we will briefly comment on the remaining six commandments, which state how they govern our lives with others. Finally, we will examine our relationships with others in chapter 9 ("Community and Holiness").

Some of the six commandments of the Decalogue are only alluded to in the Psalter. For example, there is no explicit reference to the command to honor our parents (Exod 20:12). However, in a few psalms (127, 128), family life is highlighted, which will be explored in chapter 9 ("Community and Holiness"). The Psalms do not directly cite the command not to murder (Exod 20:13). Nevertheless, we see those who follow the way of the wicked (1:6) violate this command. For example, David's enemies sought to kill him (7:2, 17:12), and the powerful exploited the vulnerable such as the widows and aliens (94:6). Clearly, our conduct must avoid murdering others. Even though David had the opportunity to assassinate King Saul, he refused to harm him (1 Sam 24: 4–5, 26:7–11). Finally, the commandment referring to adultery (Exod 20:14) is only explicitly stated once in the Psalter (50:17–18). Of course, the following psalm, written by David, addresses his

---

11. Spurgeon, *Treasury of David*, 5:139.
12. Spurgeon, *Treasury of David*, 5:143.

adultery with Bathsheba. Godly conduct involves honoring family and others by not murdering or committing sexual immorality.

There are several directives not to violate the eighth and tenth commandments, which address stealing and coveting (Exod 20:15, 17). Psalm 50:18–20 mentions these sinful behaviors. God's people must not take from others, especially those who are poor (10:3, 9; 14:4; 22:18; 26:10; 69:4). It appears that the ninth commandment regarding lying (Exod 20:16) receives the most attention in the Psalms. The psalmists frequently condemn this behavior (4:2; 5:6, 9; 10:7; 12:2, 5; 15:2–4; 26:4). Wenham suggests the psalmists are concerned about relationships destroyed by lying words while the same people honor God with their worship. Years later, James asks Christians how they could curse their neighbors and praise God (Jas 3:9–10). Our speech must honor God and others if we want to live holy lives.

We must view the Ten Commandments in light of the two paths introduced in Ps 1. In general terms, David states that the "faithful ones" (*hasidim*) turn away from evil and do good (37:27–28, 85:8, 97:10). By obeying the Decalogue, one rejects sinful conduct and chooses to live rightly with others. One's godly behavior reflects the righteous life, which is in stark contrast to the way of the wicked mentioned in Ps 1.

This same contrast of the two paths with differing lifestyles is evident in Ps 120. One pathway consists of destructive speech (vv. 2–3), which violates the ninth commandment not to lie. Likewise, actions that threaten to kill with sharp arrows (v. 4) break God's commandment not to murder (vv. 6–7). In contrast, holy living seeks peace (v. 6) and rejects the way of the wicked in favor of the pathway of the righteous (1:6). Spurgeon reminds us, "A peace-maker is a blessing, but a peace-hater is a curse."[13] We will be either blessed or cursed by God. Living peaceably with others shows respect for them because they are created in God's image.

The way God conducts himself with humanity should influence our behavior with others. Ps 111 focuses on the many ways God relates with humankind. Then, Ps 112 describes how godly people should relate to others. The description is more than a catalog of admirable virtues. While this psalm alludes to some of the Ten Commandments, the psalmist has something important to convey to us.

According to Spurgeon, these two psalms, 111 and 112, must be read alongside each other. In Ps 111, we discover how God acts toward us so that we may reflect his conduct in our behavior with others. Psalm 112 pictures a holy person who lives wisely among others by mirroring the ways God acts with his people. In addition, Spurgeon points out that both psalms

---

13. Spurgeon, *Treasury of David*, 6:7.

have the same number of verses and are written in an acrostic style. He also notes that a common theme also links the two psalms. Fearing God and his wisdom are placed at the end of Ps 111 (v. 10) and the first verse of the next psalm. Spurgeon tells us this fear is not "a slavish fear that is accursed; but that godly fear which leads to delight in the service of God."[14]

Note how Pss 111 and 112 are interrelated. We learn that God acts righteously toward others (111:3). Likewise, righteous people are expected to act rightly among others (112:3). The following verses (vv. 4–9) elaborate on their actions. First, as God acts graciously and compassionately toward us (111:4), righteous people are also expected to act graciously and compassionately with others (112:4). Second, as God has been generous in his dealings with us (111:5–6), we must act the same way with others (112:5; see also 34:8–10, 37:21). Finally, as God acts with justice (111:7), we are to behave justly or fairly in our dealings with others (112:5).

Before we leave Ps 112, we must comment on the blessings of living rightly and wisely. A blessing is mentioned for each characteristic of godly living. For those who act rightly, God prospers them (v. 3). He dispels the dark by graciously providing sunlight to those who are gracious and compassionate (v. 4). When one is generous, God will bless the individual with goodness (v. 5). Also, we should note that the psalmist twice repeats the phrase "his righteousness endures forever" (vv. 3, 9) regarding God (111:3). Spurgeon gives us insight into the way we ought to conduct ourselves: "The character of a righteous man is not spasmodic, he is not generous by fits and starts, nor upright in a few points only; his life is the result of principle, his actions flow from settled, sure, and fixed convictions, and therefore his integrity is maintained when others fail."[15]

Throughout the rest of the Psalms, the writers describe God who loves and acts with righteousness and justice (11:7, 33:5). His conduct reflects these two qualities, so he expects us to behave similarly to reflect his character. Here are a few examples of how we can display God's righteousness. The righteous must hate evil (97:11) because God hates evil and expresses his wrath every day (7:11). Also, God, as a righteous judge (7:11, 96:13), will bring "an end the violence of the wicked" (7:9). The righteous reflect God's character when they protect the rights of those who are innocent (116:5–6) and afflicted (76:9). This requires speaking and acting justly (37:30, 112:5) on behalf of the oppressed (82:3–4). Godliness demands living in ways that reflect God's character.

---

14. Spurgeon, *Treasury of David*, 5:15.
15. Spurgeon, *Treasury of David*, 5:18.

The Psalter calls on us to imitate God. Imitating God involves more than adopting a moralistic approach to holiness, which seeks to live rightly apart from dependence on God. This attempt is foolhardy when we consider who we are (sinful) in light of God's perfect nature. However, when we yield to God, who wants to transform our lives, imitating him becomes a real possibility. Spurgeon affirms that "when God makes a man upright, he makes him like himself. We are at best but humble copies of the great original."[16] Then, we can genuinely imitate God in our daily conduct (Eph 5:1-4).

To summarize, the psalmists collectively describe the ways of holiness and sinfulness introduced in Ps 1. The two groups of people, the righteous and the wicked, live very different lives. The righteous are guided by God's written word and his character, while sinful desires and interests control those who are evil, often at the expense of others. Psalm 112, in addition to the other briefly mentioned psalms, presents us with another snapshot of Ps 1, showing us how the righteous should conduct themselves. "Such persons greatly commend godliness."[17] While the wicked "waste away" and their longings "come to nothing" (112:10), the righteous experience God's blessings and flourish with his favor.

The psalmists' understanding of godly conduct is consistent with the apostles' teaching centuries later. Practical holiness involves living like Jesus (Col 3:12-14; 1 Thess. 2:10), which includes rejecting expressions of sinful behavior (Col 3:5-9; 1 Thess 4:3-7). The apostle John reminds us that we can't love righteousness and evil simultaneously (1 John 2:9-11, 15-16). Essentially, he is describing the path of holiness (Ps 1). When we live this way, we will "inherit a blessing" (1 Pet 3:9) which Peter quotes from Ps 34:12-16. We will enjoy the blessing with "good days" (v. 10), evidence of flourishing with God's favor (Ps 1:1).

Conclusion

Godly conduct is evident in many different ways throughout the Psalms. The righteous individuals in the Psalter conducted themselves before God by worshiping, obeying, and loving him, as well as studying his revealed and written word. Then, imitating God's actions toward his people, they sought to live rightly with others by honoring and respecting others. Those who live this way are on the path of holiness and will experience God's blessing and genuine happiness. According to Ps 1, this is the best way to live!

16. Spurgeon, *Treasury of David*, 5:17.
17. Spurgeon, *Treasury of David*, 5:17.

We have explored the nature of holiness and the need for our inner (both heart and emotions) and outer (conduct) life to grow in holiness. The comprehensiveness of becoming holy may be daunting, leaving us overwhelmed in this pursuit. However, there is hope! God has provided all the resources we need for spiritual growth. The remaining chapters explore the numerous ways available to us by God, which will enable us to become more like Jesus in our character and conduct.

PART II

The Path to Growing in Holiness

Chapter 6

God's Initiative in Holiness

On a snowy Sunday morning, Charles Spurgeon wandered into a small church to attend the worship service. When the preacher challenged him to turn to Jesus Christ, the fifteen-year-old boy experienced "the great change," a chapter title of his autobiography. He moved from conviction of sin to "full exhilaration" with his new relationship with Jesus. He recognized God worked in his heart to bring about this conversion in his life. He experienced forgiveness for sin and declared, "Oh, how I wondered that *I* should be pardoned.... The wonder was that it should come to *me*. I marveled that He should be able to pardon such sins as mine, such crimes, so numerous and so black."[1] He continues, "I hear his voice—it is full of sweetness, I am forgiven, I am forgiven, I am forgiven!"[2] Young Charles does not only acknowledge that God pardoned and forgave him but brought him to the point of believing: "The Holy Spirit, who enabled me to believe, gave me peace through believing. I felt as sure that I was forgiven as before I felt sure of condemnation."[3]

Charles also recognized it was God who justified him. Even though he described himself as a "lump of unworthiness, a mass of corruption, and a heap of sin," he could say,

---

1. Spurgeon, *Autobiography*, 83.
2. Spurgeon, *Autobiography*, 83.
3. Spurgeon, *Autobiography*, 83.

> I know that it is to me even to this day the greatest wonder that I ever heard of, that God should justify *me*. . . . I, who am altogether underserving, am treated as if I had been deserving. I am loved with as much love as if I had always been godly, whereas aforetime I was ungodly. . . . I know I cannot enter Heaven unless I have a perfect righteousness; I am absolutely certain I shall never have one of my own, for I find I sin every day; but then Christ had a perfect righteousness.[4]

Pardoned and forgiven, justified and righteous in Christ, fully loved and indwelled by the Holy Spirit, Spurgeon knew God is "full of grace."[5] Holiness began with God initiating the process of holiness in young Charles Spurgeon's life.

In this chapter, we will discover that the Psalms identify God's significant actions which make holiness possible in our lives. As Spurgeon once stated, "The fallen race of man, left to its own energy, has not produced a single lover of God or doer of holiness, nor will it ever do so. Grace must interpose, or not one specimen of humanity will be found to follow after the good and true."[6]

God's Covenant Relationship

Without God's enablement, we have no hope of becoming godly people. Knowing that he is holy and our nature is sinful, we don't stand a chance of growing in holiness—apart from his grace or power working in us. In theological terms, our spiritual growth is called sanctification. This personal holiness, or becoming more like Jesus in character and conduct, is impossible apart from having a right standing before God. This standing is known as justification.

Justification by God is the solid-rock foundation for our growth in the Christian life. When we enter into a new personal relationship with Jesus Christ through his one-time sacrifice on the cross, God declares us righteous in our standing in justification. We are made righteous through our position in sanctification before him (Rom 5:1–11). When we become

---

4. Spurgeon, *Autobiography*, 85.
5. Spurgeon, *Autobiography*, 85.
6. Spurgeon, *Treasury of David*, 2:434.

members of the family of God, he gives us, his adopted children, everything we need to grow in personal holiness (Eph 1:2–14). We have the assurance that God will no longer condemn us. Nor will we be separated from his unfailing love (Rom 8:34–39). With a personal relationship with Jesus, God will continue to love us in our pursuit of holiness with all of its ups and downs along the pilgrims' pathway. Now with all of his divine resources available to us, we can begin the life-long transformation process during our pilgrimage down the path of holiness, which is to become more like Jesus Christ. With the certainty of our standing before the Lord (justification), we can believe that God will continue to be with us, even when we falter and stumble in the Christian life (sanctification). Justification is undeniably the bedrock foundation for our sanctification.

Since justification was not possible until Jesus' death on the cross, it is fair to ask how the psalmists hoped to grow in holiness. They relied on a special relationship with God, who initiated a covenant with his people in the days of Abram (Gen 15). Years later, he reaffirmed this covenant relationship with King David and his descendants (2 Sam 7:8–16). God would be faithful to his people. In this context, they could experience a personal relationship with God. He affirms his unfailing father-son love relationship (2 Sam 7:14–15) with David and Solomon. Even when his people disobey him, he promises to love them unconditionally. David is understandably awed and humbled and exclaims that there is no other God like him (v. 22). This is the starting point for the psalmists and all who want to grow in their relationship with the Lord.

David refers to the special covenant relationship with God in two psalms. In Ps 25, he twice mentions the covenant (vv. 10, 14). Growing in holiness requires knowing and obeying God's ways. When we obey him, he will prosper our ways (v. 13), and he will surprisingly forgive us when we disobey (v. 11). This covenant goes beyond a contractual arrangement to an intimately personal relationship between a holy God and individuals. The Lord not only forgives, but he "confides in those who fear him" (v. 14). God shows "friendship [and] confidential intimacy"[7] just as Jesus confided to his disciples: "I have called you friends, for everything that I have learned from my Father I have made known to you" (John 15:15).

We also see how deep this relationship is in Ps 103, which mentions God's covenant. Here, David speaks of the Lord's special relationship with his people who obey him (vv. 17–18). Spurgeon comments on this covenant,

> The covenant is not legal, but it is holy. It is all of grace from first to last, yet it is no panderer to sin; on the contrary, one of

---

7. Spurgeon, *Treasury of David*, 1:395.

its greatest promises is, "I will put my laws in their hearts and in their minds will I write them"; its general aim is the sanctifying of a people unto God, zealous for good works, and all its gifts and operations work in that direction.[8]

When they disobeyed, they (like us!) often equated God's angry response with conditional love. They, along with us, needed to remember that God's actions don't betray his love for his people (2 Sam 7:14–15). Rich in Old Testament imagery, Hebrews reminds us that the father-child relationship includes discipline. Thus, "God disciplines us for our good that we may share in his holiness" (Heb 12:10). Of course, we, like David, don't enjoy or want his discipline (Ps 6:1). We can be assured that this is God's "covenant love" and he still loves us when we go through challenging times which are a part of the sanctification process.[9]

Other Psalms explicitly mention and underscore the importance of this covenant concerning our growth in personal holiness. God provides us with everything we need in life (111:5). He keeps his covenant promise to care for us because he is "holy and awesome" (v. 9). However, there are times we obey God and yet, we still go through painful times (44:17–22). In cases like this, we can call God to ask him to show his "unfailing love" by helping us according to his covenant (v. 26; 74:20; 106:44–46). Also, we can look back over the many years and recall the numerous ways God has revealed his faithful love to us (105:8–11).

Spurgeon calls Ps 89 the "Covenant Psalm."[10] Numerous times, the psalmist Ethan refers to the covenant relationship. He points back to the days of David when God established the covenant with him (v. 3). With this relationship, God promises to faithfully love his children and not violate the covenant (vv. 28, 34). So for us today, Spurgeon reminds us, "With Jesus the covenant is ratified both by blood of sacrifice and by oath of God, it cannot be cancelled or altered, but is an eternal verity, resting upon the veracity of one who cannot lie."[11] The psalmist assures us that we can walk in God's presence and he will bless us (v. 15). However, once again, like *Pilgrim's Progress*, we will go through times of "disorientation" and question God's covenant love for us (vv. 38–51). The previously mentioned psalms are instructive for how we should respond to our journey in holiness.

Since this covenant relationship with God is such a pervasive theme among God's people, it is implicit throughout the Psalms, according to

---

8. Spurgeon, *Treasury of David*, 4:282.
9. Spurgeon, *Treasury of David*, 1:57.
10. Spurgeon, *Treasury of David*, 4:23.
11. Spurgeon, *Treasury of David*, 4:31.

Spurgeon. God is our shepherd, and we are his sheep whom he cares for throughout our lives (95:7). Spurgeon comments, "Jehovah has entered into covenant with us, and from all the world beside has chosen us to be his own elect.... He is ours, and our God; ours, therefore will we love him; our God, therefore will we worship him."[12] Our relationship to him makes godly living possible. Based on the covenant, he cares for us in specific ways (84:11). Spurgeon asks, "What more can the Lord give, or we receive, or desire.... Grace makes us walk uprightly and this secures every covenant blessing to us. What a wide promise!"[13] He will give us everything we need in life, including holiness (16:5). Spurgeon explains, "He is our portion, supplying all our necessities, and our cup yielding royal luxuries; our cup in this life, and our inheritance in the life to come.... He knew that his elect would be reserved for him, and that almighty power would preserve them as his lot and reward for ever."[14]

How could David declare to be godly or "blameless" (26:1)? Spurgeon answers, "Faith is the root and sap of integrity. He who leans upon the Lord is sure to walk in righteousness. David knew that God's covenant had given him the crown, and therefore he took no indirect or unlawful means to secure it."[15] He trusted and obeyed God. When life gets bumpy, David could say that God can keep one from stumbling (116:8) or falling into sin, which is made possible by the "covenant of grace."[16] For this reason, the psalmist can say, "My feet stand on level ground" (26:12). Our confidence is in the Lord. So, Spurgeon remarks, "The even place upon which our foot stands is the sure, covenant faithfulness, eternal promise and immutable oath of the Lord of Hosts; there is no fear of falling from this solid basis, or of its being removed from under us."[17] This assurance is necessary when we face difficulties in our lives.

Jesus reminds us that by his death on the cross, we have entered into a "new covenant" with God (Matt 26:28; Luke 22:20). In Christ, we have a fuller expression of the covenant compared to what the psalmists knew. However, this does not diminish the reality of their vital and authentic relationship with the Lord. For them, this covenant relationship is foundational

---

12. Spurgeon, *Treasury of David*, 4:166.
13. Spurgeon, *Treasury of David*, 3:435.
14. Spurgeon, *Treasury of David*, 1:195.
15. Spurgeon, *Treasury of David*, 1:415.
16. Spurgeon, *Treasury of David*, 5:69.
17. Spurgeon, *Treasury of David*, 1:419.

for sanctification or personal holiness. Spurgeon asserted that "no subject is more important or is so fully the key to all theology as that of the covenant."[18]

God's Loving-Kindness

As we have explored this covenant relationship between God and his people, we have seen glimpses of his profound love for us. This unique love is a significant aspect of the covenant. The importance of this love is evident by the frequent mention of the Hebrew word *hesed* in the Psalms (of the 245 references in the Old Testament, 127 are in the Psalms). Since the Psalter contains less than 8 percent of the Old Testament, but more than half of the references to *hesed* are in the Psalter, we can see how important this word is in this collection of songs and prayers.[19] The word *hesed* is rich in meaning, translated into many English words (such as mercy, kindness, faithfulness, loyalty, steadfast love, and loving-kindness) to capture the nuances of this covenant love. This love shapes the character of the covenant, establishing it as the basis for a healthy relationship between God and his people. Since the intent of this love is to stimulate our commitment to growing in holiness, we are wise to pay attention to a few of the features of this particular kind of love described in the Psalms because:

God's Covenant Love Initiates a Relationship with Us

As previously mentioned, God initiated the formation of a covenant relationship with Abram (Gen 15) and renewed it with David and his descendants (2 Sam 7). It served as his commitment to a group of people he chose to love faithfully (Deut 7:8). David acknowledges it is God who takes the initiative to guide, instruct and confide with those in this covenant relationship with him (Ps 25:9, 12, 14). He is the lover who pursued us even though we showed no interest in him. His love is not conditioned on who we are, for sin has deeply marred us. We only love God because he first loved us (1 John 4:19). Our desire to grow in holiness is solely based on God's initiative to form a relationship with us.

---

18. Spurgeon, *Treasury of David*, 4:23.
19. Wenham, *Psalter Reclaimed*, 152.

God's Covenant Love Redeems Us

The psalmists repeatedly call out to God to save them in their troubles, which often included their enemies. They appeal to his covenant love (*hesed*), asking him to show them his unfailing love and mercy (21:7; 31:16, 21; 36:7, 10; 42:8; 44:26; 48:10; 59:16; 66:20; 85:7; 94:18; 107:8, 15, 21, 31). The psalmists also petition God to redeem them from their sins. For example, David asks the Lord not to remember the sins of his youth with justice but for God to remember him with mercy in his plight (25:7). He also asks God to blot out the current sins based on his unfailing love (51:1). The desire for holiness would be a futile pursuit if God never forgave us throughout our lives. We also would likely give up if we never sensed God hearing our cries to come and rescue us in difficult situations. Why pursue becoming like Jesus if he never responded to our calls for help? Fortunately, his love for us is unfailing.

God's Covenant Love Strengthens Us

David describes a particular time in his life when he felt "poor and needy," and his heart was wounded, leaving him feeling weak (109:22–24). He cries to God, asking for his love at such a time (v. 26). When the psalmist is the target of others' verbal taunts, he petitions God to show unfailing love to him (119:41–42). He knows this unfailing love can comfort (v. 76) and renew him (v. 149). In our spiritual pilgrimage, trials and tribulations can derail us if we don't rest in the Lord's love. When we feel like giving up, hope begins to resurface when we start pondering and acting on the fact that God loves us. When we realize the Lord is not giving up on us and offers his love, this renews and sustains us in the most challenging times.

God's Covenant Love Endures with Us

The psalmists frequently describe God's *hesed* love as "unfailing love." In other words, his love endures forever. Psalm 136 repeats the phrase "His love endures forever" twenty-six times. God's love spans the course of history from the creation of the world (vv. 4–9) to the deliverance of his people from Egypt (vv. 10–15), to the eventual arrival in the land God promised them (vv. 16–22). Though his people questioned and rebelled against God, his love endured. His love rooted in his nature (v. 1) deserves our praise (vv. 1–3, 26). When we realize that nothing shall "separate us from the love of

God that is in Christ Jesus our Lord" (Rom 8:39), we thank him with our voices and conduct.

In chapter 2, we discussed how God's work of transforming our lives originates with our inner lives and then moves outward, influencing our speech and conduct. God's covenant love has this impact on us. We are changed when we recognize his overwhelming love for us. The psalmists use *hesed* to describe their identity before God and those around them. They are the "saints" (30:5, 31:23, 52:9, 79:2, 85:9, 116:15, 132:16, 148:14, 149:9) who are increasingly becoming "godly" (4:3, 12:1, 32:6) and "faithful" (37:28, 89:19, 97:10) to God and others. They no longer live for themselves because they recognize that God has set them apart for himself and his holy purposes (4:3). The apostle Paul frequently reminds us that we are "saints" and "faithful ones" (2 Cor 1:1; Eph 1:1; Phil 1:1; Col 1:1) who God has called for his purposes (Eph 1: 11–14).

In response to God, who has set us apart for himself, we express our commitment to this love relationship by declaring our wholehearted devotion (*hesed*) or loyalty to him (86:2). For example, David is a "servant" who is faithfully devoted to God and the covenant (25:10). He shows his devoted loyalty to God by calling out to God in prayer (32:6) and praising him with others who are committed to this covenant relationship with God (52:9, 132:16, 148:14).

God's Covenant Love Calls Us to Love Others Who Share This Covenant Relationship

As God's people, we are called on to show this *hesed* love to others who share this covenant relationship. We exemplify this *hesed* love by showing kindness to those who are poor and needy (104:16). In the same spirit, Paul instructed the believers in Galatia to "do good to all people, especially to those who belong to the family of believers" (Gal 6:10). This covenant love prompts us to warn others when it is necessary (141:5). These acts of covenant love are expressions of our character, which is being transformed in the likeness of Jesus.

God's Covenant Love Does Not Mean We Are Immune from Hurt and Pain

Each of us may likely walk through the "shadow of death." However, based on God's covenant love, we can confidently claim that his "goodness and love will follow me all the days of my life" (23:6). His covenant love remains with us until our last breath because we are his saints who are precious in his sight even at death (116:5), when we enter his presence. Spurgeon offers these assuring words: "Mercy and faithfulness shall abound towards those who through mercy are made faithful. . . . There shall be mercy in every unsavoury morsel, and faithfulness in every bitter drop; let not our hearts be troubled, but let us rest by faith in the immutable covenant of Jehovah, which is ordered in all things and sure."[20] With this confidence in his unfailing love for each of us, we can press on growing in holiness.

God's Righteousness

The Psalms describe God as righteous, and he acts rightly or justly in all that he does (7:9–17, 9:8, 11:7, 34:16–22, 50:6, 51:14, 72:1–4, 82, 143:2). His righteousness is also related to his "salvation, mercy, and lovingkindness" (40:10, 85:9–10, 98:2–3).[21] It's not surprising that the Psalms indicate that God's righteousness profoundly affects our walk with him. However, given our sinful nature in light of who God is, we may question how his righteousness may affect our holiness.

A pivotal verse regarding God's righteousness is mentioned in Ps 24:5. Here, David declares, "He will receive a blessing from the Lord and vindication from God his Savior." The word "vindication" is literally "righteousness," which God grants, not by our merit but by his grace, to those who seek God (v. 6).[22] David asked a question: Who could come before God? (v. 3) No one can, apart from God, who gives us a right standing before him. Only then, with humility, can we come before him as we are with "clean hands and a pure heart" (v. 4). Here, we see how our sanctification (clean hands and a pure heart) rests on justification (to be declared righteous before a holy God). This is all by God's grace, which is the foundation for holiness. Spurgeon comments, "It must not be supposed that the persons who are thus described by their inward and outward holiness are saved by the merits of their works. . . . The present verse [v. 5] shows that in the saints grace reigns and grace alone. . . . They do not ascend the hill of the Lord as givers but as receivers, and they do not wear their own merits, but a righteousness which they have received."[23]

---

20. Spurgeon, *Treasury of David*, 1:394.
21. Diehl "Righteousness," 952.
22. Spurgeon, *Treasury of David*, 1:376. Kidner believes this verse is "akin to justification . . . he is accepted, he is helped to live an upright life" (*Psalms*, 132).
23. Spurgeon, *Treasury of David*, 1:376.

Psalm 106 gives us an important clue why God can grant a person a righteous standing before him. The psalmist provides us with a historical account of the sins of the Israelites, including idol worship. During this time, Phinehas, the grandson of Aaron the priest, killed a couple involved in sexual immorality (Num 25:1–9). God was pleased with Phinehas' action, which upheld God's honor and made atonement for the Israelites' sins (vv. 11–13). For Phinehas' deed, the psalmist states that God "credited [it] to him as righteousness" (106:31). The Hebrew word for "credited" (*hashab*) is the same word used in Gen 15:6, where God credited Abram's faith as righteousness.[24] Phinehas' and Abram's faith prompted both the killing of a couple caught in sin and the offering a son as a sacrifice to God. As a result, they were imputed or reckoned as righteous by God. This imputed righteousness, based on one's genuine faith in the Lord, was made evident by an obedient response.

David declares, "Blessed is the man whose sin the LORD does not count against him" (32:2). The verb "does not count" uses the same Hebrew word (*hashab*) found in 106:31 and Gen 15:6. One's sin is not imputed or credited to the individual, but instead, this person is counted as righteous by God ("imputed righteousness")[25] through genuine faith made evident by speaking truthfully ("no deceit"). Interestingly, Paul quotes Ps 32:1–2 in Rom 4:7–8 to make his point: God credits a person with righteousness not based on works (v. 6) but on faith (v. 9). The apostle goes on to tell us that God credits us with righteousness when we believe that God raised Jesus from the dead (Rom 4:23–24). God declares that we have a righteous standing through Jesus Christ. Though the psalmists and the people of their day could not place their faith in Jesus Christ, they still had genuine faith accompanied by their actions. The psalmists are telling us that righteousness by faith is available to those in their generation. We must understand the claims of righteousness within this theological context.

More than once, David claims he is "blameless" (18:23, 25; 15:2; 19:13; 26:1, 11; 101:2, 6). At first glance, it may appear David has a boastful, self-righteous attitude. However, when he examines his life, he can honestly say that he lived by faith, obeying God's commands within the covenant relationship (18: 21–22). Furthermore, David claims he "kept himself from sin" (v. 23) because God had searched his heart. Consequently, he was not aware of any sin in his life (17:3). Nor was he trying to deceive God or himself (32:2). "He who is pardoned, has in every case been taught to deal honestly with himself, his sin, and his God. . . . Free from guilt, free from guile,"

---

24. Brown, *New Brown-Driver-Briggs-Gesinius*, 363.
25. Spurgeon, *Treasury of David*, 2:82.

comments Spurgeon.[26] In contrast to those who are wicked by their actions and speech and rightfully deserve God's displeasure (5:5), David wants to live righteously (v. 8). There are only two ways to live (Ps 1), and he chooses the way of righteousness which reflects God's nature.

Living by genuine faith also includes daily conduct, which marks a holy life. In the Psalms (and elsewhere in the Old Testament), actions are righteous when they are according to the Torah or God's law. In Ps 15, David lists some characteristics of those who are righteous before God. Authentic faith in the Lord leads one to speak and act rightly with those around us (vv. 2–5) and to praise God (32:2, 11). David also says it is important to declare God's righteousness (faithfulness and salvation) to others (40:10). These actions in alignment with God's truth, Spurgeon explains, provide "the clear terms of reference for righteousness between man and man, and at the same time the framework within which a man may share, and go on sharing, in Yahweh's righteousness."[27] One who is considered righteous by the Lord lives according to his laws. It is inconceivable, Paul reminds us, that a person would want to take advantage of God's goodness by intentionally sinning (Rom 6:1, 15).

In light of his blameless life, David declares that God has rewarded him "according to my righteousness" (Ps 18:20). While this may appear presumptuous on his part, he expects God to reward his "grace-given righteousness"[28] according to the covenant relationship (vv. 24–25). To those who are faithful (*hasid*) to the covenant, God will be faithful or loyal (*hasad*). He will show his loving-kindness to those whose hearts and conduct reflect God's righteousness (36:10). This steadfast loving-kindness will continue for generations when people follow the covenant relationship (103:17–18) marked by faithfully loving God and others.

In conclusion, the Psalter's view of righteousness is instructive for various reasons regarding the pursuit of holiness. First, growing in holiness would be impossible apart from being declared righteous. Our confidence is based on what Christ has done for us (Rom 4:24). As Spurgeon states, the "truly humbled souls often shrink under a sense of utter unworthiness, and would not dare to approach the throne of the God of holiness if it were not for him, our Lord, our Advocate, who can abide in the heavenly temple, because his righteousness endureth forever."[29] Second, in gratitude for all Christ has done for us, we desire to love and obey God daily. We gladly offer

---

26. Spurgeon, *Treasury of David*, 2:82.
27. Seebass, "Righteousness," 355–56.
28. Spurgeon, *Treasury of David*, 1:242.
29. Spurgeon, *Treasury of David*, 1:176.

ourselves "in slavery to righteousness leading to holiness" (Rom 6:19). Jesus told his followers, "Unless our righteousness exceeds that of the Pharisees and the teachers of the law, you will certainly not enter the kingdom of God" (Matt 5:20). He is telling us, notes Spurgeon, "What is required is a greater righteousness . . . a relationship of love and obedience to God which is more than a literal observance of regulations."[30] David and the other psalmists are wise spiritual guides who reflect a passion for righteousness by loving and obeying God, which extends to those around us.

However, given that our human nature is sinful, we cannot follow God in our strength. Therefore, we need the Holy Spirit to empower us to live for him.

The Holy Spirit

God also cultivates godliness through the sanctifying power of the Holy Spirit, which is mentioned five times in the Psalter (51:11, 104:30, 106:33, 139:7, 143:10). With some of these references, Spurgeon addresses the Spirit's role in cultivating holiness.

God's Spirit gives us life. In Ps 104, the writer contrasts life without and with the Spirit. When the Spirit is removed, creatures die (v. 29) and in contrast, the Spirit creates earth with life (104:30a). The Spirit (*ruach*) was present when the world was created (Gen 1:2). When God formed the first human being, Adam came into existence through God's "breath (*ruach*) of life" (Gen 2:7). This point is not lost on Spurgeon, who remarks that God's Spirit goes forth to "create life in nature even as we see him in the realms of grace," which refers to his work in humanity.[31] God's Spirit creates new spiritual life (regeneration) whereby we are born again (John 3:1–8).

The Psalmist also states that when the Spirit is sent, he "renew[s] the face of the earth" (104:30b). Spurgeon speaks of the spring season following the winter season.[32] The morning dew, the mountain snow, and the rains refresh and renew the earth after a long winter or a scorching summer. Spurgeon uses the imagery of nature in Ps 65:10 to portray the Spirit's work in our lives. Like the rain on a farmer's field, Spurgeon notes, the Spirit is actively "beating down high thoughts, filling our lowly desires, softening the soul, and causing every holy thing to increase and spread."[33] God's Spirit even brings renewal to dry bones (Ezek 37:1–10). What he does with

---

30. France, *Matthew*, 116.
31. Spurgeon, *Treasury of David*, 4:310.
32. Spurgeon, *Treasury of David*, 4:310.
33. Spurgeon, *Treasury of David*, 2:94.

old bones, he deals similarly with our human nature. While our bones get more aged, God's Spirit renews our nature so that we become more like Jesus (2 Cor 3:18—4:16). When we look to him who was perfect, we may get discouraged in our pursuit of godliness. Still, Spurgeon encourages us: "In perfection this holiness is found only in the Man of Sorrows, but in a measure it is wrought in all his people by the Holy Ghost."[34] As we submit to the Spirit, our lives will gradually reflect Jesus.

God's Spirit watches over us. The psalmist acknowledges God's omnipresence through the Spirit, making it impossible to run away from him (139:7). The awareness of God's presence makes us very conscious of how we live before him. The fact that he sees everything we do should encourage and challenge us to pursue holiness. Spurgeon warns us, "We must be, whether we will it or not, as near to God as our soul is to our body. This makes it dreadful work to sin; for we offend the Almighty to his face, and commit acts of treason at the very foot of his throne."[35] We are more apt to refrain from deliberately sinning when we are conscious of God's Spirit watching and knowing what we are doing. Realizing that "our presence is ever in his presence"[36] contributes to our growing sanctification. Thus, we ought to revere the Spirit's presence in our lives. David describes God's Spirit as "good" (143:10). Spurgeon comments, "His essence is goodness, kindness, holiness." While David longed for peace and communion with the Lord, he could not achieve this through his effort. As he needed the Spirit's help, we also know the Holy Spirit will "guide and conduct us to his own dwelling place in the country of holiness."[37]

God's Spirit convicts us of sin. In our pursuit of holiness, we can't overlook the reality that our sin does grieve the Holy Spirit. So that we avoid affecting God in this way, his Spirit graciously convicts of sin. Spurgeon reflects on David's experience in Ps 38:

> There is, perhaps, no Psalm which more fully than this describes human nature as seen in the light which God the Holy Ghost casts upon it in the time when he convinces us of sin. I am persuaded that the description here does not tally with any known disease of the body. It is very like leprosy, but it has about it certain features which cannot be found to meet in any leprosy described either by ancient or modern writers. The fact is, it is a spiritual leprosy, it is an inward disease which is here described,

---

34. Spurgeon, *Treasury of David*, 1:177.
35. Spurgeon, *Treasury of David*, 6:260.
36. Spurgeon, *Treasury of David*, 6:260.
37. Spurgeon, *Treasury of David*, 6:338.

and David paints it to the very life, and he would have us to recollect this.[38]

If we want to cultivate and enjoy our relationship with God, we must respond to the Spirit's convicting work in our lives. The psalmist expresses his heart's desire: "I will listen to what God the LORD will say" (85:8). Spurgeon remarks that if we want to "enjoy communion with God" we must "avoid all that would grieve the Holy Spirit; not only the grosser sins, but even the follies of life must be guarded against by those who are favoured with the delights of conscious fellowship. We serve a jealous God, and must needs therefore be incessantly vigilant against evil."[39] When we are conscious of our committed sin, we can't minimize or deny it, but we must agree with God's Spirit about the grievous nature of sin. Our confession of sin must be honest, as was David's in Ps 51. Spurgeon paraphrases David's thoughts, "Not only have I sinned this once, but I am in my very nature a sinner. . . . I naturally lean to forbidden things. Mine is a constitutional disease."[40] Rather than denying his sin, David "is sick of sin as sin; his loudest outcries are against the evil of his transgressions, and not against the painful consequences of it."[41] We may fear or be reluctant to tell God what we have done wrong, but fortunately, God does not disown us for our wrongdoing.

God's Forgiveness

The psalmist declares, "If you, O LORD, kept a record of sins, O Lord, who could stand?" (130:3). The answer? No one! But God does forgive! Spurgeon comments,

> This is the fruitful root of piety. None fear the Lord like those who have experienced his forgiving love. Gratitude for pardon produces far more fear and reverence of God than all the dread which is inspired by punishment. If the Lord were to execute justice upon all, there would be none left to fear him; if all were under apprehension of his deserved wrath, despair would harden them against fearing him: it is grace which leads the way to a holy regard of God, and a fear of grieving him.[42]

---

38. Spurgeon, *Treasury of David*, 2:203–4.
39. Spurgeon, *Treasury of David*, 2:452.
40. Spurgeon, *Treasury of David*, 2:403.
41. Spurgeon, *Treasury of David*, 2:402.
42. Spurgeon, *Treasury of David*, 6:119.

God's Initiative in Holiness 105

With confidence in God's forgiveness, the conviction of our sin should prompt us to confess it before God. "Sins of omission, commission, and rebellion we ought to acknowledge under distinct heads, that we may show a due sense of the number and heinousness of our offences," instructs Spurgeon.[43] While confession should be genuine, Asaph knows the human tendency not to be honest before God (78:36). As a result, Spurgeon notes, the people's "skin-deep repentance was a film too thin to conceal the deadly wound of sin.... There was no depth in their repentance, it was not heart work."[44] The effect is dismal if we are unwilling to acknowledge and confess our sin to God. David tells us it is possible our whole being will wilt under the oppression of unconfessed sin (32:3-4). While this description may appear an exaggeration, experience tells us how nagging guilt gnaws away at us in our thoughts, emotions, and behavior.

When we confess, we are assured of God's forgiveness (32:1-2, 5), and our hearts are changed. Confession isn't always easy, but we must do it to pursue holiness. Spurgeon remarks that it is "beneficial to us to own it [sin], for a full confession softens and humbles the heart. We must as far as possible unveil the secrets of the soul" for our growth in holiness.[45] David, a "man after God's heart," knew that confession contributes to personal holiness. With the admission of sin comes the joy of forgiveness (51:8) and a desire for a pure or holy heart (v. 10). David shows us the actual value of confession. Acknowledging our sin before God assures us of forgiveness (1 John 1:9), but if we are motivated to confess to avoid feeling guilty, we will short-circuit what God has in mind.

When David confesses, he asks God to renew him in his heart's deep or "secret parts." This renewal requires the work of the Spirit (51:11), who enables us to live with "uprightness of holiness [and] will not enslave but emancipate us; for holiness is liberty, and the Holy Spirit is a free Spirit."[46] Our confession of sin is a part of the process under the Spirit's transforming power so that we may be conformed to the image of Jesus Christ. With this in view, our confession shouldn't only include our sinful actions and thoughts but the areas where we have failed to act or speak in ways that would be pleasing to God. Genuine confession is a step in the right direction along the pathway to growing in holiness.

Our confession and desire for a renewed heart, accompanied by a God who forgives without "sin offerings," increase our longing to obey the Lord

---

43. Spurgeon, *Treasury of David*, 4:365.
44. Spurgeon, *Treasury of David*, 3:339.
45. Spurgeon, *Treasury of David*, 4:81, 83.
46. Spurgeon, *Treasury of David*, 2:405.

(Ps 40:6–10). Rather than doing so out of sheer duty, David declares God's law is in his forgiven heart, and now he delights in obeying the Lord (vv. 6–8). Spurgeon remarks, "Herein is the essence of obedience, namely, in the soul's cheerful devotion to God."[47] Because he has forgiven us, we live with gratitude to God. But, yes, admittedly, our desire to obey God wanes from time to time. Commenting on the unfaithfulness of God's people in Ps 78:8, Spurgeon notes that our hearts are "fickle as the winds, and changeful as the waves."[48] We may be ashamed to confess repeatedly the same sin or new sins, but God, in his mercy, knows and loves us. A lifestyle of obedience is rooted in the awareness of God's continual forgiveness of our sins. Being filled with gratitude for his forgiveness cultivates a life of holiness when we obey the Lord. As Spurgeon said, "The life of faith, hope, holy fear, and true holiness is produced by a sense of living and walking before the Lord."[49]

Conclusion

The New Testament echoes the Psalms' central tenets regarding God's initiative to make our growth in holiness possible. We cannot achieve personal holiness apart from what God has done for us. He took the initiative to enter into a relationship with us through the death of his Son, Jesus Christ. By this, we entered a new covenant marked by a new ongoing love relationship with God. We were given a new righteous standing before God, which makes growing in holiness a distinct possibility. For the guilt of our sin, we experienced God's forgiveness upon the confession of our sin. Finally, the indwelling Holy Spirit allows us to enjoy his abiding presence and transforming power. His covenant, righteousness, forgiveness, and indwelling Spirit are indicators of God's grace extended to us, providing the foundation for us to mature spiritually in our character and conduct.

The foundation for holiness has been established. Now, we can enter into a life of holiness with the resources, including Scripture, which he has provided for us.

---

47. Spurgeon, *Treasury of David*, 2:238.
48. Spurgeon, *Treasury of David*, 2:332.
49. Spurgeon, *Treasury of David*, 5:69.

Chapter 7

Scripture and Holiness

Charles Spurgeon loved the Bible! He read and studied it during the week. Twice on Sundays and during the week, he preached from the Bible. On one occasion, he "focused strongly on the need for purity and Christlikeness. As the message unfolded, he put special emphasis on the phrase in Romans 13:14, 'put . . . on the Lord Jesus Christ'. . . . He not only preached *about* Christlikeness, he seemed to actually *embody* that quality, even as he spoke."[1] In addition to preaching, Spurgeon used Scripture to write commentaries and devotional books to encourage individuals and families in their spiritual lives. He trained pastors to teach the Bible to their congregations through the college he established. He raised funds so itinerant preachers could go to the neglected and remote areas of the country to distribute Bibles and other literature. Through all these means of making Scripture known, Spurgeon believed it could change people's lives to become more like Jesus Christ. Regarding holiness, "Spurgeon's sermons, with their vast worldwide circulation, prompted many to greater dedication."[2] The word of God contributes toward our growth in personal holiness.

---

1. Morden, *C. H. Spurgeon*, 107–8.
2. Bebbington, *Holiness*, 100.

The previous chapter discussed how God makes holiness growth possible for us. However, this does not mean we should rest on our laurels and coast into heaven. On the contrary, Spurgeon cautions us, "We are not pardoned that we may henceforth live after our own lusts, but that we may be educated in holiness and trained for perfection."[3] The issue before us is: what can I do to grow in holiness? The psalmist asks the question in 119:9, which is, how can anyone have a pure life? In response, he tells us that God's word is necessary to cultivate personal holiness.

It's important to consider why Scripture, including the Psalms, is indispensable for holy living. As the reader may recall, chapter 1 instructs us that the Psalms serve as a pathway to holiness. Spurgeon comments, "The Bible must be your chart, and you must exercise great watchfulness that your way may be according to its directions. . . . With the greatest care, a man will go astray if his map misleads him; but with the most accurate map, he will still lose his road if he does not take heed to it."[4] Scripture supplies us with the right directions for holy living, and then we must follow the route. The pursuit of holiness requires a commitment "to obey the Lord and walk uprightly will need all our heart and soul and mind." Knowing what the Bible says about the right path to follow is one thing. Then we must cultivate a "holy watchfulness in his heart."[5]

The Nature of Scripture for Personal Holiness

Since it is God's will for Jesus' followers to grow in holiness, the nature of Scripture contributes to our holiness. The Psalms utilize several terms and word pictures to describe the nature of Scripture which shape our lives in this manner.

Scripture Is Qualitatively Perfect

Regarding Ps 18:30 ("his way is perfect"), Spurgeon remarks, "The gospel is perfect in all its parts, and perfect as a whole: it is a crime to add to it, treason to alter it, and felony to take from it."[6] As a result, Scripture is "perfect, reviving the soul" (19:7), whereby we are turned to "God and to holiness"

---

3. Spurgeon, *Treasury of David*, 2:84.
4. Spurgeon, *Treasury of David*, 5:157.
5. Spurgeon, *Treasury of David*, 5:158.
6. Spurgeon, *Treasury of David*, 1:272.

Scripture and Holiness

and our soul is "moved and renewed." In contrast to human philosophies, God's truth "works a transformation."[7]

Scripture Has the Quality of Purity

Psalm 19:9 describes God's fear as pure within the context of his laws and precepts, which are perfect and right (vv. 7–8). Since God is pure, his revelation is consistent with his nature and contributes to our holiness. Spurgeon states, "The doctrine of truth is here described by its spiritual effect, [namely] inward piety, or the fear of the Lord; this is clean in itself, and cleanses out the love of sin, sanctifying the heart in which it reigns."[8] We also know that God's word is pure because life's experiences have tested it over time. Commenting on Ps 119:140 ("Your promises have been thoroughly tested"), Spurgeon writes, "It is truth distilled, holiness in its quintessence. In the word of God, there is no admixture of error or sin. It is pure in its sense, pure in its language, pure in its spirit, pure in its influence, and all this to the very highest degree—'*very* pure.'"[9]

Scripture Possesses the Quality of Light

The Bible is a "lamp" that supplies divine light so that we know the pathway to holiness (1:6, 119:105). Scripture is not given to "astound us with its brilliance, but to guide us by its instruction."[10] Biblical teaching is a helpful guide along God's pathway, cultivating personal holiness. On the practical nature of Scripture, Spurgeon comments, "It is true the head needs illumination, but even more the feet need direction, else head and feet may both fall into a ditch. Happy is the man who personally appropriates God's word." Thus, if we want to grow in godliness, we must use Scripture "personally, practically, and habitually."[11]

Scripture Is Inherently Right

Psalm 19:8 informs us that Scripture rests on God's righteousness. Therefore, if we want to grow in holiness, we will wisely follow his right ways. We

---

7. Spurgeon, *Treasury of David*, 1:272.
8. Spurgeon, *Treasury of David*, 1:273.
9. Spurgeon, *Treasury of David*, 5:391.
10. Spurgeon, *Treasury of David*, 5:342.
11. Spurgeon, *Treasury of David*, 5:342.

can only conclude as Spurgeon does: "As a physician gives the right medicine, and a counsellor the right advice, so does the Book of God."[12] Related to being right, Scripture is truthful (33:4; 119:142, 151). We can be assured that God's revelation contains truth because his nature is true (119:160). Spurgeon astutely reminds us that "his law is the truth, the very essence of truth, truth applied to ethics, truth in action . . . they [Scriptures] are not only true, but the truth itself. We may not say of them that they contain the truth, but that they are the truth."[13] However, truth exists not only to be grasped but followed. Spurgeon reminds us, "Virtue is truth in action, and this is what God commands. . . . We may . . . be quite sure that we are in the right way; for God's precepts are right and true."[14] By knowing and obeying the truth, individuals can be assured that "they are walking in a way consistent" with Scripture (119:142).[15]

Scripture Contains God's Wisdom

The psalmist declares that Scripture is wise because it gives him more insight and understanding than all his teachers and the elders (119:99–100). Spurgeon defines wisdom as "knowledge put to practical use."[16] Scripture instructs how to live wisely on the pathway to holiness. Therefore, the psalmist hates all life's wrong or evil paths which would lead him away from God (vv. 101–104). Biblical wisdom contributes to godly living if we are willing to study the Bible for its understanding and allow this practical knowledge to rule our lives. When we obey Scripture, then "a holy life is the highest wisdom and the surest defense"[17] to cope with the Lord's adversaries.

Therefore, it should be evident that the Bible reflects God's character—perfect, pure, true, right, and wise. Thus, the nature of Scripture gives us the confidence to grow in holiness because God's written revelation provides us with the necessary and correct information to become holy people.

---

12. Spurgeon, *Treasury of David*, 1:273.
13. Spurgeon, *Treasury of David*, 5:391.
14. Spurgeon, *Treasury of David*, 5:403.
15. Spurgeon, *Treasury of David*, 5:391.
16. Spurgeon, *Treasury of David*, 5:330.
17. Spurgeon, *Treasury of David*, 5:330.

The Role of Scripture for Personal Holiness

How does the Bible specifically contribute to growth in holiness? For some, holiness is equated with good behavior, which seeks to avoid sin (moralism). They consider the psalmist's words, "I have kept myself from the ways of the violent" (17:4), as the totality of holiness. Godliness is measured by steering clear of sinful people and their ways. However, Jesus tells us that our godliness must exceed the Pharisees' external godliness (Matt 5:20). There is more to holiness than outward conformity to God's standards.

Neither should holiness be equated with attaining a high degree of biblical knowledge. While knowing the Bible is invaluable, we are also expected to obey Scripture (78:7). Spurgeon reiterates this thought: "The design of teaching is practical; holiness towards God is the end we aim at, and not the filling of the head with speculative notions."[18] Commenting on the psalmist's statement, "I have chosen the way of truth" (119:30), Spurgeon remarks, "There is a doctrinal way of truth which we ought to choose . . . and then there is a practical way of truth, the way of holiness, to which we must adhere whatever may be our temptation to forsake it."[19] Biblical doctrine is practical.

The psalmists emphasized this relationship between biblical truth and obedience with the various terms they used to describe Scripture. For example, Ps 119:168 uses both "precepts" and "statutes," which Spurgeon distinguishes. He associates the precepts with the practical aspects of Scripture, while the statutes are related to the doctrinal portions of the Bible. He points out that some pay great attention to doctrine but not the practical dimension. Of course, others stress the practical aspect while they exclude the doctrinal truths.[20] The Bible provides sound doctrine with its practical instruction informing us about how to grow in holiness. While we must express holy living in applicable terms, we must be careful to refrain from adopting self-management approaches that exclude any dependence on the Holy Spirit. While we must take practical steps to avoid yielding to sin, obedience without a changed inner life by God's Spirit will be limited.

Therefore, we must pay attention to our hearts, which influence our thoughts, attitudes, and behaviors. Psalm 119:70 contrasts an individual with a calloused heart and one who loves God's truth. The latter has a tender heart for God, which consequently creates new choices in life. Spurgeon comments,

---

18. Spurgeon, *Treasury of David*, 3:332.
19. Spurgeon, *Treasury of David*, 5:192.
20. Spurgeon, *Treasury of David*, 5:425.

> Holiness in the heart causes the soul to eat the fat of the land. To have the law for our delight will breed in our hearts the very opposite of the effects of pride; deadness, sensuality, and obstinacy will be cured, and we shall become teachable, sensitive, and spiritual. How careful should we be to live under the influence of the divine law that we fall not under the law of sin and death.[21]

A spiritually changed heart is vastly superior to obedience motivated by self-management techniques.

When God supernaturally works in our interior life, our attitude toward Scripture radically changes. The psalmist exclaims that he "finds great delight" in God's commands (112:1). Spurgeon reminds us,

> The man not only studies the divine precepts and endeavours to observe them, but rejoices to do so: holiness is his happiness, devotion is his delight, [and] truth is his treasure. He rejoices in the precepts of godliness, yea, and delights greatly in them. . . . Cheerful obedience is the only acceptable obedience; he who obeys reluctantly is disobedient at heart, but he who takes pleasure in the command is truly loyal.[22]

We obey the precepts of Scripture because our heart is rightly motivated by a delight in God's truth.

Holiness stemming from a changed heart gladly follows the way of righteousness. Reminiscent of Ps 1, Ps 119:1 mentions the "ways" of those who obey God. Scripture is like a chart or a "map of the road" for our spiritual journey.[23] Spurgeon elaborates on this in Ps 119:33: "He would know that path of holiness which is hedged in by divine law, along which the commands of the Lord stand as signposts of direction and mile stones of information, guiding and marking our progress. The very desire to learn this way is in itself an assurance that we shall be taught therein, for he who made us long to learn will be sure to gratify the desire."[24] The aim is not only to understand God's ways but to practice their "daily use."[25] Knowing and doing are two elements of holiness.

Of course, it is naïve to think we always want to obey the Bible. Instead, we are tempted to follow many other detours, which lead us on paths that lead us away from obeying God. To minimize this problem, we need to

---

21. Spurgeon, *Treasury of David*, 5:273.
22. Spurgeon, *Treasury of David*, 5:13.
23. Spurgeon, *Treasury of David*, 5:141.
24. Spurgeon, *Treasury of David*, 5:208.
25. Spurgeon, *Treasury of David*, 5:208.

know God's way well enough to differentiate it from other destructive paths (17:4). Echoing *Pilgrim's Progress*, Spurgeon remarks, "That heavenly Book which lies neglected on many a shelf is the only guide for those who would avoid the enticing and entangling mazes of sin; and it is the best means of preserving the youthful pilgrim from ever treading those dangerous ways."[26]

God's word keeps us from doing wrong and guides us to practice what the Lord desires. The psalmist declares, "I have not departed from your laws" (119:102). Spurgeon notes, "God's instruction has a practical effect—we follow his way when he teaches us, and it has an abiding effect—we do not depart from holiness."[27] By developing the habit of obeying God's laws, we grow in holiness. Since Scripture is an integral means for holy living, a humble submission of obedience is necessary. We discover the true delight of following God by turning away from the temptations of sin.

Our Response to Scripture for Personal Holiness

With a passion for pursuing God and holiness, Scripture increasingly shifts our attention, priorities, and time toward becoming more like Jesus Christ. Our response to his written revelation contributes to our growth in holiness.

Revere Scripture

A posture of reverence for Scripture is foundational to personal holiness. Psalm 119 provides us with several reasons why this is so.

One, God's precepts and laws are far more valuable than anything else. The psalmist declares, "The law from your mouth is more precious to me than thousands of pieces of silver and gold" (v. 72), which he reiterates in verse 127. This love is a "burning affection for his [God's] holy precepts" because they are "better than any earthly thing . . . better than the best sort of the best earthly thing."[28] Spurgeon suggests that the psalmist highly valued God's laws because its' promises don't vanish like our possessions. The psalmist exclaims, "My heart is set on keeping your decrees to the very end" (v. 112). Spurgeon comments, "His whole heart was bent on practical, persevering godliness. He was resolved to keep the statutes of the Lord with all his heart, throughout all his time, without erring or ending."[29] As we near

---

26. Spurgeon, *Treasury of David*, 1:217.
27. Spurgeon, *Treasury of David*, 5:331–32.
28. Spurgeon, *Treasury of David*, 5:370.
29. Spurgeon, *Treasury of David*, 5:345.

the end of our lives, we may realize our wealth is meaningless in contrast to the promise of seeing Jesus, the incarnate Word.[30]

Two, Scripture has an inherent value to it. The psalmist states that he hates "double-minded men" and then exclaims, "I love your law" (v. 113). He contrasts the "wavering, changing opinion of men" and the "divine revelation" which does not change with the times. It's no wonder that he loves God's written word. Spurgeon states, "When we love the law it becomes a law of love, and we cling to it with our whole heart."[31] A love for Scripture, which does not fluctuate when a culture changes, shapes our priorities and actions so that we desire to obey God. Spurgeon explains why we should love Scripture:

> The law is God's law, and therefore it is our love. We love it for its holiness and pine to be holy; we love it for its wisdom and study to be wise; we love it for its perfection and long to be perfect. Those who know the power of the gospel perceive an infinite loveliness in the law as they see it fulfilled and embodied in Christ Jesus.[32]

A reverence for Scripture is foundational if we are committed to growing in holiness.

Three, we should revere God's truth rather than loving evil. The psalmist mentions the relationship between God's perspective of evil and loving his statutes (119:119–120). We should love his word because he hates sin. Or, to paraphrase Spurgeon, we would not highly revere God's written revelation if we knew he treated sin lightly. Thus, we view Scripture with awe (v. 20) or a "filial fear which leads to reverence and obedience."[33] Love for God's written revelation consequently shapes our pursuit of holiness. The psalmist declares he hates "every wrong path" (v. 128) and equally loves what is right. When the psalmist declares his love for God's statutes, he obeys them (v. 167). We value Scripture, not for selfish reasons, but we recognize the benefit of following his will. Spurgeon comments, "We not only reverence but love the law, we obey it out of love, and even when it chides us for disobedience we love it nonetheless."[34] Love for God's laws motivates us to obey him rather than loving evil in society.

---

30. Spurgeon, *Treasury of David*, 5:274.
31. Spurgeon, *Treasury of David*, 5:355.
32. Spurgeon, *Treasury of David*, 5:330.
33. Spurgeon, *Treasury of David*, 5:358.
34. Spurgeon, *Treasury of David*, 5:330.

Four, we have a great delight in Scripture. The psalmists frequently refer to "delighting" in God's word (112:1; 119:24, 35, 47, 70, 77, 92, 143, 174). The psalmist who reveres God delights in what he has communicated to us (112:1). This attitude to God and his revelation is foundational to our growth in godliness. The believer "not only studies the divine precepts and endeavours to observe them but rejoices to do so: holiness is his happiness, devotion is his delight, truth is his treasure. He rejoices in the precepts of godliness, yea, and delights greatly in them."[35]

When we love God, we love his truth and delight in it (119:47). Spurgeon explains this relationship between loving and delighting in God's commands. The psalmist

> never failed to delight himself when he was musing on the word of the Lord. He declares that he loved the Lord's commands, and by this avowal, he unveils the reason for his delight in them: where our love is, there is our delight. . . . All the Psalm is fragrant with love to the word, but here for the first time love is expressly spoken of. It is here coupled with delight.[36]

This delight reflects the longing of one's heart.

We delight in God's commands because they provide the path to holiness (119:35). Spurgeon remarks, "The holiness we seek after is not a forced compliance with command. . . . He who delights in the law should not doubt but what he will be enabled to run in its ways, for where the heart already finds its joy the feet are sure to follow."[37] More specifically, we delight in God's wise counsel, which guides us along the path of holiness (119:24). This wisdom is far superior to the so-called delights offered by society (119:70). Delighting in God's truth also sustains us when we are tempted to quit pursuing holiness (119:92). From personal experience, Spurgeon confesses, "We should have felt ready to lie down and die of our griefs if the spiritual comforts of God's word had not uplifted us; but by their sustaining influence we have been borne above all the depressions and despairs which naturally grow out of severe affliction."[38]

The psalmist utilizes other terms to express this delight. God's word is sweet (v. 103) and brings joy to the heart (v. 111). Scripture is also wonderful (119:129) because it provides motivation and practical means by "instructing, strengthening, and comforting the soul."[39]

35. Spurgeon, *Treasury of David*, 5:15.
36. Spurgeon, *Treasury of David*, 5:229.
37. Spurgeon, *Treasury of David*, 5:210.
38. Spurgeon, *Treasury of David*, 5:316.
39. Spurgeon, *Treasury of David*, 5:376.

Delighting in God and his truth is fundamental to our growth in holiness. This delight reflects our attitude toward him and our priorities as followers of Jesus Christ. We reject any teaching that is antithetical to biblical truth, and instead, we delight in his counsel and grace, enabling us to become more like Jesus. A serious commitment to pursuing holiness demands a genuine reverential love for God's precepts. Delighting in Scripture motivates us to love God, hate sin, and become serious about growing in holiness.

Know Scripture

A commitment to pursuing godliness is buttressed by knowing God's truth. Throughout the Psalter, the desire to know God's will for us is tied to practical holiness or obedience. For example, we need to have an adequate understanding of God's precepts to reject ("hate") the wrong ways to live before God (119:104).

We need to study the Bible so that we may know and understand what God has communicated to us. We shouldn't seek warm hearts for God devoid of biblical truth. Neither should we seek biblical knowledge with no love for God.[40] Spurgeon quipped, "We care neither for devout dunces nor for intellectual icebergs."[41] In other words, we are to be "God-fearing and God-knowing" and "possess both devotion and instruction."[42] Spurgeon advises us to know God's commands so we may obey them. "You must take heed to your daily life as well as study your Bible, and you must study your Bible that you may take heed to your daily life."[43] The application of scriptural truth contributes to the process of growing in holiness.

Our acquired biblical knowledge has to be applied so that we may obey God. Therefore, our minds must be enlarged with "sacred knowledge" to become "proficient" in the "holy practice" of obeying Scripture.[44] Spurgeon states, "The best understanding is that which enables us to render perfect obedience and exhibit intelligent faith."[45] Therefore, our prayer should echo the psalmist who prayed, "Teach me to do your will" (143:10). "This is the best form of instruction, for its source is God, its object is holiness, its spirit

---

40. Spurgeon, *Treasury of David*, 5:288.
41. Spurgeon, *Treasury of David*, 5:290.
42. Spurgeon, *Treasury of David*, 5:290.
43. Spurgeon, *Treasury of David*, 5:157.
44. Spurgeon, *Treasury of David*, 5:287.
45. Spurgeon, *Treasury of David*, 5:369.

is that of hearty loyalty."[46] Biblical knowledge and obedience go hand in hand. "Only those who are taught of God can be holy." Our pursuit of understanding should motivate us to become "obedient and holy."[47]

This relationship between knowing Scripture and practical holiness is evident throughout Ps 119. We need to be taught biblical truth so that we may obey God's instructions (v. 33). We steer away from evil to follow the written revelation given by God, our teacher (vv. 101–102). We need to learn scriptural truths so that "we do not depart from holiness."[48] There is no ambiguity here about how we go about growing in holiness. God does not expect us to determine our own course of direction for growing in godliness. Instead, by learning his decrees which are "practical," we are shown the way or "path of holiness" (vv. 30, 32, 35).[49]

We expand our knowledge of the Bible by various means. In our quiet times with the Lord, we gain new insights by reading and studying Scripture. Our insight into God's truth is also enlarged through the hard knocks in life. The psalmist was tormented by people who were callous and unfeeling. He says it was good to be afflicted "so that I might learn your decrees" (vv. 70–71). Learning occurs in the context of the challenges of daily life. As Spurgeon comments, "The truth to be learned by adversity is good for the humble. Very little is learned without affliction. If we be scholars we must be sufferers . . . God's commands are best read by eyes wet with tears."[50] At other times, our disobedience teaches us painful lessons. The psalmist also confesses he was "laid low in the dust," possibly caused by his wrongful actions (119:25). He then tells the Lord, "teach me your decrees" (v. 26) because he recognizes God's will is the best way to live. We must imitate the psalmist who "wished to know all the mind of God" because he "pined after holiness."[51] The psalmist's desire to know Scripture must be combined with meditation (v. 27), to which we next turn our attention.

Meditate on Scripture

While knowing the Bible is very important, our growth in holiness is hindered if we don't meditate on its truths (119:48). Spurgeon undoubtedly knew the value of this practice: "Meditation is the soul of religion. It is the

46. Spurgeon, *Treasury of David*, 6:337.
47. Spurgeon, *Treasury of David*, 5:287–88.
48. Spurgeon, *Treasury of David*, 5:331–32.
49. Spurgeon, *Treasury of David*, 5:208.
50. Spurgeon, *Treasury of David*, 5:273.
51. Spurgeon, *Treasury of David*, 5:190.

tree of life in the midst of the garden of piety, and very refreshing is its fruit to the soul which feeds thereon."[52] In other words, meditation which focuses on God and his written revelation brings vitality to our lives so that we become more like Jesus.

As previously mentioned, the Psalter's preface (Ps 1) provides an overview of the rest of the psalms with its themes, including meditating on Scripture. In addition to this psalm, Ps 119 contains eight references to meditating on God's truth. As it was for the writers of the psalms, we must consider meditation one of the essential rhythms to practice.

Spurgeon describes meditation as thinking and musing on Scripture.[53] We commonly do this during our "quiet time" before moving on with the flurry of the day's activities. However, the psalmist states he meditates on God's word "day and night" (1:2, 119:97). Spurgeon comments, "He takes a text and carries it with him all day long; and in the night-watches, when sleep forsakes his eyelids, he museth upon the word of God. In the day of his prosperity he sings psalms out of the word of God, and in the night of his affliction he comforts himself with promises out of the same book."[54] We may be accustomed to meditating on Scripture, but the psalmist also practiced this during the night (119:147–148). It wasn't a technique to fall back to sleep but a way to ponder on troubles. He meditated on God's promises to address his particular circumstances. We have to admit that our minds must focus on many important matters which arise during the day. So, the psalmists' practice of meditating on Scripture day and night may seem impractical and unrealistic.

Nevertheless, the psalmists invite us to meditate on Scripture, perhaps more than we presently do. We must meditate on Scripture when we encounter perplexing issues and demanding situations. If the psalmists meditated on God's truth throughout the day, we have to ask ourselves: how is meditation related to growth in holiness? Not surprisingly, the psalmists provide us with some clues.

We meditate on the Bible because of its great value to us. We have already mentioned delighting in God's truth. The psalmists twice identify a direct connection between delighting in Scripture and meditating on it (1:2, 119:15–16). Spurgeon remarks on this attitude of delight and the meditation on Scripture, "He who has an inward delight in anything will not long withdraw his mind from it. . . . To some men meditation is a task; to the man

---

52. Spurgeon, *Treasury of David*, 4:311.
53. Spurgeon, *Treasury of David*, 1:2.
54. Spurgeon, *Treasury of David*, 1:2.

of cleansed way it is a joy."[55] Related to delighting in Scripture is a "love" for God's word, which motivates us to meditate on it (119:48, 97, 113). Each of these verses refers to the interplay between meditating and loving Scripture. The psalmist desired God's laws because he loved them and meditated on God's truths. Spurgeon insightfully comments, "This was both the effect of his love and the cause of it. He meditated on God's word because he loved it, and then loved it the more because he meditated in it."[56] What we love dramatically affects our personal holiness. As James Smith cautions us, "We can *think* our way to holiness—sanctification by information transfer" (italics his). While we cannot dismiss knowledge, he continues by saying, "you are what you *love*" (italics his).[57] Loving God's precepts enables us to grow in holiness.

Meditation on Scripture enables us to know God's will and live accordingly. The psalmist asks for understanding or a "deep insight into the practical meaning" of Scripture (119:27). Blind obedience is not preferable, Spurgeon warns us, because "God would have us follow him with our eyes open."[58] Meditation fosters an understanding of God's ways (119:15) so that we can walk in obedience to God and his commands (119:1). Thus, meditation contributes to personal holiness. If we want to obey his truth, we must "plan to keep the word of the Lord much upon our minds . . . and only by daily communion with the Lord by his word can we hope to learn his way, to be purged from defilement, and to be made to walk in his statutes."[59] Obeying God's commands requires meditation or thoughtful reflection on what God is saying to us and responding by talking to God ("daily communion"). We reflect on the applicability of Scripture so that we can respond in a way that will honor the Lord by our obedience.

Meditation on the Scriptures enables us to be wise in daily life. The psalmist states, "I will have more insight than all my teachers" (119:99). When we are wronged and tempted to retaliate, God instructs us on how to respond wisely (119:23, 78, 97). However, meditating on Scripture will be severely limited to a mental exercise without a change in our character. For this reason, the psalmist states that he has "hidden [God's] word in my heart" (119:11). We often associate "hiding God's word" with Scripture memory, but for the psalmist, he has more than this in mind. Spurgeon states that we shouldn't consider meditation a "mere feat of the memory,

---

55. Spurgeon, *Treasury of David*, 5:161.
56. Spurgeon, *Treasury of David*, 5:330.
57. Smith, *You Are What You Love*, 4, 7.
58. Spurgeon, *Treasury of David*, 5:190.
59. Spurgeon, *Treasury of David*, 5:141.

but as a joyful act of the affections."[60] Since Scripture is a treasure we love and delight in, we store its truths in our hearts. With God's truth immersed in our being, we have a greater possibility of living wisely. This is practical holiness.

Meditation enables us to consciously avoid sinning against God. In Psalm 119:11, the psalmist gives us another reason for meditating on Scripture. He does not want to sin against God, says Spurgeon, but comments, "He can never have enough of meditation upon the mind of God. Loving subjects wish to be familiar with their sovereign's statutes, for they are anxious that they may not offend through ignorance."[61] Not sinning against God requires more than remembering a Bible verse. "No cure for sin in the life is equal to the word in the seat of life, which is the heart. There is no hiding from sin unless we hide the truth in our souls."[62] The psalmist sought to do this because he "was after holiness."[63] David expresses the same sentiment in Ps 37. He wants God's law in his heart so that "his feet do not slip" (v. 31). Thoughtful meditation on God's truth exposes sin in our lives and protects us from yielding to sin.

Meditation is a means for growth in holiness. In Ps 119:97, the writer states that he loves God's laws and meditates on it. Meditating on the truths allows them to soak into our softened hearts. For this reason, David could say, "Your law is within my heart," which motivated him to do God's will (40:8). Spurgeon explains why our love for God and his word contribute to our holiness. "We not only reverence but love the law, we obey it out of love, and even when it chides us for disobedience we love it nonetheless. The law is God's law, and therefore it is our love. We love it for its holiness, and pine to be holy; we love it for its wisdom, and study to be wise; we love it for its perfection, and long to be perfect."[64]

These comments show the relationship between meditating on Scripture and holiness. We take our meditative insights on biblical truths and thoughtfully integrate them with the events of our daily lives. Keeping God before us throughout the day and responding correctly to everyday challenges enables us to grow in holiness. Our motivation for meditation focuses on knowing Scripture and growing in holiness. These two areas are inextricably related.

---

60. Spurgeon, *Treasury of David*, 5:159.
61. Spurgeon, *Treasury of David*, 5:230.
62. Spurgeon, *Treasury of David*, 5:159.
63. Spurgeon, *Treasury of David*, 5:159.
64. Spurgeon, *Treasury of David*, 5:330.

Allow Scripture to Convict

By meditating on Scripture in our minds and hearts, God reveals specific areas where sin has occurred. Growth in holiness without the conviction of sin is an impossibility. Our natural inclination is to hide our sins from God and others by one means or the other. God's truth has to confront our denials and convict us of our sin whereby we say, "Forgive my hidden faults" (19:12). Spurgeon adds, "By the law is the knowledge of sin, and in the presence of divine truth, the psalmist marvels at the number and heinousness of his sins. He best knows himself who best knows the word."[65]

It is crucial to allow Scripture to make us aware of the deceitful practices (119:29) which pose the genuine danger of leading us astray from God's will. Thought patterns may have deceived us, as well as behaviors and attitudes which we assumed were quite acceptable. Scripture has to expose the lies which have fooled us and led us down a dead-end road.

God's laws also chasten or discipline us where we have erred in our lives (94:12). The psalmist describes a person "who is under the teaching and training of the Lord. . . . The book and the rod, the law and the chastening, go together, and are made doubly useful by being found in connection. . . . The afflicted believer is under tuition, he is in training for something higher and better, and all that he meets with is working out his highest good."[66] The conviction of divine truth is a painful process of learning from God's word, but a needed one to build godly character.

Obey Scripture

With awe for God and his revealed truth, a genuine desire to know and meditate on it, and an increased awareness of our need to align our lives to the truth, we are rightly positioned to obey his will for us. The Bible reveals his perfect will which provides for us a "practical way of truth, the way of holiness, to which we must adhere whatever may be our temptation to forsake it."[67] Scripture is intended for "practical use, and therefore it must be kept or followed."[68] This obedience to God requires our lives to be conformed to his truth. Therefore, we want to echo the psalmist's words: "I obey your precepts" (119:100).

---

65. Spurgeon, *Treasury of David*, 1:274.
66. Spurgeon, *Treasury of David*, 4:145.
67. Spurgeon, *Treasury of David*, 5:192.
68. Spurgeon, *Treasury of David*, 5:141.

However, we must not be under any illusions about obeying God's will. Due to the influence of sin in our lives, the process of aligning ourselves to Scripture is a lifelong pursuit. Instantaneous holiness is not achievable since spiritual maturity is certainly not learned in a day. We need to embrace "habitual holiness" as the biblical perspective because the "holy life is a walk, a steady progress, a quiet advance, a lasting continuance."[69] Since holiness requires habits, such as reading and meditating on Scripture, we have to decide to obey if we want to grow in holiness (119:101). We must be intentional about this holy pursuit. Developing holy habits demands that we be "careful," "zealous," and "self-denying."[70] Cultivating these healthy habits also demands that we repudiate known sins if we are serious about spiritual training. "There is no treasuring up the holy word unless there is a casting out of all unholiness."[71]

It is possible to align our lives to Scripture if our minds, will, and heart are in a posture of reverence and humility before the Lord. Such a person is "deeply bowed down by a sense of his weakness and need of grace . . . he does desire to be in all things conformed to the divine will."[72] We need God's grace to work in us "to will and act according to his good purpose" (Phil 2:13). With this dependence on God, he instills in our lives the desire to obey Scripture. Spurgeon comments on our desires,

> True godliness lies very much in desires. As we are not what we shall be, so also we are not what we would be. The desires of gracious men after holiness are intense. . . . What a blessing it is when all our desires are after the things of God. We may well long for such longings. . . . David had such reverence for the word, and such a desire to know it, and to be conformed to it, that his longings caused him a sort of heart break, which he here pleads before God. . . . God reveals his will, and our heart longs to be conformed thereto. . . . He who always longs to know and do the right is the truly right man.[73]

This commitment to obey God's will is a mark of one growing in holiness.

With this renewed desire for God and his revealed word emerging in our lives, we are better able to obey. Obedience is comparable to a track athlete who competes in a race. The psalmist declares, "I run in the path of your commands" (119:32). Spurgeon exclaims, "The heart is the master;

---

69. Spurgeon, *Treasury of David*, 5:141.
70. Spurgeon, *Treasury of David*, 5:143.
71. Spurgeon, *Treasury of David*, 5:331.
72. Spurgeon, *Treasury of David*, 5:212.
73. Spurgeon, *Treasury of David*, 5:173.

the feet soon run where the heart is free and energetic. Let the affections be aroused and eagerly set on divine things, and our actions will be full of force, swiftness, and delight."[74]

Our obedience is also marked by joy. The psalmist finds delight in obeying God's word (119:35). Spurgeon remarks,

> The holiness we seek after is not a forced compliance with command, but the indulgence of a whole-hearted passion for goodness, such as shall conform our life to the will of the Lord. . . . If so, the outward path of life, however rough, will be clean and lead the soul upward to delight ineffable. He who delights in the law should not doubt but what he will be enabled to run in its ways, for where the heart already finds its joy the feet are sure to follow.[75]

The joy we experience in our hearts is also where the law, or God's word, resides (40:8). Spurgeon correctly observes, "Herein is the essence of obedience, namely, in the soul's cheerful devotion to God."[76] This view of holiness does not take the fun out of living but brings zest and unparalleled joy to the believer's life. This individual "not only studies the divine precepts and endeavours to observe them, but rejoices to do so: holiness is his happiness, devotion is his delight, truth is his treasure. . . . Cheerful obedience is the only acceptable obedience; he who obeys reluctantly is disobedient at heart, but he who takes pleasure in the command is truly loyal."[77]

Conclusion

Scripture is a means of grace for our personal growth in holiness. The very nature of Scripture lends itself to the cultivation of our spiritual maturity. God's word is perfect in its purity, rightness, and truth. Scripture's intent includes the means to cultivate "practical holiness" so that we can become more like Jesus Christ. In order to see this become a reality, we need to be fully engaged with Scripture. We read the Bible to know it and then meditate on its truths to appropriate them in the interior regions of our lives. As Scripture percolates in our hearts, the Holy Spirit reveals specific shortcomings; we confess them so that God can continue transforming our desires and thoughts. With God renewing us, we have a new longing

---

74. Spurgeon, *Treasury of David*, 5:193.
75. Spurgeon, *Treasury of David*, 5:210.
76. Spurgeon, *Treasury of David*, 2:238.
77. Spurgeon, *Treasury of David*, 5:15.

to enthusiastically and wholeheartedly obey God. Here, we discover and experience an essential means to holiness. This is the best and wisest way to live. As Spurgeon says, "To love holiness, to have the motives and desires sanctified, to be in one's inmost nature obedient to the Lord—this is the surest method of making the whole run of our life efficient for its great ends."[78]

When God's truth speaks into our lives regarding those areas which need to be transformed to be more like Jesus, we have to talk to him about these matters. Our progress on this path to holiness continues through communion with God. It is the topic of prayer to which we now turn our attention.

---

78. Spurgeon, *Treasury of David*, 2:177–78.

Chapter 8

Prayer and Holiness

Charles Spurgeon was a man of prayer. He spent time praying alone in the mornings and evenings and with his wife and two sons. In addition to scheduled times during the day, he also enjoyed brief prayers (sometimes one sentence) to cultivate his fellowship with the Lord. One day, when Spurgeon was walking in the woods with a friend, he said, "Come, let us pray!" The two men kneeled and prayed before rising and proceeding with their walk.[1] This example of extemporaneous prayer typified Spurgeon's life. He once said, "Some of us could honestly say that we are seldom a quarter of an hour without speaking to God."[2] For him, one's prayers did not have to be lengthy, but they had to come from the heart. Other times, Spurgeon spent time being quiet before God. "I like sometimes in prayer, when I do not feel I can say anything, just to sit still and look up."[3] Contemplative prayer was essential, as were verbalized prayers. It is not surprising that Spurgeon gives us insight into the Psalter's emphasis on prayer, which deepens our walk with God.

1. Dallimore, *Spurgeon*, 178.
2. Morden, *C. H. Spurgeon*, 86.
3. Morden, *C. H. Spurgeon*, 86.

In the last chapter, we considered how Scripture cultivates a holy life. We genuinely benefit when we think about what God has said to us through the Bible and then talk to him about what he has revealed to our hearts and minds. The psalmist does this in Ps 119:148–149. First, he exclaims, "My eyes stay open through the watches of the night that I may meditate on your promises." Then he uses God's promises to express his prayer to the Lord, "Hear my voice." In this chapter, we will explore the various types of prayer and the ways that prayer contributes to personal holiness.

For a long time, the Psalms have been considered a prayer book. David, who penned more psalms than other writers, describes himself as "a man of prayer" (Ps 109:4). Within the Psalter itself, the writer ends book two with these words: "This concludes the prayers of David son of Jesse" (72:20). Commenting on this verse, Derek Kidner states, "It seems from this verse that the word *prayers* was the earliest collective term for the Psalms" (italics his).[4] The Psalter has been a source of prayer throughout the millennia. Peterson states, "The Psalms were the prayer book of Israel; they were the prayer book of Jesus; they are the prayer book of the church."[5] For example, many of the monastic orders have several times of prayer using the Psalter throughout the day.[6] The practice of doing so is undoubtedly understandable when we consider the wide range of human experiences discovered in the Psalms. They "establish perspectives and lines of vision and patterns of communication between ourselves and the Lord" covering "the whole range of the spiritual experience of God's people in every age, ours as much as any."[7] It is no wonder that "the Psalms speak for us."[8]

I am indebted to J. I. Packer and Carolyn Nystrom, whose book *Praying: Finding Our Way through Duty to Delight* has provided a framework that describes seven types of prayer. This chapter will explore five categories: brooding, searching, praising, asking, and complaining. In addition, contemplating prayer will be discussed toward the end of the chapter. These categories describe prayer as a typical daily experience in the Psalms.

Brooding Prayer

The very first psalm identifies a relationship between reading Scripture and meditating on it (1:2). In the previous chapter, meditation is defined as

4. Kidner, *Psalms*, 277.
5. Peterson, *Working the Angles*, 35.
6. Foster, *Prayer*, 110.
7. Packer and Nystrom, *Praying*, 216, 49.
8. Peterson, *Working the Angles*, 38.

musing on the biblical text. The idea of "brooding" also captures the idea of ruminating on Scripture. It is "thinking in God's presence, thinking before the Lord, thinking about the Lord and our life in his world, by his grace, under his sway."[9] The focus is on Jesus Christ and how he impacts us so we can lead godly lives.

While meditation reflects on Scripture and how it applies to our lives, we diminish the value of meditation when we exclude prayer from the process. Throughout the Psalter, a close relationship exists between Scripture and prayer. Referring to Ps 119:145–152, Spurgeon suggests that this section focuses on various aspects of prayer.[10] The psalmist states he meditates on God's promises (v. 148), but he also calls out to God because he has placed his hope in Scripture (vv. 145–147). Dwelling on God's laws lead him to brood in prayer (v. 149). The point is not lost to Spurgeon. "David at length broke through his silence, arose from his quiet meditations, and began crying with voice as well as heart unto the Lord his God. . . . It is instructive to find meditation so constantly connected with fervent prayer: it is the fuel which sustains the flame."[11]

We often rush into prayer without carefully considering what we are asking from God. As a result, our prayers may not align with his will when we hastily pray like this. Spurgeon addresses this issue, saying, "We too often rush into the presence of God without forethought or humility. We are like men who present themselves before a king without a petition, and what wonder is it that we often miss the end of prayer?"[12] Meditating on Scripture allows for informed brooding in prayer so that our conversation with him aligns with his will. For this reason, brooding "is directed thinking, a basic discipline for all of our living and especially for our praying."[13] When our prayers align with God's will, he responds accordingly.

If we are honest, we aren't always able to articulate our thoughts to God. So, David calls out to God, "Give ear to my words, O Lord, consider my sighing" (Ps 5:1). This sighing may be understood as the "unuttered longings which abide as silent meditations."[14] This brooding is the essence or the "spirit of prayer" which is appropriate when words fail to express

---

9. Packer and Nystrom, *Praying*, 71.
10. Spurgeon, *Treasury of David*, 5:401.
11. Spurgeon, *Treasury of David*, 5:402.
12. Spurgeon, *Treasury of David*, 1:46.
13. Packer and Nystrom, *Praying*, 69.
14. Spurgeon, *Treasury of David*, 1:45.

what is on our hearts. But, whether we pray with or without words, the heart must still be informed by God's revealed will in Scripture.[15]

Our brooding in prayer is also encouraged by the frequent (seventy-one times!) use of *selah* throughout the Psalms. Commenting on the first *selah* (3:2), Spurgeon remarks that this is an opportunity to pray about what we have meditated on in the biblical text. When we see *selah*, he encourages us to pay greater attention to the previous and following verses. *Selah* calls us to pause and brood over the truths in prayer (21:2). At other times, *selah* reminds us to brood over our sinfulness (32:5) before talking to God about such matters. Or, *selah* may be used to reflect on God's goodness to us (32:7). The Psalms provide us with built-in opportunities to brood on the text so that we may pray according to the truths of Scripture.

Since brooding prayer is rooted in the Bible, it becomes the foundation for the other prayers discussed in this chapter. We search our hearts based on what we learn about ourselves revealed in Scripture. We adore God, who reveals himself to us in the Bible, and we complain to him when he apparently fails to act according to his nature. Our requests before God are brought into alignment with his will as we learn more about his will made known to us in Scripture. We now turn to the role of searching prayers, which contribute to our personal holiness.

Searching Prayer

If we want to pursue a life of holiness, it is necessary to come before God, asking him to probe every area of our lives. In this regard, the Psalms assist us in this spiritual examination.

Psalm 15 describes an individual who has the integrity of character and lives accordingly. How can we become such people? At the end of this psalm, Spurgeon challenges his readers, "Let us betake ourselves to prayer and self-examination, for this Psalm is as fire for the gold, and as a furnace for silver."[16] Growing in godliness requires searching the interior regions of our lives and then taking these matters to God in prayer. We must hold these two aspects in tandem. Without this dual relationship, we can become preoccupied with introspection on our shortcomings, which may lead to discouragement and hopelessness. To guard against falling into this dark hole, we turn to God, who offers us hope in prayer.

The way we approach self-examination is essential. In Ps 4:4, David instructs his readers to "search your hearts and be silent." Spurgeon advises

---

15. Spurgeon, *Treasury of David*, 1:45.
16. Spurgeon, *Treasury of David*, 1:178.

that we take time to slow down and be quiet so that we may review our past actions and think about the consequences of what we have done or said. Then, we can talk to God about these matters.[17] However, we often need to create space to have this kind of conversation with the Lord. The inclusion of *selah*, which follows verse four, serves as a solemn reminder to slow down enough so that we can ruminate on what we have said and done to dialog with the Lord. The psalmist reminds us that this self-examination must be taken seriously and cannot be rushed. When we consider the busyness of our lives, the distractions around us, and the internal pressures we face, we quickly realize it is a great challenge to silence our hearts. If we take self-examination seriously, we must be intentional when approaching this time of searching our lives. We must create space in time and our hearts for a spiritual checkup to occur.

We are wise to take this spiritual inventory with others. With the intent to mature spiritually, our invitation to ask God to search us turns this into a sacred exploration of our lives. David prayed, "Search me, O God, and know my heart" (139:23). Spurgeon elaborates on what David is asking God, "He will have God himself search him, and search him thoroughly, till every point of his being is known, and read, and understood. . . . He challenges the fullest investigation, the innermost search: he had need be a true man who can put himself deliberately into such a crucible." With a specific purpose in mind, David is open to God searching his life. He wants the Lord to examine his inner life ("my heart and anxious thoughts") and his outer life with its behaviors (vv. 23–24). Our prayer should be, "If there be such an evil way, take me from it, take it from me. No matter how dear the wrong may have become, nor how deeply prejudiced I may have been in its favour, be pleased to deliver me therefrom altogether, effectually, and at once, that I may tolerate nothing which is contrary to thy mind."[18]

This search process may be somewhat intimidating when we realize that God knows us all too well (139:1). "The Lord knows us as thoroughly as if he had examined us minutely, and had pried into the most secret corners of our being."[19] His search is a penetrating and thorough examination of our lives. We want him to do this, not because he already knows everything about us, but because we want every area of our lives to become more like Jesus. While the Spirit's probing into our lives may feel threatening to us, Spurgeon assures us that God's searching is not like a police officer looking for stolen goods, nor is God searching for something he does not already

---

17. Spurgeon, *Treasury of David*, 1:35.
18. Spurgeon, *Treasury of David*, 6:266.
19. Spurgeon, *Treasury of David*, 6:258.

know about us. Instead, God is like a loving heavenly father who wraps his arms around us and lovingly strokes us with his gentle hand.[20]

If we are open to God searching our lives, we must willingly accept what he reveals. This acceptance requires true humility so that we honestly agree with him regarding who we are.[21] This honest response to God, known as confession, is essential to our growing spiritual maturity. Spurgeon reminds us that being honest with ourselves is the best course to adopt because "self-deception and hypocrisy bring no blessedness."[22] Humility engenders honesty, but honesty also fosters humility. A "full confession softens and humbles the heart. . . . We must as far as possible unveil the secrets of the soul."[23] Confession is good for the soul if we want to grow in holiness.

With humility, we can confess sins that weren't initially apparent to us (139:23–24) and sins we are very aware of in our lives (Ps 51). In the latter case, David knows he ultimately sinned against God (v. 4) and confesses his sin before him (vv. 1–5). He does so not because he was caught but because of the sin itself. "It is not the punishment he cries out against, but the sin . . . he is sick of sin as sin; his loudest outcries are against the evil of his transgression, and not against the painful consequences of it."[24] With a broken and contrite heart (v. 17), he confesses his sin to God, who is gracious and loving (v. 1). Confidence in God's forgiveness gives one the boldness to confess before the Lord. As Spurgeon aptly puts it, "Pardon of sin must ever be an act of pure mercy, and therefore to that attribute the awakened sinner flies."[25] Confession of sin with greater humility allows us to experience God's forgiveness with renewed hope for spiritual growth.

To address our sins, God has to purify us. David asks God to do spiritual work in him so that he may have a pure heart (51:2, 7, 10). Disgusted by his sin, David wants to be made clean. God will genuinely cleanse our inner life with its motives, affections, and attitudes, which will change our daily lives. For fundamental changes to occur, the heart is the starting point. "The affections must be rectified first, or all our nature will go amiss. The heart is the rudder of the soul, and till the Lord take it in hand we steer in a false and foul way. . . . Renew a right spirit within me."[26] Our heart must undergo the process of transformation throughout life if we want to become more

---

20. Spurgeon, *Treasury of David*, 6:260.
21. Packer and Nystrom, *Praying*, 129.
22. Spurgeon, *Treasury of David*, 2:82.
23. Spurgeon, *Treasury of David*, 6:83.
24. Spurgeon, *Treasury of David*, 2:402.
25. Spurgeon, *Treasury of David*, 2:402.
26. Spurgeon, *Treasury of David*, 2:405.

like Jesus Christ. Asking God to search our hearts, followed by our genuine confession of sin, makes it possible to have a pure and undivided heart of love for God and others (86:11).

When we ask God to search and reveal what is in our hearts, we are more inclined to do his will. Our petitions are less selfish and more in line with God's desires. We now turn to approaching God with our requests which will cultivate spiritual growth in our lives.

Asking Prayer

Many of us will admit that we come to God with requests far more than we do with adoration. Our requests are commonly motivated by valid personal interests such as healing, finding a job, or purchasing an antique car. However, how many of our prayers are centered on our personal growth in holiness? The Psalter aids us in this pursuit in two specific ways. One, the psalms shape our request for God to change us so that we may be more like Jesus. Holiness is cultivated in our attitudes and motivations, which influence our actions and words. Two, the psalms redirect our prayers to move us from personal ambitions to a greater alignment with God's will. We grow in holiness when we relinquish our willful desires and gladly surrender to God's purposes. These two expressions of piety are evident in the psalmists' requests before God.

Psalm 119:36 offers us general guidance regarding what we ask God in prayer. We should turn our hearts to his will and "not toward selfish gain."[27] Is it wrong to be given life's simple pleasures? Spurgeon offers wise insight here. The issue is not so much the *object* of our desire but the *reason* for our heart's desire. Even if the object is seemingly unimportant, we still have to pay attention to our hearts to protect ourselves from coveting, which is a sin.[28] We have to ask God to change the inclination of our hearts. As Spurgeon says, "Holiness of heart is the cure for covetousness."[29] Being attentive to this insight shapes our hearts and requests before God.

However, not all petitions focus on possessions or status. The psalmists frequently ask God for protection and deliverance from their enemies. For example, in Ps 86, David asks the Lord to save and guard his life (v. 2). Many times, we have similar requests when we travel or face precarious situations. Does such a prayer reflect a selfish heart that violates a move toward holiness? Not necessarily. This psalm instructs how to make such

---

27. Spurgeon, *Treasury of David*, 2:210.
28. Spurgeon, *Treasury of David*, 5:210.
29. Spurgeon, *Treasury of David*, 5:210.

requests which move us closer to God's heart and purity. First, the psalmist recognizes his "poor and needy" condition (v. 1). This phrase is found seven other times throughout the Psalter (35:10, 37:14, 40:17, 70:5, 74:21, 109:22). We need to see ourselves as God sees us. We are needy followers of Jesus who must daily depend on his grace. With this quality of heart and a holy posture before God, we present our requests to him. Second, the psalmist explicitly asks God to replace his needy condition by being filled with joy (v. 4). As we discovered in chapter 4, joy is one of the qualities of a holy life. David does not only want the Lord to spare his life but to change him to reflect God's joy. God, the source of genuine happiness, can uproot our fears. Third, the psalmist asks the Lord to instruct him so that he may know God's will and act on it with an "undivided heart" (v. 11). Such requests reflect growth in godliness.

When we come with a singular heart for God with specific requests, we relinquish our will to his timing and purposes. Spurgeon remarks, "I lay aside all willfulness and only desire to be informed as to thy holy and gracious mind. Not my way give me, but thy way teach me; I would follow thee and not be willful. I will walk in thy truth."[30] How can we learn to relinquish our willful prayer requests to God's will? We can gradually surrender willingly to God when we know and experience his mercy (86:3), compassion (v. 15), and abundant love (vv. 5, 13, 15). As David Benner eloquently states, "surrender is foundational to Christian spirituality and is the soil out of which obedience should grow. Christ does not simply want our compliance. He wants our heart. He wants our love and he offers his. He invites us to surrender to his love."[31] Relinquishing our willfulness and surrendering to God's love is a mark of personal holiness.

Sometimes, God seemingly fails to listen and respond to our many requests. Like the psalmist, we "cry out to you, O Lord" (130:1). Several times, we see the psalmists crying out to the Lord for his help (3:4, 18:6, 30:8, 31:17, 77:1, 118:5, 119:147). They are desperate because their situations are vividly urgent and they demand a response from God. Yet, surprisingly, they simply wait on God (130:5–6). Doing this often feels like a frustrating experience for us. Rather than feeling encouraged and gaining strength while continually waiting (27:14), we feel disappointed because God has not acted. How can we grow in holiness while waiting for him to respond to our prayer requests? The psalmists tell us that we are to wait on God and his word (119:147–148, 130:5). We are to trust him and take him at his word.

---

30. Spurgeon, *Treasury of David*, 3:466.
31. Benner, *Surrender to Love*, 10.

When we practice the discipline of waiting on God, our trust deepens, and our patience grows as we learn (once again!) to submit to God's good and perfect will. Also, the psalmists permit us to cry out to God rather than be passive about our situation. Calling out to God, who can deliver us, is an act of faith and growth in holiness.

Ultimately, our requests aren't for our interests but for God to reveal himself to others. Admittedly, David asks God to rescue him (86:2, 16), but asks for a purpose greater than his own interests. He wants his enemies to see the Lord's goodness and thereby be ashamed (v. 17). David would experience divine power by being delivered, and, by comparison, his opponents would recognize their limited strength. But, of course, God's goodness to his people often involved God defeating their enemies (68:1). David explicitly requests God to do this. This request looks pretty selfish in light of David asking God to bring happiness and rejoicing to his people (v. 3). However, his petition is not for the sake of personal or national happiness. He wants God to uphold his holiness by defeating those who have embraced evil and hate him. When our requests express hatred for sin and a desire for God to be exalted, our prayers reflect our piety.

The ultimate goal of the psalmists' prayers is to see God's glory revealed. Psalm 67:1 expresses the writer's request for the Lord to bless his people. Again, this prayer appears to be selfish. However, the psalmist reveals the real purpose behind this request (vv. 2–3). He longs to see people around the globe praising God. Praying for God to be honored worldwide pleases the Lord of the universe (57:5).

Presenting our requests to God is a means for growth in personal holiness. Therefore, asking God to respond to our requests tests our hearts. Is my heart right before God? Do I depend on him by waiting for him to act? When it dawns on us that our requests have been motivated by willful impatience, we have the opportunity to learn "willing surrender" and patience by waiting on God's response.[32] Are my requests seeking to honor the Lord? When we realize our prayers are preoccupied with our agenda, we can ask God to redirect our hearts. Then, we give God our prayer requests with an undivided heart devoted to his will. Our prayer requests become a means to grow in holiness.

We have to admit that there are those times in our lives when it is challenging to surrender to God's purposes. We find ourselves complaining to God about what we hear and see happening in our lives and society. Yet,

---

32. Packer and Nystrom state, "Mature people are, among other things, persons who have learned to wait. God is in the business of maturing us in Christ, and this lesson is integral to adult Christianity" (*Praying*, 224).

surprisingly, our complaining before God does not place a question mark on our holiness but is an exclamation of our walk with the Lord.

Complaining Prayer

The phrase "How long?" occurs nearly twenty times throughout the Psalter. We resonate with the psalmists because we often find ourselves complaining. We find comfort in knowing these ancient writers also complained. We may also feel guilty knowing that the Psalms have instructed us to wait on God. Complaining seems to contradict waiting on God because we assume complaining indicates a lack of personal godliness. However, can our complaints contribute to personal piety rather than seeing them as a lack of spiritual maturity? Since the Psalms frequently mention prayers of complaint, it behooves us to touch on some of them to see how they cultivate godliness. To aid us, the authors of *Praying* place the complaining prayers in four categories: opposition, deprivation, isolation, and depression[33]. These four descriptions will be applied to the Psalms as they relate to holiness.

Opposition

On one occasion, David states that his enemy is defeating him (13:2, 4). Four times David cries out, "How long?"(vv. 1–2). He expresses grief because of the enemy surrounding him. Spurgeon comments, "We may not complain *of* him, but we may complain *to* him."[34] After complaining to God, David asks him for discernment to see his divine hand in this situation (v. 3). David expresses trust for divine insight and God to act amid the opposition (vv. 5–6). He is voicing honest feelings and his dependency on God with his complaints.

Deprivation

In one situation, David groans, "How long, O Lord, how long?" (6:3, 6) because he is in physical pain (v. 2). David elaborates on his loss of health in other psalms as well (Ps 38:3, 5, 7–8, 10–11, 13–14, 17). We may assume this complaint reflects a lack of godliness, and we feel guilty for doing so. However, David trusts God by turning to him in this prayer. He mentions that the Lord hears him and can respond by his unfailing love (vv. 4, 9).

---

33. Packer and Nystrom, *Praying*, 194–99.
34. Spurgeon, *Treasury of David*, 2:446.

With his complaint, "the psalmist is conscious that he has not exaggerated, and therefore appeals to heaven for a confirmation of his words."[35] When we are deprived of health, healthy relationships, and a generous savings account, we are reminded of our dependency on the Lord. These situations are opportunities to develop deeper trust by praying to him. Our complaints of deprivation are opportunities to grow in holiness as we wait to see how God will provide for us.

Isolation

The psalmists experience acute loneliness because many rejected them (88:8, 18), and they feel abandoned by God (42:9, 69:17, 77:7–8). Experiencing isolation is incredibly painful. We must acknowledge that we may periodically feel this way because it is a part of human existence. The psalmists not only honestly express their feelings but also exercise faith when they feel rejected by God. Knowing his love is rock-solid (42:8–9; 69:13, 16), this is the time to apply biblical knowledge to particular situations. We grow in our walk with him by acting on what we know about the Lord. When we voice our complaints, we can do so while placing our hope in him (42:11). Also, when we feel alone, telling God about our complaints is an opportunity to express our need for his presence to be with us. We often take the Lord's closeness for granted—until it feels like he has gone AWOL. It is then that we need his nearness. When we complain to him about the feeling of abandonment, our hunger for fellowship with him further promotes our growth in holiness.

Depression

The psalmists are frequently distressed (4:1, 25:18, 35:26, 69:29, 77:2, 102:2) by life's circumstances. Sometimes, their distress is very intense, accompanied by grief and impending death (18:4–6, 31:9, 55:17–18, 57:6). In these cases, they are in a very dark place in their lives (88:5–6). The pain is so deep that words fail, and we can utter nothing except to cry to God (77:1, 88:1–2). Fortunately, groaning "can sometimes say more than tongues."[36] Sometimes, the psalmists complain by questioning God (77:7–9, 88:14). When we feel he has rejected us, we can be encouraged instead of ashamed of such thoughts. "The questions are suggested by fear, but they are also the cure for fear. It

---

35. Spurgeon, *Treasury of David*, 2:200.
36. Spurgeon, *Treasury of David*, 5:305.

is a blessed thing to have grace enough to look such questions in the face, for their answer is self-evident and eminently fitted to cheer the heart."[37] Feeling rejected by God becomes an opportunity to pause and notice signs of his covenant love (77:11–20). We can do this by meditating on Scripture and reflecting on past experiences in prayer. These two acts strengthen our faith in the Lord, knowing he accepts and loves us. Furthermore, when we feel rejected by God, this can drive us into deeper conversations with him (88:13). Rather than dismissing our complaints about feeling rejected, we can come to the Lord without fear of him rebuking us.

We have seen that our prayers of complaint can foster spiritual growth. This is because they express honesty just as Jesus did in the garden of Gethsemane.[38] In addition, our complaints drive us deeper into prayer seeking his presence and insight into our plight. Our complaints aren't necessarily an expression of cynical questioning but the longing for God to act on our behalf. We may not know how long it will be before God responds, but our coming to him is an expression of faith that he hears and will eventually act. With our complaints, our conversations and fellowship go deeper with the Lord. Personal holiness is nurtured at such times.

Praising Prayer

How is one's holiness related to praising God in prayer? In Ps 101:1–2, David praises God and commits to a life of integrity. He does not make this commitment in a moment of exuberance. Instead, he resolves to live with integrity in light of God's character. Praise per se does not deepen our piety, but it does when God is the object of our praise. Praise to God shouldn't be an irrational emotion but a response based on "sufficient and constraining reasons" and the depths of personal experience.[39] We want to live a righteous life because our hearts and thoughts are in awe of the many facets of God's nature.

The Psalms are filled with praise to God by individuals and congregations assembled for worship. We will examine worship by the community of believers and its role in personal holiness in chapter 9. This chapter explores praising the Lord in our personal prayer life. Praise includes adoration for who God is (such as his love and justice) and thanksgiving for what he has done for us (such as redeeming and forgiving us). These are the songs of praise that engender godliness in four specific ways.

---

37. Spurgeon, *Treasury of David*, 3:314.
38. Packer and Nystrom, *Praying*, 192–94.
39. Spurgeon, *Treasury of David*, 2:22.

Praise in Prayer Puts a Check on Egotism

All too often, we like to take credit for what we have accomplished. We feed our ego, but intentionally or unintentionally push God to the sidelines. Then, we come before God in prayer and realize how wrong we were to exclude God by personally taking all the credit. We confront our pride when we admit that God is behind our successes, and we should praise him. When David escaped from Saul, he gave God credit and thanked him for making his deliverance possible (18:32–36). If we begin the day with prayer before setting out with the day's activities, David's example reminds us to leave our egotistical pride at the door and depend on God's resources.

Praise in Prayer Cultivates Gratitude

Our circumstances frequently stress us. David was no exception. In one situation, his enemies appear to be just around the corner, and David cries out for God's mercy (28:2) and justice on the perpetrators of evil (vv. 4–5). The Lord intervenes and spares David, who praises him for his mercy (vv. 6–7). Unfortunately, we know all too often of our failure to thank God for answering our prayers. Spurgeon admonishes us for the lack of gratitude we express to God. "God's mercy is not such an inconsiderable thing that we may safely venture to receive it without so much as thanks. We should shun ingratitude and live daily in the heavenly atmosphere of thankful love."[40] This holy habit would cultivate gratitude as we see God at work around us and would prompt us to thank him. Joyful praise, adoration of God's attributions, and an awareness of divine activity throughout the day are marks of holiness.

On another occasion, David praises God, who has delivered him from his enemies (9:1, 3–6). The first verse suggests various reasons why gratitude expressed to God contributes to our growth in godliness. One, God gets the credit rather than us ("I will praise you"). Two, gratitude fills and shapes our hearts ("with all my heart"). Praise to God shouldn't be half-hearted when one has experienced God's goodness. Three, expressing gratitude in our honor to God generates other gratefulness in our lives ("tell of all your wonders"). By encouraging this attitude, we will discover that "gratitude for one mercy refreshes the memory as to thousands of others."[41] We are filled with thankfulness as we consider God's forgiveness, the benefits of salvation, and

---

40. Spurgeon, *Treasury of David*, 2:22.
41. Spurgeon, *Treasury of David*, 1:97.

how God has changed our lives.[42] Cultivating the practice of praising God in prayer is a corrective to ingratitude and a means to shape a grateful heart for all God has done for those who call out to him.

Praise in Prayer Redirects Our Hearts

When we pray to God, fear, guilt, and shame may fill our hearts. David certainly experienced these feelings. Psalm 34 is David's commentary on 1 Sam 21:10–22:1, which describes his foolish actions and his escape. Fear filled his heart (v. 12), but God miraculously spared his life even though he did not trust the Lord in this precarious situation. Later, when he expresses his thoughts in Ps 34, he does not complain to God about this frightful situation but instead praises God (vv. 1–2). David is overwhelmed by God's mercy even when he fails to trust the Lord.

Rather than grumbling and complaining about our plight, Spurgeon encourages us to follow the psalmist's practice: "What a blessed mouthful is God's praise. . . . If we continually rolled this dainty morsel under our tongue, the bitterness of daily affliction would be swallowed up in joy."[43] Thinking good thoughts is not a self-help approach. Instead, by focusing on God and his mercy for us, we redirect our hearts from complaining to praising him in our prayer times. Glorifying God is a mark of holiness.

In Ps 51:14–16, David praises God for his righteousness. After experiencing the devastating impact of sin—which controlled his heart—he now gives thanks—with a broken and pure heart—to God for the forgiveness extended to him (vv. 10, 17). He expresses similar thoughts in Ps 103. David praises God for his holy character (v. 1), followed by numerous expressions of his love—including forgiveness, deliverance, and compassion.

When sin dominates our hearts, we are unlikely to be praising God for his holiness. But, on the other hand, when our hearts are aligned with God's heart, we will spend time in prayer, praising him for his holiness. Spurgeon offers this insight, "It is instructive to note how the Psalmist dwells upon the *holy* name of God, as if his holiness were dearest to him; or, perhaps, because the holiness or wholeness of God was to his mind the grandest motive for rendering to him the homage of his nature in its wholeness."[44] Praising God in prayer for his holiness reflects the high value we want for our lives.

---

42. Spurgeon, *Treasury of David*, 1:97.
43. Spurgeon, *Treasury of David*, 2:122–23.
44. Spurgeon, *Treasury of David*, 4:275–76.

Praise in Prayer Sustains Us

In Ps 42:11, the writer is feeling very discouraged. When we feel like this, it's hard to think clearly and to persevere. While we will never be immune from discouragements, this psalm points us away from hopelessness and shows us a different way to live. We can find hope in the Lord whom we praise (vv. 5, 11). This hope fosters our spiritual maturity because we move from our particular plight to focus on God, with whom we have a personal ("my") relationship. Spurgeon remarks, "Note well that the main hope and chief desire of David rest in the smile of God. His face is what he seeks and hopes to see, and this will recover his low spirits, this will put to scorn his laughing enemies, this will restore to him all the joys of those holy and happy days around which memory lingers. This is grand cheer."[45] At least, until the next disappointment comes along.

Unlike the writer in Ps 42, David does not express any feelings of discouragement in Ps 145. Instead, he commits to praising God daily for the years ahead (vv. 1–2). This resolve solidifies his loyalty to the Lord, who is his king. Spurgeon comments, "When we cannot express all our praise just now, it is wise to register our resolution to continue in the blessed work and write it down as a bond: 'I will extol thee.'"[46] While we may be reluctant to make a commitment that we may break, developing the habit of daily praise will sustain us during the difficult days ahead of us. The path to growing in holiness could be smoother, but bumpy with challenges and periodic setbacks. However, our time in prayer praising God sustains us for the long haul while we become more like Jesus.

The writer of Ps 71 recognizes the need to prepare well for the future. In old age, when physical strength fades and complaints of aging increase, he commits to praising God and thanking God for his power (vv. 9, 14, 18). Praise in our prayer life nurtures our spiritual growth despite growing weaker. This posture of thankfulness sustains those who are elderly as well as those who are younger. We can encourage youth by telling them about God's faithfulness shown to us throughout many years (vv. 15–16, 18). Public declaration of God's goodness will ring genuine to others when we have practiced praising God in private. Nurturing holy intimacy with God by praising him in the prayer closet will result in others observing a holy life characterized by the testimony of thankfulness to God. Yes, prayer with praise cultivates and expresses a life of holiness.

---

45. Spurgeon, *Treasury of David*, 2:273.
46. Spurgeon, *Treasury of David*, 6:375.

Contemplating Prayer

Much of our discussion on prayer has centered on conversing with God with our requests, complaints, and praise. While it is important to talk to God, it is also essential that we be silent in his presence. Silence is golden because we enjoy being in the presence of another and listening to what the other has to say. The psalmists touch on both of these aspects.

When two lovers are together, they thoroughly enjoy sitting beside each other—without talking! David expresses this thought at the beginning of Ps 65 with the words "praise awaits you" (v. 1). Admittedly, the meaning of this statement is somewhat ambiguous. However, Spurgeon and others believe David is referring to silent worship in God's presence. After considering various options, he concludes, "When the soul is most filled with adoring awe, she is least content with her own expressions, and feels most deeply how inadequate are all mortal songs to proclaim the divine goodness."[47] Contemplative prayer allows us to sit quietly in the presence of God and adore him. This imagery is akin to Moses, who stood in God's presence. As we spend time with the Lord, we are transformed by the Holy Spirit into the image of Jesus Christ (2 Cor 3:12–18).

With healthy conversations, one has to be silent to listen. Close friendships are built on talking and listening to each other. There are various aspects of listening to God. We need to be quiet while he searches our hearts to expose what needs to be addressed by us. When we meditate on Scripture, we need to be silent to let God speak his truth into areas that require change. We also need to be quiet to hear what the Lord has to say to us in response to our requests, complaints, and praises to him. Growing in holiness requires a listening posture before God, who speaks through Scripture and the Holy Spirit, and reminds us of our friendship (John 10:16, 27; 15:15). The Psalter also instructs us to assume a silent and listening posture before Jehovah God, who has a relationship with his people. Like human relationships, we grow and are changed by this intimacy with God, our heavenly Father. It is no wonder that Spurgeon valued this type of prayer in his own life and commented on it more than once in the *Treasury of David*.[48]

---

47. Spurgeon, *Treasury of David*, 3:89–90. Kidner states, "It may sometimes be the height of worship, in other words, to fall silent before God in awe at his presence and in submission to his will" (*Psalms*, 248).

48. Morden states that Spurgeon's interest in contemplative prayer is due to the influence of some writers within the Quaker, Catholic, and High Church traditions. As a result, Spurgeon had a "mystical strain in his prayers" (*Communion with Christ*, 146, 149–54).

It takes wisdom to know when to speak and when to be silent in prayer. There are times when it is best not to be quiet before God. In Ps 39, David is silent and doesn't say anything to God. As a result, he became increasingly upset before he spoke (vv. 2–3). In this situation, his silence was detrimental because he did not voice his anguish before listening to God. In contrast, on another occasion, David tells us that his "soul finds rest in God alone" (62:1). The word "rest" has the idea of "silence" or "silent waiting."[49] While some might question the role of silence in prayer, there is value in it. Spurgeon comments on David's silence, "The presence of God alone could awe his heart into quietude, submission, rest, and acquiescence."[50] In this silence, we intentionally hold back any rebellious words or thoughts to allow God's grace "to bring down the will and subdue the affections."[51] Being silent before God allows us to hear from him and do his will. Besides, there may be nothing more eloquent than the "patient silence of a child of God."[52] Silent prayer contributes to growing in holiness.

Conclusion

The Psalms provide us with a rich resource for our prayer life so that we may grow spiritually in our relationship with God and others. Prayer is a transformative means of his grace when we sit in his presence, allowing him to search and speak (through Scripture and the Holy Spirit) into those areas of our lives that need to be changed. We can move from listening to conversing with him by heartily praising and asking him about our concerns. Adoration, thanksgiving, and supplication involve more than an approach to daily devotions. They align our hearts and minds with our holy God. By continuing with these types of prayer, we shape our hearts and minds by developing habitual practices which confront daily whatever is opposed to God's way of living.

However, we can't grow in holiness on our own, even if we spend time reading Scripture and praying. We need others to encourage and challenge us in our walk with Jesus Christ. Community life—a means of holiness—is the focus of the next chapter.

---

49. Spurgeon, *Treasury of David*, 3:50. Kidner supports this translation mentioned in the *Treasury of David* (*Psalms*, 239).
50. Spurgeon, *Treasury of David*, 3:50.
51. Spurgeon, *Treasury of David*, 3:50.
52. Spurgeon, *Treasury of David*, 3:50.

Chapter 9

Community and Holiness

Due to increasingly poor health, Spurgeon would leave damp London in January to spend four to six weeks in Mentone, situated on the French Riviera. There, he could enjoy a degree of anonymity and solitude while recuperating. This retreat also provided "a close evangelical community for encouragement, worship, edification, and warm fellowship."[1] With a number of his close friends, he would speak on a passage of Scripture, and then they would sing a few hymns and celebrate the Lord's Supper together in his hotel room. On some occasions, his brother or son would join him and on his last visit to Mentone, his wife, Susannah, was able to join him for the first time before he passed away three months later. During his many stays at this resort town, he also enjoyed times with visitors such as George Mueller and Hudson Taylor. Community life was essential to Charles Spurgeon, whether with his congregation in London or with a small group of friends.[2]

We have been examining various ways we grow in our relationship with God. We spend time in solitude reading Scripture and conversing with him. In an individualistic culture, we may wrongly assume that we can grow in

---

1. Nettles, *Living by Revealed Truth*, 621–22.

2. Nettles, *Living by Revealed Truth*, 608, 647–48; Dallimore, *Spurgeon*, 232; Morden, *C. H. Spurgeon*, 157–58.

holiness on our own with God's help. However, the psalmists remind us we need others who can also contribute to our spiritual growth. Taylor claims the Psalter is a "fundamentally communal book where individuals find their place in the world of faithfulness and faithlessness within the context of the community."[3] He mentions the psalmists' use of words such as "assembly," "congregation," "neighbors," and "friends." He concludes, "For the psalmist there is no autonomous spirituality."[4] While there is a place for a person to spend time alone with God, community life is also essential to holiness. The Psalms describe the community of God's people as the *"hasidim"* which refers to the godly who are faithful and devoted to serving the Lord.[5]

This chapter will explore the religious, family, and neighborhood communities mentioned in the Psalter. These communities may be wholesome and life-giving, while others may be factious and mean-spirited. Community life may be marked by religious activities or by the daily ordinariness of life. Through this diversity, these communities contribute to our growth in godliness in various ways.

The Worshiping Community

Living at a time when we can live stream church services, we may find it more comfortable sitting at home in our pajamas while enjoying a cup of coffee. Why bother going to all the effort going to a church service when we can sit at home? The Psalms challenge us to worship with God's people willingly. These are a few key observations regarding how the worshiping community nurtures personal holiness.

Community Worship Is the Norm

Throughout the Psalter, we see God's people gathering in the sanctuary to worship God (134:2, 150:1). David declares, "In the congregation I will praise you," and he reiterates this a few moments later, "From you comes my praise in the great assembly" (22:22, 25). Again, he states that "in the great assembly I will praise the Lord" (26:12). Praising God with the community of God's people is a hallmark of David's spirituality (35:18, 40:9, 68:26–27). Not surprisingly, he encourages us, "Praise God in the great congregation; praise the Lord in the assembly of Israel" (68:26). This is the testimony of

---

3. Taylor, *Open and Unafraid*, 15.
4. Taylor, *Open and Unafraid*, 15.
5. Brown, *New Brown-Driver-Briggs-Gesinius*, 339.

the psalmists. "I will extol the LORD with all my heart in the council of the upright and in the assembly" (111:1; 33:1–3, 102:22). As the Psalter comes to a close, it does so with a crescendo of congregational praise. "Sing to the LORD a new song, his praise in the assembly of the saints," and we do so with everything we have (149:1, 150). Thus, God's people are called to community worship. The psalmist challenges us, "Let them exalt him [God] in the assembly of the people" (107:32).

The early church met on the "first day of the week" (Acts 20:7), or on Sundays, to commemorate Christ's resurrection. We are instructed, "Let us not give up meeting together" (Heb 10:25), because others enrich our spiritual growth. God uses people to encourage us and "spur" us on toward "love and good deeds" (v. 24). We can't grow in holiness if we remain in isolation from other believers.

Community Worship Informs Us Who God Is

Left on our own, we are prone to focus on our needs. However, community worship draws our attention to what should be our primary focus—namely, God's qualities. When we praise God for his attributes, this worship reminds us, with our limitations, of his infinite resources for our spiritual growth.

Worshiping God's holiness (29:2, 96:9) reminds us how we should come before God in worship. Focusing on his holiness challenges us not to approach worshiping God with a casual attitude. Instead, praise to a mighty and awesome God cultivates a greater reverence for him (89:7, 29:1). Spurgeon asserted that "irreverence is rebellion," and in contrast, the thoughts of God's grace "tend to create a deeper awe of God; they draw us closer to him, and . . . the more humbly we prostrate ourselves before his Majesty."[6] Spurgeon also reminds us that personal holiness is a "sister to holy fear."[7] This awareness of God's holiness informs us that, in comparison to him, we are finite and weak. With an attitude of reverence before God, we can worship him with "holy motives and in a holy manner." In turn, we grow in "inward purity and outward holiness."[8] Our corporate worship before a holy God catalyzes holy living.

In Ps 95, the congregation is called on to declare that God is King and Creator (vv. 3–5). Then, the worshiping community collectively bows down and kneels in humble adoration to God (v. 6). "We are to worship in such style that the bowing down shall indicate that we count ourselves to

---

6. Spurgeon, *Treasury of David*, 4:26.
7. Spurgeon, *Treasury of David*, 4:26.
8. Spurgeon, *Treasury of David*, 2:30.

be as nothing in the presence of the all glorious Lord. . . . It is seemly that an adoring heart should show its awe by prostrating the body, and bending the knee."[9] Similarly, when Peter realized Jesus knew the Sea of Galilee with its fish better than he did, Peter fell to his knees, recognizing his sinfulness (Luke 5:8).

Singing about God's greatness is a splendid way to humble ourselves before our Creator. We must depend on his care because we are his feeble and helpless sheep (95:7, 100:3). It's important to note that the psalmist refers to the "flock." We are a community of sheep reminding ourselves of our interconnectedness to one another. Therefore, we must follow God together along the "paths of righteousness" (23:3). However, when we collectively refuse to follow him, our hearts are hardened (95:8). We can avoid this plight by adoring God and humbling our hearts as a community of God's people. Softened hearts before God, our King and Creator, lead us along the path to holiness.

Whatever attributes of God we worship, we should ponder on how they shape our character and how we express ourselves in daily life. For example, when we praise God for his covenant love, this should prompt us to ask God to fill us with his love so that we might covenant to love others as we walk through life with them.

Community Worship Reinforces Godly Values[10]

In Ps 26, David has come to the house of God to worship him with many others (vv. 5, 8, 12).[11] He has decided to worship based on love (v. 8) and a rejection of evil (vv. 4–5). He values holiness (vv. 6, 11) and highly prioritizes worshiping God. "God's worship requires us to be holy in life. . . . We see from this verse that holy minds delight in the worship of the Lord, and find their sweetest solace at his altar; and that it is their deepest concern never to enter upon any course of action which would unfit them for the most sacred communion with God."[12] When we hear the call to worship by those who are "upright in heart" (32:11), it is appropriate to ask God to examine our hearts (26:2) to reveal if we value holy living.

---

9. Spurgeon, *Treasury of David*, 4:166.

10. Smith states, "Worship is the heart of discipleship if and only if worship is a repertoire of Spirit-endued practices that grab hold of your gut, recalibrate your *kardia*, and capture your imagination" (*You Are What You Love*, 83).

11. Kidner points out that the word "great assembly" is plural, and thus, there are "multitudes of fellow believers" who are worshiping God with David (*Psalms*, 137).

12. Spurgeon, *Treasury of David*, 1:417.

When we gather with others to worship God with hymns and songs which focus on his nature, this should cause us to ask, "Are my values, priorities, and decisions in alignment with his righteousness, love, justice, and forgiveness?" Community worship creates the opportunity for us to ask such a question. A positive response reinforces our commitment to personal holiness through community worship.

Community Worship Reminds Us of God's Goodness

When we meet to praise God, we express thankfulness for the many ways he has cared for and loved us. The Psalms were written for congregational worship to point people to the Lord's goodness shown to them throughout their history. These thanksgiving songs give us an account of the past and a challenge for the present. That is, they are a call to holiness.

Several psalms recount God delivering his people from Egypt and preserving them during their years of wandering in the wilderness. After Ps 81 briefly summarizes Israel's past, God rebukes them for their ingratitude and rebelliousness (vv. 11–12), and they are called on to listen to God once again (vv. 8, 13). Psalm 107 graphically describes the many times God rescued his people who had rebelled against him. Psalm 111 reiterates the same theme of God's many acts of deliverance. Hearing of God's rescue based on his loving-kindness, giving thanks to him is the only appropriate response (81:1–2, 107:31–32). Since he is worthy of praise, we should praise him with the right attitude (111:1, 10). "Holy reverence of God leads us to praise him, and this is the point which the psalm drives at, for it is a wise act on the part of the creature towards his Creator. . . . Practical godliness is the best of wisdom."[13]

Finally, Pss 113 to 118 celebrate God's deliverance of his people from Egypt in Moses's day and a few related themes. These psalms commonly begin and end with "praise the LORD," the English equivalent of the Hebrew word *hallelujah*. Congregations and families would read these Hallel ("praise") Psalms during Passover, thanking God for what he did on their behalf.[14] This annual congregational celebration was a formative experience filling hearts and minds with gratitude for all God had done for them. With this attitude, obeying God is not burdensome but a joyful privilege. Moreover, recounting past experiences of God's goodness to his people is a formative means to cultivate a holy life.

---

13. Spurgeon, *Treasury of David*, 5:5.
14. Bowling, "Hallel," 19.

While it is beneficial for a congregation to have a historical community perspective of God's goodness, we can't underestimate the value of the individual who has experienced God's faithfulness. David thanks God for rescuing him (30:1–3). He then invites the people to respond appropriately—by praising the Lord (v. 4). Hearing stories of what God has done in one's individual life is a powerful testimony of his love, and a means to strengthen one's faith. For these two reasons, God calls us to praise him. Spurgeon challenges us to "let your holiness constrain you to sing. You are his saints—chosen, blood bought, called, and set apart for God; sanctified on purpose that you should offer the daily sacrifice of praise."[15] As holy people of God, it is only appropriate that we praise "his holy name" (v. 4). In light of this, Spurgeon comments, "Holiness is an attribute which inspires the deepest awe, and demands a reverent mind; but still give thanks at the remembrance of it. 'Holy, holy, holy!' is the song of seraphim and cherubim; let us join it—not dolefully, as though we trembled at the holiness of God, but cheerfully, as humbly rejoicing in it."[16]

The call to the community of faith to worship the Almighty God is intended to have a profound spiritual impact on our personal lives. Ephesians 5:19 reminds us to "speak to one another with psalms, hymns, and spiritual songs." Filled with the Holy Spirit (v. 18), our worship encourages others. With others, we cultivate our love for Christ and strengthen our faith walk with him. We need one another to grow in Christlikeness.

The Mentoring Community

Those who mentor others help them grow in various areas, whether in knowledge, personal growth, or specific skills. In the Christian context, mentoring relationships include teaching truths of the Christian faith, instructing and modeling how to grow as a disciple of Jesus Christ, learning to share the gospel with others, and leading home Bible studies.[17] Those who are newer in their walk with Jesus can look to others who can mentor them so that they may grow in spiritual maturity.

Throughout the Bible, we see mentoring taking place. As they go about the day, parents intentionally teach their children about God's laws (Deut 6:7–9). This teaching might occur while sitting at home or going about the daily tasks (v. 7). In addition to teaching, mentoring involves modeling,

---

15. Spurgeon, *Treasury of David*, 5:44.
16. Spurgeon, *Treasury of David*, 2:45.
17. Clinton and Stanley, *Connecting*, 47–85.

which influences others as they observe us (vv. 8–9). The early church continued the practice of mentoring others.

The early church continued the practice of intentionally mentoring others. For example, the apostle Paul mentored Timothy, a young man, and an emerging church leader. Also, mature men and women taught and shaped the lives of younger men and women regarding various areas of life (Titus 2:4–8). Those who want to grow in holiness need to surround themselves with men and women who are spiritually mature and who are willing to share their biblical knowledge, experience, and gifts with them.

It shouldn't surprise us that the Psalter also touches on mentoring others and how they should do this. But, again, this is a part of fostering spiritual maturity within the community of faith.

Mentoring by Telling God-Stories

While there is a place to teach others propositional truths, we can't minimize the impact of hearing stories of what God has done in the past. Telling stories is a powerful medium for remembering, learning, and shaping lives. Spurgeon knew by experience that storytelling "produces a more vivid impression on the mind than any other; to hear with the ears affects us more sensitively than to read with the eyes."[18] Attentively listening to godly parents and grandparents captivates and inspires a younger generation to pursue following Jesus Christ.

Various psalms touch on intergenerational storytelling. One of the writers tells us, "when I am old and gray," he wants to declare God's power "to the next generation" (71:18). In Ps 44, the writer recounts the intriguing stories his generation heard from their fathers (vv. 1–3). They listened to stories about God defeating surrounding nations so that his people could flourish. When the older generation told these stories, they didn't take the honor but gave credit to God. The stories the younger generation hear shape their view of life and God. These are the best stories to pass on to the next generation. "Those who are taught to see God in history have learned a good lesson from their fathers, and no son of believing parents should be left in ignorance of so holy an art."[19]

In Ps 78, Asaph wants to tell some parables (v. 2) to his generation and the next generation (vv. 3–4). He hopes the parents will pass on these stories to their children, who will eventually tell their stories to the following generations (vv. 5–6). So, here we have four generations, including the children

---

18. Spurgeon, *Treasury of David*, 2:299.
19. Spurgeon, *Treasury of David*, 2:300.

and the great-grandparents! Regardless of the number of generations, Asaph does not believe these old stories are outdated. On the contrary, they are significant enough that the younger generation must hear them. However, as we will discover, Asaph does not want to be known simply as a storyteller.

Spurgeon made two suggestions regarding the importance of storytelling. "Around the fireside fathers should repeat not only the Bible records, but the deeds of the martyrs and reformers, and moreover the dealings of the Lord with themselves both in providence and grace."[20] He also recommended reading stories from apparently "dull, dry task books"[21] which contain historical models of believers whom we can pattern our lives as we pursue growing in godliness.[22] In addition to *telling* stories verbally and non-verbally (reading), we are also responsible for *listening* to others within the community of faith who can mentor us in our relationship with Jesus Christ. Listening to others is an opportunity to learn from older people who can mentor us in pursuing personal holiness.

Mentoring with a Holy Purpose

While listening to stories of the past may be enthralling, the psalms point us to an essential reason for sharing these accounts. Undoubtedly, hard times will come our way from time to time. The writer of Ps 44 describes the very difficult afflictions God's people are going through. We naturally ask questions about God's lack of response during these times. We can become resentful and angry at his apparent lack of concern for us. In situations like this, it is encouraging to recount the stories of God's past faithfulness and ask him once again to show his unfailing love (v. 26). This can sustain us even when we realize that our suffering, including the possibility of death, may be God's will for us. Being mentored by seasoned believers who have undergone the most painful experiences encourages us to persevere and grow in godliness. Their spiritual maturity enables us to see the importance of holding on to those past stories of God's faithful love.

Asaph also had a reason for recounting past stories of how God had revealed himself to his people. Spurgeon suggests God uses "parables" (78:2) or analogies to trace "the story of Israel and the lives of the believers."[23] Asaph wanted the present and future generations to learn from the past and apply the lessons to their current situations (vv. 6–7). He wanted them to

20. Spurgeon, *Treasury of David*, 3:331.
21. Spurgeon, *Treasury of David*, 3:331.
22. Clinton and Stanley, *Connecting*, 147–54.
23. Spurgeon, *Treasury of David*, 3:331.

trust in the Lord because he, who was faithful in the past, would continue to be faithful to the present generation. Spurgeon warns us, "Those who forget God's works are sure to fail in their own. He who does not keep God's love in memory is not likely to remember his law. The design of teaching is practical; holiness towards God is the end we aim at, and not filling the head with speculative notions."[24] Learning about God's work throughout the centuries includes drawing practical lessons from the past that we can apply to our present lives. These historical lessons will contribute to growth in our walk with Jesus Christ.

Suppose we don't learn these lessons for personal godliness. In that case, we will likely fall into the same trap of stubbornness and rebelliousness that earlier generations have fallen into (v. 8). Hearing past stories of continued disobedience and the consequences should prompt us to love and follow the Lord. Effective mentoring includes sharing the inspiring stories of God's goodness and the painful ones that serve as somber warnings for us. We need the community of believers to encourage and warn us along the path of holiness. Their wise words require listening attentively to what others are saying.

Mentoring by Modeling Godliness

The mentoring process is short-circuited when we learn biblical truths, but don't see them modeled by others. So, it is not surprising that the Psalms call believers to model the truth. To become like Jesus, we need godly examples to follow.

Psalms 112 and 128 explicitly refer to modeling a godly life and its impact on family relationships. Holy living is evidenced by fearing or reverencing God and delighting in his commands, leading to living with his favor (112:1; 128:1, 4). Spurgeon's comments are critical to consider in the context of mentoring others.

> This fear of the Lord is the fit fountain of holy living; we look in vain for holiness apart from it; none but those who fear the Lord will ever walk in his ways.... It is idle to talk of fearing the Lord if we act like those who have no care whether there be a God or no, God's ways will be our ways if we have a sincere reverence for him: if the heart is joined unto God, the feet will follow hard after him. A man's heart will be seen in his walk, and the blessing will come where heart and walk are both with God.[25]

---

24. Spurgeon, *Treasury of David*, 3:332.
25. Spurgeon, *Treasury of David*, 6:97.

One who exemplifies a godly life can expect family relationships to be blessed (112:2, 128:3). Spurgeon emphasizes that "family blessedness comes from the Lord. . . . To the Lord alone we must look for it. . . . There must be the blessing of God, the influence of piety, the result of holy living."[26] We should consider this blessing to be something other than an iron-clad guarantee. Having a godly family, Spurgeon wisely notes, "It must be understood as a general statement rather than a promise made to every individual, for the children of the godly are not all prosperous, nor all famous." Neither do they all follow the Lord. He continues, "Nevertheless . . . the children of the righteous man commence life with greater advantages than others, and are more likely to succeed in it, in the best and highest sense."[27]

Mentoring by God's Enablement

David declares, "I will walk in my house with blameless heart. I will set before my eyes no vile thing" (101:3). But, in the very place he made this personal promise, he betrayed it—with tragic results.[28] Spurgeon warns us,

> Piety must begin at home. Reader, how fares it with your family? Do you sing in the choir and sin in the chamber? Are you a saint abroad and a devil at home? For shame! What we are at home, that we are indeed. He cannot be a good king whose palace is the haunt of vice, nor he a true saint whose habitation is a scene of strife, nor he a faithful minister whose household dreads his appearance at the fireside.[29]

Then, Spurgeon reminds us that "we are no better than David."[30] We need the Holy Spirit to empower our lives if we want to resist sin and model a consistent godly life. Effective mentoring by others includes hearing past stories of God's working in people's lives and examples of godliness. Also, if we want to follow exemplars of godliness, we need God's Spirit to enable us to imitate them.

Psalm 127 reminds us that God must be involved in our spiritual growth. Three times the word "vain" is used (vv. 1–2). Our efforts will be futile if we don't depend on him and seek his divine favor in our activities. Parents who face the demands of raising children know too well their

---

26. Spurgeon, *Treasury of David*, 6:99.
27. Spurgeon, *Treasury of David*, 5:16.
28. Kidner, *Psalms*, 391.
29. Spurgeon, *Treasury of David*, 4:240.
30. Spurgeon, *Treasury of David*, 4:240.

shortcomings and continual need for God's help. This dependence on God is an opportunity for the parents to grow in their walk with Christ. At the same time, through their parents' lives and the Holy Spirit working in them, children can also grow spiritually with a passion for Jesus. Family life is "domestic spirituality," which provides the setting for each person to grow in "domestic holiness."[31]

The Neighboring Community

For most followers of Christ, most of the time is spent not in structured religious activities but in the routines and rhythms of daily interactions with people in the home, workplace, residential environments, and church settings. They are our neighbors. The Psalter refers to diverse groups of people we frequently associate with during the week. Some of them are followers of God mentioned in the Songs of Ascent or Pilgrim Songs (120–134). Groups primarily sang these psalms of people as they traversed the gradual climb to Jerusalem to celebrate the religious feasts. But until they arrived, they had the daily grind of packing, loading, and unloading. Psalm 84 is a description of this journey. Is it possible for us to grow in holiness whereby we love God and others amid life's daily challenges? The Psalter provides us with the answer.

Sacred Companion Relationships

Developing close friendships is challenging in an individualistic culture with high mobility. Yet, we need sacred companions who will journey with us for our spiritual growth, and we must do the same with others. Psalm 84 describes the spiritual journey, including others who accompany us on this pilgrimage. They long for the time when they can be in God's presence (vv. 1–4), and when they arrive, it is a great experience (vv. 10–11). But until then, life can be somewhat arduous along the way. There are the desert-like times in life ("the Valley of Baca") that are draining (v. 6). However, these fellow pilgrims discover God's power so that they gain increasing strength while on their journey (vv. 5, 7). They also experience refreshing, "even in the dreariest part of the road."[32] As they trust God, they experience his blessing of protective care (v. 11).

---

31. Stevens, *Disciplines of the Hungry Heart*, xii, 35–42.
32. Spurgeon, *Treasury of David*, 3:434.

Marriage expresses community life when one's spouse is a sacred companion. Psalm 128 speaks of the husband's wife, who is like a "fruitful vine" because she brings their children into the world (v. 3). Spurgeon wisely notes that not all wives bear children, but they may still be "fruitful." He sensitively notes, "Good wives are also fruitful in kindness, thrift, helpfulness, and affection. If they bear no children, they are by no means barren if they yield us the wine of consolation and the clusters of comfort. Truly blessed is the man whose wife is fruitful in those good works, which are suitable to her near and dear position."[33] Ray Rhodes's inspiring account of Susannah Spurgeon's life reveals how she both comforted Charles during the difficult times and ministered to poor pastors through her Book Fund and Pastors' Aid Fund. And he encouraged his wife during her prolonged period of illness. In her words, she and Charles were "two pilgrims treading this highway of life together, hand in hand, heart linked to heart."[34]

Sacred companions may include a spouse, adult children, parents, and friends who know us well. We need them to nurture, encourage, impart wisdom, and share our life's struggles and joys. Through them, we have the real possibility of growing in holiness. And they need us too. When those times come when we feel overwhelmed by their needs, we grow in spiritual maturity when we realize our dependence on the Lord's resources. We grow in holiness when others journey with us in life and when we depend on God's strength.

Shalom Relationships

The daily news and personal experiences painfully remind us how difficult it is to live in harmony with others. To those who live in Jerusalem, David calls for them to live in peace with one another (122:6–8). When he urges people to pray for the peace of Jerusalem (v. 6), he is not referring to the cessation of hostilities with international enemies. Instead, he calls upon the city's residents to live in peace with one another (vv. 7–8; Heb 7:2). The God-given name of the city, Jerusalem, also reminds the people to have wholesome (*shalom*) relationships with one another. This community life represents the true essence of living in peace.

Wholesome relationships require hard work. In another psalm, David challenges the people to "seek peace and pursue it" (34:14). Spurgeon knew God's people do not always live peaceably with each other. He notes, "In a church one of the main ingredients of success is internal peace; strife,

33. Spurgeon, *Treasury of David*, 6:98–99.
34. Rhodes, *Susie*, 220.

suspicion, party-spirit, division—these are deadly things."[35] The apostle Paul appeals to his readers in the first-century church to "live in peace" with one another (2 Cor 13:11). We can only do this through the influence of the Holy Spirit in our lives (Gal 5:22).

Living in peace with those around us is another way to grow in holiness. When others have a factious spirit, we need to depend on the Spirit's power to live peaceably among them. Unfortunately, we may be the ones who pick fights and become divisive. When this is the case, we need to heed the warning of others who call us out for our behavior and attitudes. Their call for us to love authentic people can move us to grow in personal holiness. Growth in this area of our lives allows us to bring God's peace to others. His peace, a mark of holiness, fills our hearts, overflowing with those we meet. With his peace, our experience of wholeness influences our walk as sacred companions with others.

Unified Relationships

Psalm 133, another Pilgrim Song, reminds us that we must live in unity. Living in harmony brings refreshing among God's people (v. 2), including those who are different from us (v. 3).

We, along with Spurgeon, know that unity is not easily achieved. "How many families are rent by fierce feuds, and exhibit a spectacle which is neither good nor pleasant!"[36] Learning to live in unity is an opportunity to grow in holiness. Since the relationships among the holy triune God reflect unity (John 17), we must pursue relational unity—a mark of godliness. United with Christ, we are called on to live in harmony with one another (Rom 15:5; 1 Cor 1:10; Phil 2:1–4; Col 2:2). When others are divisive, we may be more prone to retaliate or withdraw and not love them. We need the Holy Spirit to pursue unity with them at such times. Other times, our attitudes and conduct may contribute to divisiveness. When people challenge us, we can repent and ask God to change our hearts and behavior. These real-life situations are opportunities to grow in holiness.

Loving Relationships

The psalmists are realistic about life. David frequently mentions the loss of close friendships he once enjoyed. He had friends who turned against him

---

35. Spurgeon, *Treasury of David*, 6:29.
36. Spurgeon, *Treasury of David*, 6:167.

for one reason or another. Some now avoid him altogether (31:11b, 38:11, 88:8), and others oppose him (41:9; 55:13, 20). Whatever the reason, the loss of a close friend is a dark experience (88:18). David tells us of another painful loss involving family members who don't want to have anything more to do with him. Being alienated and treated like a stranger by the family is profoundly hurtful (69:8). His son, Absalom, rejected him by quietly building a conspiracy to overthrow his father as the king (2 Sam 15). Even David's close advisor, Ahithophel, also turned against him (2 Sam 15:12, 16:21–23). Centuries later, Jesus, on the night Judas betrayed him, quotes David, who said, "Even my close friend . . . he who shared my bread, has lifted up his heel against me" (41:9; John 13:18).

At first glance, hurtful and broken relationships seemingly have little to do with personal godliness. However, when this happens to us, Jesus tells us to love others, including those who strongly oppose us (Matt 5:43–45). Then he concludes, "Be perfect, therefore, as your heavenly Father is perfect" (v. 48). Jesus' statement is strikingly similar to Lev 19:2: "Be holy, because I, the LORD your God, am holy." Jesus is not speaking about perfectionism but about becoming more like God in our character and conduct.[37] Holiness is, says France, a "life totally integrated with the will of God, and thus reflecting his character."[38] We express holiness by loving those who hate us. Spurgeon reminds us, "Our Lord spake evil of no man, but breathed a prayer for his foes; we must be like him."[39] We grow in holiness when we depend on and are controlled by the Holy Spirit, who makes it possible to exercise the fruit of the Spirit, including love (Gal 5:22). Paul not only wrote about this but practiced it. When individuals deserted him, he asked God not to hold their behavior against them (2 Tim 4:16).

Conclusion

This chapter has also reminded us of the importance of being an integral part of a community. Yet, we need those times alone with the Lord in Scripture reading and prayer. Bonhoeffer eloquently states, "Let him who cannot be alone beware of community. . . . Let him who is not in community beware of being alone. . . . Each by itself has profound perils and pitfalls. One who wants fellowship without solitude plunges into the void of words and

---

37. Carson, *Matthew*, 160–61.
38. France, *Matthew*, 129.
39. Spurgeon, *Treasury of David*, 1:178.

feelings, and the one who seeks solitude without fellowship perishes in the abyss of vanity, self-infatuation and despair."[40]

We need to be in a community with others if we are serious about growing in holiness. When we worship with others, we exalt Christ, who wants to reign in our lives by drawing us away from a preoccupation with self-interests.

We also need individuals of any age who can speak into our lives for personal growth and maturity. With the areas in our lives we are aware of and the blind spots others are fully aware of, we need others to listen, advise, instruct, and pray for us. Equally important, we need people who model what it means to be like Jesus in character and conduct. We need them to contribute, intentionally or unintentionally, to our growth in godliness.

Finally, we need sacred companions who walk alongside us in this spiritual journey through life. They give us strength when we are weary and discouraged. Their pursuit of peace and unity becomes a model for our growth in holiness. When we have a factious spirit, they challenge and inspire us to change, enabling us to grow in godliness and become more like Jesus. If we are serious about pursuing holiness, we will resolve to live in peace and unity with others.

---

40. Bonhoeffer, *Life Together*, 77–78.

Chapter 10

Life's Trials and Holiness

Not long after arriving in London to commence his pastoral ministry at New Park Side Baptist Church, the media got wind of the unique preaching style of Charles Spurgeon, a twenty-year-old sensation. While others flocked to hear this young man, the newspapers viewed him as a charlatan. They described his preaching style as "vulgar," "theatrical," in "bad taste," and "ranting." The criticisms deeply hurt Spurgeon, partly because he was very sensitive.[1]

While he received negative coverage by the media, the 1854 cholera epidemic in London occupied much of Spurgeon's time. This plague, which killed forty thousand people in the city, did not spare his congregation from casualties. He spent countless hours caring for the sick and conducting numerous funeral services. He commented, "Family after family summoned me to the bedside of the smitten and almost every day I was called to visit the grave."[2] After spending countless hours, day and night, consoling the sick and bereaved, he admits, "I became weary in body, and sick at heart. . . . I felt or fancied that I was sickening like those around me."[3]

Spurgeon faced another traumatic trial in his life. At the first service held

---

1. Dallimore, *Spurgeon*, 67–69.
2. Spurgeon, *Autobiography*, 281.
3. Spurgeon, *Autobiography*, 281.

at the Surrey Gardens Music Hall, with twelve thousand people packed into the ten-thousand-seat auditorium, a shout in the audience caused people to rush for the exits. Seven people died, and many were seriously injured when the commotion ended. Spurgeon fainted a few times in the ensuing days, and went through what he called a "horror of great darkness."[4] Every day, he relived the horrible event and replayed the details over and over in his mind. He couldn't think clearly, and prayer seemed impossible. God seemed very distant from him. This tragedy became the most memorable crisis which would affect the rest of his life.[5] This event affected him physically and emotionally.

Near the end of this life, Spurgeon found himself in the center of a theological controversy. His conviction regarding the authority of Scripture created strained and broken relationships among his ministerial peers, financial supporters, and former students. Even his brother, James, brought him great heartache during this controversy. These relational conflicts exacerbated his physical suffering and hastened his death at age fifty-seven. He also suffered emotionally. He lamented, "The strain has nearly broken my heart already, and I have had all I can bear of bitterness."[6]

In addition to these trials, for half his life, he was also afflicted with painful gout and kidney disease. At times, he had to limit his movement to his house. Consequently, he was away from his pulpit for several consecutive Sundays, including a five-month absence. He also had to be painfully separated from his dear wife, Susannah, when he went to Mentone, France, for several weeks to recuperate from his health issues. Unfortunately, due to her prolonged poor health, which was a great concern to her loving husband, she could not travel with him.

Given his sensitive nature and the severity of his trials, it shouldn't surprise us that Spurgeon suffered emotionally. Being sick for five weeks, he admitted that he experienced mental depression. Some have suggested that Spurgeon also experienced spiritual depression, feeling God had abandoned him without healing his diseases. He could identify with

---

4. Morden, *C. H. Spurgeon*, 70.
5. Morden, *C. H. Spurgeon*, 70–72.
6. Dallimore, *Spurgeon*, 216.

Asaph's words: "Has God forgotten to be merciful?" (Ps 77:9).

Through all these challenging trials, Spurgeon continued to be faithful to the Lord and the ministry. With just reason, his problems "had kept his faith bright, drawing him closer to his suffering savior [and] closer to others."[7] At the end of his life, he said to his wife, Susannah, "Oh wifey! I have had such a blessed time with my Lord."[8]

Whatever hardships Spurgeon may have faced, some believe trials are an aberration of the Christian life. When they come to Ps 1 and read about the "blessed" life (v. 1), they do not associate this life with adversities. For them, experiencing trials contradicts a life blessed by God. Those who hold this stance can become bitter because they believe God has dealt them an unfair hand. They committed their lives to him, faithfully obeyed him, and sought to serve him to the best of their ability. Seeking to follow the Lord, they believe the trials which have come their way shouldn't happen to them. In their opinion, they don't equate trials with a blessed life.

Rather than viewing trials as a contradiction or an aberration of the Christian, the Psalms offer us a radically different perspective. The hard times are par for the course. They are one way of experiencing God's blessing in this life. While we don't usually equate a good and prosperous life with trials, they contribute to our spiritual growth. Speaking from personal experience, Spurgeon remarks, "It is often for the soul's health that we should be poor, bereaved, and persecuted. Our worst things are often our best things. . . . There is a blessing concealed in the righteous man's crosses, losses, and sorrows. The trials of the saint are a divine husbandry, by which he grows and brings forth abundant fruit."[9] The blessing of fruitfulness or prosperity mentioned in Ps 1 includes trials that contribute to our holiness. We develop "this-worldly holiness that is lived out in the midst of pain and conflict of the world."[10] It is worth paying attention to the psalmists' attitude toward trials so we can learn from them and grow in holiness.

The writers of the psalms knew very well that God's people face many troubles in life (34:19). If David, a man after God's heart, experienced many hardships and afflictions (132:1), we should realize and accept the fact that

---

7. Morden, *Communion with Christ*, 259.
8. Morden, *C. H. Spurgeon*, 167.
9. Spurgeon, *Treasury of David*, 1:2.
10. Bloesch, *Holy Spirit*, 320.

neither are we immune from trials. The Psalms don't provide room for a romantic view of life without struggles for those who are serious about their commitment to God.

The psalmists express three broad types of trials they faced in their lives. First, they met enemies who hated them and threatened them with death. This hatred is usually not based on wrongdoing on the psalmists' part but because they associated themselves with God (38:19–20). Pain is also acutely felt when family or close friends reject us (3, 31:11, 38:11). "It is very hard when those who should be the first to come to the rescue are the first to desert us."[11] Second, the psalmists experienced personal afflictions, such as physical ailments and deprivation of food. Finally, the psalmists' trials were triggered by a profound sense that God had abandoned them. These three categories, which we also experience, provide us with several insights regarding how we can grow in holiness.

Holiness through Relational Trials

Trials and Groups of People

Many of the psalms describe David and other psalmists facing adversities from their enemies (25, 35, 52:1–4, 56:1–2, 57:1–4, 59, 140:1–5). While David faced enemies outside of Israel (1 Chr 18:1–10), he also faced them from within his own country. For example, Ps 59 depicts King Saul trying to kill David, and Ps 35 may refer to the same threat, or it may refer to the insurrections David faced at a later time when he was king. These attacks included physical threats to his life and verbal accusations (35:3–4, 7).

Some of the most painful trials mentioned in the Psalter include the family conflict between David and his son Absalom along with his allies. Psalm 3 has the caption "a Psalm of David, when he fled from his son Absalom" in some Bible versions. It is believed that David wrote this psalm describing this painful experience when he had to flee from Absalom (2 Sam 15). His son turned against him and recruited many others from David's ranks (such as Hushai and Ahithophel). Those close to David became his foes (3:1). On top of this, his adversaries claimed that God had abandoned him and he was no longer the rightful king (v. 2).

The accusations against David were painful because they were slanderous. If he wrote Ps 119 (as Spurgeon believed), he mentions princes slandering him and then facing people's "scorn and contempt" (vv. 22–23). One historical example of a false and defamatory charge against David is

---

11. Spurgeon, *Treasury of David*, 2:201.

described in Ps 7. The heading mentions Cush, a Benjamite from Saul's tribe. Many of David's enemies came from this tribe (2 Sam 16:5–13; 20:1–2, 6). As previously mentioned, many references to his adversaries came not from neighboring countries but from God's covenant people. In this particular psalm, David is wrongfully accused of conspiring against Saul. Trials may come from those who want no association with God, but they also come from people who have professed allegiance to the Lord. Adversities include the possibility of losing one's life, but losing one's reputation is also devastating.

Trials and Human Limitations

We don't always cope with hardships when we go through them. Our limitations may include some or all of the breadth of life—physical, emotional, relational, and spiritual. For example, as king, David had at his disposal vast resources, such as chariots and horses (20:7). However, these powerful assets are nothing compared to God's strength. Many other times, David was on the run without military supplies. Psalm 63 describes a situation like this when he appears alone. Stripped of most everything, he was reminded again of his limitations and his need to trust in the Lord (v. 11). Trials are a "severe mercy," revealing our need to depend on God and his resources. Recognizing our dependence on God in difficult times is a significant step forward in our spiritual growth.

Trials and Self-Examination

Our trials are also an opportunity to ask ourselves if sin has been the cause of our afflictions. When accusations smear David, he raises the issue of whether or not he is guilty of wrongdoing (7:3–4). He uses others' threats for his spiritual well-being by asking God if their charges are valid. By doing this, he concludes that he is innocent because he has pursued a life of integrity (v. 8).

On other occasions, when David faces enemies who vigorously hate him, he believes his sin may cause their antagonism (25:18–19). So he cries out to God, asking him to "take away all my sins." Although our first reaction might be to ask God to confront our adversaries, David wisely asks God to deal with him first. Rather than absolving ourselves of any responsibility for the reaction of others, we should resolve to reflect on the ways we may have contributed to the painful situation. We may discover that we cause our troubles because of our sinful attitudes, words, and actions. When we are willing to confront our sin, it can be said, "Blessed is the man to whom sin is more unbearable than disease."[12]

Trials, especially in the area of relationships, provide an invaluable opportunity to ask ourselves: have I contributed to the conflict which has angered and antagonized others? By examining our lives, aided by Scripture and the Holy Spirit, we can discover whether or not we have wronged others by our actions and words. Though it may be painful, this opportunity for personal soul-searching gives us the possibility of confronting the sin that caused the conflict. When there is sin, and we deal with it, we may be able to restore the relationship with those who were angry at us. Whether reconciliation in human relationships occurs or not, we move on with a right relationship with the Lord, further growing in holiness.

Trials and Trusting in God

It is not unusual to hear people say that it is wrong to complain about their trials to God. They refer to the Israelites who grumbled against both Moses and the LORD (Exod 16:2, 7–9) or to the first-century church (Phil 2:14; Jas 5:9). To avoid sinning by complaining about their adversities, they deny or downplay their feelings about the misfortunes. Rather than adopting these problematic approaches, David suggests an alternative. He tells us, "I pour out my complaint before him [God]; before him I tell my trouble" (142:2; 64:1). David, a man after God's heart (1 Sam 13:14), complains to the Lord!

Is there any difference between grumbling and complaining? Psalms 64 and 142 help to clarify this question. David turns to God, who knows his way (142:3), and asks him for protection from his enemies (64:1). He complains to the Lord, knowing that he can act. In contrast, grumbling involves questioning God and his apparent lack of concern and care for his people (Exod 16:3). Simply put, complaining focuses on the conditions, and grumbling questions God himself. So, the psalmists, like David, are examples of how we may legitimately complain about our trials to the Lord.

Moreover, our trust in God can grow when we turn to him, even with our complaints. We see this in the two psalms already mentioned. When David asks God to protect him, he has to trust the Lord to fight on his behalf (64:7–8). When he feels alone, he expresses confidence in God's power to rescue him (142:6–7). God sees David's trials, and he will respond.

The psalmists sometimes begin their descriptions of their trials with a tone of desperation. Their situation is a matter of life or death, and they turn to God, trusting him to spare their lives (17:10–15, 140:1–5). Psalm 59

---

12. Spurgeon, *Treasury of David*, 1:397.

portrays David facing a real threat from his enemies, Saul and his cronies. Once again, David turns to the Lord, "Deliver me . . . deliver me" (vv. 1–2). This cry is one of desperation, but not without hope. His trust is evident in the way he talks to God. David says, "O my Strength, I watch for you; you, O God, are my fortress, my loving God" (v. 9a). By trusting him (and not taking matters into his own hands), David can let God deal with the situation (vv. 9b–13). At the end of the psalm, he, by faith, exclaims that he will praise God, who will intervene on his behalf (vv. 16–17). Spurgeon encourages us, "The greater our present trials the louder will our future songs be, and the more intense our joyful gratitude. Had we no day of trouble, where were our season of retrospective thanksgiving?"[13] David's confidence in God rests in the history of his people. God delivered and preserved his people when the Israelites sought to escape from their Egyptian captors (66:6–7). For this, the psalmist praises God (v. 9). Spurgeon states that this is a "great reason for gratitude but much more when we are called to undergo extreme trials."[14] Trials allow us to relinquish our hold on painful situations and trust God to actively work through these circumstances. They become an opportunity to cultivate gratitude as we see God intimately involved in our adversities. Trusting and praising God are signs of growing in holiness.

We may not find ourselves facing adversity as severe as the nearness of death. However, other fears may paralyze us or evoke reactions that are detrimental to us and others. We discover another way to respond when David is slandered and his words are twisted (56:2, 5). He wasn't ashamed to admit that he was afraid (v. 3a). As Spurgeon comments, David "feared but that fear did not fill the whole area of his mind."[15] Before God, he could still acknowledge that "I will trust in you" (56:3b–4). Then, he remarkably states, "I will not be afraid" (v. 4). During our trials and fears, our trust in the Lord can deepen and our fears can be reduced. God uses problems to enable us to grow in holiness.

Trusting God during hardships also tests our patience. In Ps 13, we see David again facing his enemies (v. 4). He comes to God and asks four times the inevitable question: how long (vv. 1–2)? We can be impatient with God, chafing at his apparent lack of action during a difficult life season. When we feel God is sleeping (7:6), we create more difficulty for ourselves. However, our impatience is an opportunity to further cultivate our trust in God's love (13:5). Becoming more patient requires discipline, which requires dependence on the Holy Spirit (Gal 5:20). Patience is another mark of holiness!

13. Spurgeon, *Treasury of David*, 3:18.
14. Spurgeon, *Treasury of David*, 3:110–11.
15. Spurgeon, *Treasury of David*, 2:465.

It reflects a trusting attitude toward God and waiting for his timing during our trials.

Waiting on God means we commit our trials to his providence. David does not take it upon himself to repay those imposing these hardships on him. He does not take matters into his own hands for three reasons. One, he prays for his opponents (35:13–14). Spurgeon notes that David mourned and humbly "prayed for his enemy, and made the sick man's case his own, pleading and confessing as if his own personal sin had brought on the evil."[16] Spurgeon captures David's sentiment: "I wished no worse to them than to myself."[17] While trials test our love for our enemies, they are also a God-given opportunity to love them as God does. Two, David wants God's righteousness to be known (v. 28). Honoring God's character was more important to him than seeking personal revenge. Rather than going after those who have made life difficult, this is the opportunity to choose to honor God. Three, growing in holiness involves yielding our egos so that God receives the glory through his actions. This point leads us to the following insight.

Trials and Experiencing God's Character

Relying on God's nature during trials is a common theme throughout the Psalter. David is a sterling example of this, which is evident throughout his psalms. Rather than boasting in his personal or military might, he relied upon the "name of the LORD our God" (20:7). His name represents the nature of God who, as Spurgeon affirms, is "the self-existent, independent, immutable, ever-present, all-filling I AM."[18] There are a few outstanding qualities of God's nature that the psalmist mentions during his painful experiences.

In Ps 25, David uses six terms to elaborate on the severity of his trials (vv. 16–18). We might assume that he would naturally question God's character. However, David does not, and instead, he affirms his confidence in who God is. He trusts in God's "integrity and uprightness" to protect him (v. 21).

The psalmists often mention God's faithful love. In Ps 52, David confronts those who use their power to destroy the righteous (vv. 1–4). Amid these threats, he makes the remarkable claim that he is flourishing during this troublesome situation (v. 8a). David could say this because he trusts in God's unfailing love (v. 8b). In Ps 57, he says his trial is like a disaster

---

16. Spurgeon, *Treasury of David*, 2:143.
17. Spurgeon, *Treasury of David*, 2:143.
18. Spurgeon, *Treasury of David*, 1:303.

because his enemies intend to kill him (vv. 1, 3, 4, 6). Once again, David trusts God's love and faithfulness (vv. 1, 3). Confidence in God's character provides the strong assurance he needs during this overwhelming situation. This assurance is all he needs to worship the Lord in the most unlikely time (v. 7). David's praise to God in adversity is also evident in Ps 63:9–11. His response to God is remarkable, considering the intensity of the trial. People seek to destroy him (v. 9). Nevertheless, he trusts in God's love, which spurs him to enthusiastically worship the Lord (vv. 3–5, 7). In the most challenging times, we can grow in holiness by knowing and increasingly relying on God's nature.

Complementary to God's love is his justice. When David faces the rage of his enemies, he asks God to judge them, or exercise "justice" (7:6). The Hebrew word (*mihspat*) has the meaning of "judgment" and "justice." He can expect God to judge with justice because he is "righteous" (v. 17). The Hebrew word (*tsedeq*) is translated as "righteous" or "just."[19] Rather than an angry, counterproductive reaction to those who might slander him, he wisely trusts God to act justly on his behalf.

God's strength is also essential for David when he asks for protection from his enemies (3:3). His trust in the Lord prompts him to call upon God, who hears him (v. 4). David is also confident that he can fall asleep and wake up in the morning, knowing that the Lord is protecting him (v. 5). With this confidence, he boldly asks God to deal with those who are attacking him. This event drives David to focus on God's character, which gives him the confidence to rest well because he depends on the Lord's protection. Trials allow us to know God better and deepen our trust in him, whether sleeping or praying (vv. 5, 7). He is the one who "daily bears our burdens" (68:19) during our trials.

Trials and Empathy

When David writes about his hardships, he occasionally cries out to God to save his people in their troubles (25:22). He also asks God to be "their shepherd and carry them forever" (28:9). David knew how God had been his shepherd during difficult times (23:1, 4). He wanted his people to experience the same shepherd's care he had personally known. Spurgeon states, "Sorrow had taught the psalmist sympathy and given him communion with the tried people of God; he therefore remembers them in his prayers."[20] When the apostle Paul went through a tough time, he could comfort others

---

19. Brown, *New Brown-Driver-Briggs-Gesinius*, 841, 1048–49.
20. Spurgeon, *Treasury of David*, 1:397.

because he experienced God's comfort (2 Cor 1:3–4). So likewise, our pain allows us to empathize and minister to those who are undergoing afflictions. This loving attitude is a mark of growing holiness in one's life.

Trials and Commitment to God

In Ps 69:5–12, David's zealous passion for God inflamed people's hostility toward him ("zeal for your house consumes me" v. 9). Spurgeon comments, "Zeal for God is so little understood by men of the world, that it always draws down opposition upon those who are inspired with it; they are sure to be accused of sinister motives, or of hypocrisy, or of being out of their senses."[21] Many years later, the twelve disciples would recall David's words regarding zealousness when Jesus had driven out all the sellers, money changers, and everything else (John 2:13–17). John Calvin once said, "Where zeal for integrity and holiness is not in force, there neither the Spirit of Christ nor Christ himself are present."[22]

When we hold unswervingly to God's standards, we shouldn't be surprised if we encounter adverse reactions from our contemporary culture. Negative responses shouldn't be due to our foolish belligerence but because of our association with an unswerving commitment to Jesus Christ (John 15:18–20). These trials further test our faith and create an opportunity to grow in godliness.

Trials and Repentance

Unfortunately, we aren't always faithful to Jesus Christ because we yield to sin's influence. Then, we face the consequences of our actions. Some of our trials are brought on by deliberately disobeying God. Throughout Ps 78, we are painfully reminded of God's people who repeatedly turned away from him by continuing to sin (vv. 10, 17, 32, 40, 56–57). Many times, God, in his mercy, continued to show his love to them. However, when they chased after other gods, the Lord's anger was aroused toward his people. As a result, he withdrew his power (v. 62), and they experienced defeat, death, and grief (vv. 62–64). They brought about their own trials. Yes, at an earlier time, they did eagerly seek God (v. 34), but then they did a turnaround only to "flatter him with their mouths, lying to him with their tongues" (v. 36, 62:4). Their hearts were not loyal to God (v. 37).

---

21. Spurgeon, *Treasury of David*, 3:178–79.
22. Bloesch, *Holy Spirit*, 318.

It shouldn't be surprising that God tests our hearts during these trials. Asaph describes an account of a time when God tested his people (81:7; Exod 17:7; Num 20:13). After the people had quarreled with Moses, God miraculously provided water for them. Exodus 17:7 informs us that Moses gives this location two names, Meribah (a place of quarreling) and Massah (a place of testing). The last name represents the people testing God when they asked, "Is the LORD among us or not?" (v. 7). By trying him, they believed God passed with flying colors because he supplied them with water. But, in reality, God was testing them (81:7), and they miserably failed the test because they critically questioned him.

God wants loyal hearts, and when our hearts wander away from him to pursue our idols, he will discipline us (Heb 12:7–9). Although he does this out of his love, our trials may be painful (v. 11). His goal is for us to return to him, not with flattering words, but with a firm, wholehearted commitment. Spurgeon remarks, "Tribulation brings us to God, and brings God to us. Faith's greatest triumphs are achieved in her heaviest trials. It is all over with me, affliction is all over me; it encompasses me as a cloud, it swallows me up like a sea, it shuts me in with thick darkness, yet God is near, near enough to hear my voice, and I will call him."[23] With this posture, we can "share in his holiness" (v. 10). "The aim of God's chastisement of his people is to produce in them a holy character like his own."[24] Trials provide an opportunity to grow in personal holiness.

Trials and Obedience to God

With genuine repentance, we are rightly positioned to obey the Lord After failing the test with him (81:7), Asaph tells us what God expects from his people. We are to listen to him, which involves following his ways (vv. 8, 13). Spurgeon reminds us, "Since God does not forsake us in our need, we ought never to forsake him at any time."[25] If we obey him, Ps 81 reminds us that he will give us everything we need to sustain and satisfy us (vv. 10, 16). In Ps 60, David expresses the same line of thinking. After God disciplines us (vv. 1–3), he will help his people whom he loves (v. 5). This love relationship is expressed by giving the land he promised to his people (vv. 6–7). God did not let them down.

The apostle Peter, who experienced and wrote about life's trials (1 Pet 1:6–9), knew that personal holiness requires obeying and depending on

23. Spurgeon, *Treasury of David*, 3:40.
24. Morris, *Hebrews*, 138.
25. Spurgeon, *Treasury of David*, 3:401.

God's power (v. 15; 2 Pet 1:3). Our obedience reflects his power at work in our lives.

Holiness through Emotional Trials

David expresses the deep inner anguish he frequently experienced. We can draw a few observations from his accounts.

Trials Are Very Real

Psalm 6 is a poignant example of David's inner malady. He paints his miserable condition as "weak," "sick at heart," and that his "bones are in agony" (vv. 2–3). He also weeps profusely (vv. 6–8). On another occasion, he describes an inner anguish afflicting him (31:7, 10). In addition to feeling weak (vv. 9–10), he is in distress and filled with sorrow and grief, affecting his whole body (v. 9). In Ps 38, he depicts some of the same symptoms. He is racked with sores and pain (vv. 3, 5, 7, 10, 17), and he also feels inner anguish (vv. 6, 8). These accounts illustrate the interconnectedness between our lives' physical and emotional spheres. One who is very discouraged or depressed shouldn't be surprised when the body also suffers.

Asaph gives an account of his inner life trials in Ps 77. He doesn't dwell on his physical afflictions but on emotional despondency. He is in distress, and his "spirit grew faint" (vv. 2–3). Even when he seeks and remembers God, he still does not find solace. He is in a dark place of despair. Spurgeon, who knew his share of physical and emotional trials, comments with insight,

> The best of men know the depth of this abyss.... He mused and mused but only sank the deeper. His inward disquietudes did not fall asleep as soon as they were expressed, but rather they returned upon him, and leaped over him like raging billows of an angry sea. It was not his body alone which smarted, but his noblest nature writhed in pain, his life itself seemed crushed into the earth. It is in such a case that death is coveted as a relief, for life becomes an intolerable burden. With no spirit left in us to sustain our infirmity, our case becomes forlorn; like man in a tangle of briars who is stripped of his clothes, every hook of the thorns becomes a lancet, and we bleed with ten thousand wounds. Alas, my God, the writer of this exposition well knows what thy servant Asaph meant, for his soul is familiar with the

way of grief. Deep glens and lonely caves of soul depressions, my spirit knows full well your awful glooms![26]

Emotional suffering may afflict anyone regardless of one's godliness. Finger-pointing does not alleviate the pain but only accentuates it.

Trials Have Various Sources

Though David was on the run in the wilderness, there appears to be no lack of supplies, such as food or water, which we might expect him to mention. Instead, he refers to his enemies as a source of emotional and physical suffering (6:7; 31:11, 13, 15). David also clearly recognizes that his sin and its guilt create personal suffering (38:3–4). In addition, he knew that the covenant between God and his people stated that disease could be a sign of divine anger (Deut 28:21–22; Isa 1:6). By personal experience, he understood that sin brought both illness and eventual death to his newborn son (2 Sam 12:13–15, 18).

Trials Cultivate Holy Lives

When we face adversities, we can get stuck in self-pity and continue living despondently. Is it possible for God to use such personal low points for transformation for growth in holiness? Fortunately, the psalmists who are spiritual guides direct us to him.

First, trials should make us aware of our sins. When we acknowledge our sins, we benefit spiritually. In Ps 38, David does not rationalize or deny his sin. When Nathan confronts him with sin, he immediately admits it (2 Sam 12:1–13). One might skeptically suggest that David confessed because he was caught red-handed. However, David even wants God to search and reveal any sin he was unaware of in his heart (139:23–24, 4:9). The trials that come into our lives should sensitize us to any sin we may have committed.

Second, trials humble us. When we experience success, we can become proud (107:38). When we do, God humbles us through oppression, calamity, and sorrow (v. 39). The psalmist reminds us that we must take "heed of these things and consider the great love of the LORD" (v. 43). God uses trials to break our pride and self-sufficiency so that we return to the one who truly loves us. A humble heart grateful for God's love is integral to a holy life.

Third, trials allow us to be receptive to God's discipline. David recognizes God might be disciplining him (6:1). At first glance, it seems he is

---

26. Spurgeon, *Treasury of David*, 3:313.

asking the Lord not to discipline him. However, he qualifies his request by asking God not to discipline him in anger but with his mercy (vv. 2, 4). As already mentioned, discipline is God's means to restore us to a healthier spiritual condition. With trials, God uses suffering and pain for his redemptive purposes.

Fourth, severe trials undoubtedly create anguish and pain in our whole being (vv. 2–3). As Spurgeon has wittily remarked, "Soul-trouble is the very soul of trouble."[27] It is very appropriate to ask God to heal our wounded hearts (6:2). Rather than remaining resentful and embittered, growth in holiness occurs when we are open to God's curing of the wounds. When we have been deeply hurt, inner healing moves us along the path to growth in holiness.

Fifth, a proper response to trials ultimately deepens our relationship with the Lord. David is aware that God has heard and has compassionately answered his crying prayer (6:8). Sometimes, our trials are so painful that words fail us when we try to express our thoughts to God. Rather than feeling guilty about this, Spurgeon encourages us "to think of tears as liquid prayers."[28] It is encouraging to know that God understands what is on our hearts. Trials allow us to go deeper in our prayer life when we grieve before the Lord. These afflictions can also deepen our commitment to obey the God. The psalmist admits, "Before I was afflicted I went astray, but now I obey your word" (119:67). His comments align with Spurgeon's sentiment, "Sweet are the uses of adversity, and this is one of them; it puts a bridle upon transgression and furnishes a spur for holiness."[29]

Holiness through Spiritual Trials

Numerous psalms describe individuals who feel abandoned and rejected by God. We may feel the same when we believe God doesn't act on our behalf.

Spurgeon entitles Ps 22 as the "Psalm of the Cross" because it most graphically points to Jesus Christ, who his heavenly Father forsook on the cross (Matt 27:46). Of course, whatever divine abandonment we may sense pales in comparison to Jesus' experience. Nevertheless, our situation can be frightful and alarming. With David, who wrote this psalm, we may feel God has forsaken us and is unwilling to respond to our cries (vv. 1–2). These are dark days when we feel as helpless and powerless as a worm (v. 6).

---

27. Spurgeon, *Treasury of David*, 1:57.
28. Spurgeon, *Treasury of David*, 1:59.
29. Spurgeon, *Treasury of David*, 5:271–72.

Many of the same feelings are expressed in Ps 44. Here, God does not respond to his people (v. 23a). It seems God has fallen asleep. To make matters worse, they are experiencing "misery and oppression" (v. 24). God, who is compassionate, now appears insensitive to their plight. One can understandably conclude that God has rejected his people and gone into hiding (vv. 9, 23b–24). In such times, Spurgeon acknowledges, "It is hard, indeed, in the midst of persecution to see the reason why we are left to suffer so severely."[30] We may not only feel puzzled but angry at God. The *Deus absconditus* is a painful trial to go through.

We may wonder how God's apparent absence might contribute to our spiritual growth when such a trial seemingly hinders our holiness. The following are some suggestions to aid us in this area. One, rather than appearing distant, Jesus is empathetic when we feel God has deserted us. He knows abandonment at the very deepest level with his heavenly Father. Besides, the divine silence accomplished the divine purpose of redemption. Though God's silence with us is a great trial, we can believe he is working out his purposes in our lives. Two, we have to accept what we know is true (God is with us), and not trust our senses which may tell us something entirely different (God has abandoned us). David mentions the word "trust" three times to remind us of past generations, who trusted God, who delivered them and did not disappoint them (22:4–5). The "dark night of the soul" is a painful experience, but God assures us that he is attentive to us and is at work in us.

Conclusion

We need adversities in life to continue the process of growing in the image of Jesus Christ. Trials and holiness are inseparable. With the insight gained by personal experience, Spurgeon insightfully comments, "Often our trials act as a thorn hedge to keep us in the good pasture, but our prosperity is a gap through which we go astray. If any of us remember a time in which we had no trouble, we also probably recollect that then grace was low and temptation was strong." Then he adds, "Truth to be learned by adversity is good for the humble. Very little is to be learned without affliction."[31]

With the hardships that come along, God wants us to recognize our limitations and depend on him. This recognition occurs as we cultivate our prayer life, learn to wait on the Lord, and discipline ourselves to examine our hearts. Despite any hopelessness, trials ultimately allow us to

---

30. Spurgeon, *Treasury of David*, 2:306.
31. Spurgeon, *Treasury of David*, 5:271, 273.

grow in our dependency and intimacy with Jesus. In turn, we become more like him.

Our adversities are the crucible testing our responses. If we respond well, this is a mark that we are growing in holiness. Spurgeon has the last word: "It is a rich sign of inward grace when the outward walk is changed, and when ungodliness is put far from our actions."[32]

---

32. Spurgeon, *Treasury of David*, 1:1.

Chapter 11

Nature and Holiness

Growing up in a rural setting, young Charles Spurgeon greatly appreciated nature, which stayed with him throughout his life. He had "an insatiable love of the created order, [a] near-delirious fascination with it and joy in it."[1] After moving to London, he would periodically escape city life, go to the countryside, and enjoy walking in the woods. He cared for his rose garden and other flowers in his home backyard. He loved them so much that he knew their botanical names in English and Latin. He also enjoyed various creatures; he had a goldfish pond and a beehive at his home. Fascinated by bees, he marveled about them in the *Treasury of David*.[2] After hearing about a case of animal cruelty, he also wrote a strongly-worded article criticizing cruelty to animals.

His love of nature was also rooted in the belief that the created world belonged to God. Spurgeon developed many analogies between nature and biblical truths. Tom Nettles notes, "The washing of sheep, the dropping of moisture from a wall, the deadness of trees, a mouse in the field, the singing of birds in flight, the activities of bees all provided theological reflection and fodder for his sermons."[3] God's involvement with nature also taught Spurgeon to discern the hand of God. For example, in rural life, he

1. Nettles, *Living by Revealed Truth*, 160.
2. Spurgeon, *Treasury of David*, 3:51.
3. Nettles, *Living by Revealed Truth*, 160.

saw firsthand how people looked to God to supply suitable weather for their crops and food for their cattle. Nettles comments, "Nothing in all of God's creation could fail to speak a word about its maker, sustainer, and redeemer or fail to show the creature's dependence on its immutable and self-existent source."[4]

God intends his created order to be enjoyed and encourage our spiritual growth. Spurgeon clearly understood the connection between nature and holiness. The Psalms move us in this direction by learning more about God revealed through nature and appropriately responding to him, the Creator of the universe.

Throughout the Psalter, the writers frequently refer to the vast array of God's creation with its living creatures and plant life, the land and sea, and then beyond, including the sun, moon, and stars. However, the Psalter does not refer to nature as an apologetic, providing reasons why a person should believe there is a living God. Instead, the psalmists' descriptions of nature contribute to a general revelation of God, whom we see more clearly through Scripture. As Millard Erickson puts it, "The psalmist who saw a declaration of the glory of God in the heavens saw it clearly because he had come to know God from the special revelation, but what he saw had always been genuinely and objectively there."[5]

The psalmists viewed the vastness of nature as another means to stir God's people to respond appropriately to him. Rather than relegating creation to an unimportant role, true spirituality includes the created order as another means to grow in holiness. When we recognize who God is through his creation, it causes us to see who we are in our relationship with him and how we should respond accordingly. We will explore the psalmists' references to nature from this perspective. We will discover that nature can contribute to our holiness and is another way to shape our lives to become more like Jesus Christ.

This chapter will discuss the psalmists' understanding of God's attributes revealed through creation and how God expects us to respond. These responses have explicit and implicit ramifications for our pursuit of holiness.

---

4. Nettles, *Living by Revealed Truth*, 160; Dallimore, *Spurgeon*, 185.
5. Erickson, *Christian Theology*, 171.

Truths about God through Nature

The Psalter teaches us about God through two ways we can approach his creation—literally and metaphorically. The latter is a figure of speech that compares two entities to identify their similarity. Most of the metaphors are derived from nature.[6] For example, rocks are frequently used as a metaphor to instruct us about God's created order (18:2, 31, 46; 19:14; 28:1; 31:3; 42:9; 62:2; 71:3; 89:26; 144:1). God is strong and unmovable in a chaotic world. Other metaphors describe God as the sun (84:11) and our shade (121:5). He is also like a mother bird protecting her chicks (91:1). When God speaks, his words are like honey (19:10).

The Psalms' metaphors related to nature are intentional. Leland Ryken suggests metaphors are used for specific reasons which provide insight into the relationship between creation and God.[7] First, metaphors express the "emotional side of religious experience."[8] For example, the taste of honey is sweet, expressing how good God and his word are to us. Also, metaphors move us from the abstract to the concrete. God's protection is abstract until we picture a mother bird covering her young brood with her massive wings. Third, metaphors of nature illustrate the mysteriousness of God's transcendence. When he speaks from heaven, it is like a raging sea storm (93:3). Finally, the Psalms' use of metaphors with nature illustrates how "spiritual reality is incarnate in this world." Ryken points out that metaphors enable spiritual realities, such as God's providence, in everyday life. The spiritual truth of God providentially watching over us is interwoven with physical entities such as the sun and shade (121:5). By using metaphors, "the Psalms let us know that religion is earthly as well as heavenly."

The many metaphors drawn from nature deepen our understanding of and appreciation for God. With awe, we are stirred to love and obey him, cultivating personal holiness. Now, we focus on the relationship between God and the world he created.

God Is the Creator of Nature

Psalm 104:1–26 provides the most descriptive account of God creating the world in the Psalter. Or, as Spurgeon puts it, "It is a poet's version of Genesis."[9] The psalmist generally follows the creation account in Gen 1.

---

6. Ryken, "Metaphors in the Psalms," 20.
7. Ryken, "Metaphors in the Psalms," 9–29.
8. Ryken, "Metaphors in the Psalms," 18.
9. Spurgeon, Treasury of David, 4:301.

He does not wait until the end of his account of creation, but at the very outset, he shouts out, "O Lord my God, you are very great; you are clothed with splendor and majesty" (v. 1). It is God who gets the praise and not the creation,[10] unlike contemporary society, which largely exalts nature with barely a thought about God.

The psalmist describes God as "the Maker of heaven and earth, the sea, and everything in them" (146:6). Then the writer adds the phrase, "the Lord who remains faithful forever," which is an immediate contrast to human mortality (vv. 3–4). Since he "determines the numbers of stars and calls them each by name" (147:4), God is faithful to his creation which rightfully belongs to him (95:4–5).

The writer of Ps 136:5–9 describes God actively creating the sun, moon, stars, and Earth. For each of these heavenly bodies, the psalmist responds with a hearty "His love endures forever," a phrase repeated twenty-six times. While we may gloss over this repetitive phrase, Spurgeon explains how each of God's creative acts reflects his love. For example, by raising the land above the water (v. 6), humanity will not be destroyed by global flooding (except in Noah's day). Or, by creating the sun and the moon (vv. 7–8), his love provides us with predictable orderliness of days, months, and years. The moon and stars (v. 9) reveal God's love by guiding ships on the sea and providing light to those on land.[11]

In addition to the heavenly bodies, God created the animals and designed them to be in rhythm with the rest of creation. The psalmist uses the lion to illustrate his point (104:20–23). When night arrives, the lion begins to search for his food, and when the sun rises, he sleeps. Likewise, as the day begins, people rise and work until the evening. Reflecting on this interplay between the beasts and humans, Spurgeon asks who could domesticate the lion. "The sun suffices to do it. He is the true lion-tamer."[12] The daily rhythm of the nocturnal animals and the daytime activities of humans point to his well-ordered design for life on earth. God is supremely wise.

God's creative activity culminated with the origination of humans. Psalm 139 describes some of the intricate details of being knit and woven before we are born (vv. 13, 15). Or, as Spurgeon puts it, the body is "embroidered with great skill.... What tapestry can equal the human fabric?"[13] The intricate details of the human body also reveal the grandeur of God's creation. The complexity and functions of each organ, the blood, DNA,

---

10. Spurgeon, *Treasury of David*, 4:302.
11. Spurgeon, *Treasury of David*, 6:206–7.
12. Spurgeon, *Treasury of David*, 4:308.
13. Spurgeon, *Treasury of David*, 6:263.

hormones, and chemicals point to one simple but profound truth: we are "fearfully and wonderfully made" (v. 14)! It is equally remarkable that God created the first humans from the soil of the earth (Gen 2:7). We are very much related to God's nature as we are a unique part of his creation.

As majestic as the snowcapped Canadian Rocky Mountains are, the creation of a man and woman is the pinnacle of everything God brought into existence. Psalm 8 informs us that God gave humans a unique role in his created order, which exalted us above all the other living creatures. David makes his case with two affirmations. First, when one considers the beauty of God's creation, one might assume humans, made from dust, would rank least among his creation. In verse 4, David asks, "Who are human beings?" Spurgeon comments, "Well might the Psalmist wonder at the singular exaltation of man in the scale of being, when he marked his utter nothingness in comparison with the starry universe."[14] Yet, God is mindful of us and cares for us (v. 4). He pays attention to us and will remember us as he tenderly provides for us. Second, God has crowned us "with glory and honor" (v. 5b), which refers to women and men made in God's image (Gen 1:26). He has appointed people as rulers, with authority and dominion over his creation (vv. 7–8; Gen 1:28), which includes working and caring for the land (Gen 2:15).

God's creation reveals his majesty, love, wisdom, orderliness, and creativity. These and other attributes, which describe God's nature concerning his creation, are expressions of his glory (8:1; 19:1). As Spurgeon says, "The whole creation is full of his glory and radiant with the excellency of his power; his goodness and his wisdom are manifested on every hand."[15] In addition to referring to God's glory in these two psalms, Spurgeon points to God's glory in Ps 24. His glory is associated with his strength and might (vv. 8, 10). Along a similar line, when Jesus changed water into wine, he revealed his glory or attribute of power over nature (John 2:11). God's creation is a revelation of his glorious character.

In Ps 94, we note that those who oppose God minimize who he is (v. 7). The psalmist challenges these "senseless ones" about their foolishness (v. 8). God hears and sees because he is the one who created our ears and eyes; he even knows our thoughts (vv. 9, 11). In contrast to those who rule out a divine creator, it is wise to accept God as the Creator (v. 8). This biblical view of God allows us to see his love, wisdom, care, and involvement in all of his creation. This realization is humbling and intended to cultivate personal

---

14. Spurgeon, *Treasury of David*, 1:32.
15. Spurgeon, *Treasury of David*, 1:29.

holiness growth by adoring, loving, and obeying him. The natural world is God's means for supernatural work in our lives.

God Is the Sustainer of Nature

Various psalms portray God tenderly caring for his creation. In Ps 147, we see God sustaining his creation. He provides rain for vegetation to grow and food for the animals (vv. 8–9). He also "gives food to the hungry," who are oppressed (146:7). For all our ingenuity, we, like the rest of God's creatures, are ultimately dependent on him. This is beautifully pictured in Ps 104, which tells of God opening his hand to feed the animals at just the right time (vv. 27–28). Their very existence depends on God (v. 30). In Ps 65, David describes how God sustains his creation (vv. 9–13). "He is represented here as going round the earth, as a gardener surveys his garden," Spurgeon asserts, " and as giving water to every plant that requires it, and that not in small quantities, but until the earth is drenched and soaked with a rich supply of refreshment."[16] Under the care of the Gardener, the land produces an abundance of grain crops for people and grass for animals. The writer of Ps 85 sums it up, "The LORD will indeed give what is good, and our land will yield its harvest" (v. 12).

The psalmists do not allow us to adopt a deistic view of God, who is distant and uninvolved in our world. If we do this, a mechanical view of the world that operates exclusively by the laws of nature asserts itself.[17] The Psalms deny this perspective by affirming God caringly and generously sustains his created world. This realization should humble us when we realize that the world does not center on us. God cares for all of his creation, of which I am a part. Because God "gives food to every creature," the psalmist exclaims, "His love endures forever" (136:25). In light of the Psalms, Jesus' words about his Father feeding the birds and clothing the fields with grass shouldn't surprise us (Matt 6:26, 30). He sustains us because he loves his creation.

We can't sustain our lives apart from God. As pilgrims in this world, we depend on him for each breath we take. In three of the Songs of Ascent, the pilgrims' songs refer to the LORD, who is the "Maker of heaven and earth" (121:2, 124:8, 134:3). Since he has complete control over nature, God sustains us through our life's journey. A healthy dose of God's role as sustainer calls us away from our futile efforts to grow in spiritual maturity apart from him. We can only become like Jesus with his presence and transforming

---

16. Spurgeon, *Treasury of David*, 3:93.
17. Macdonald, "Deism," 304–5.

power. We need the Lord and his unlimited resources to sustain us daily in our relationship with him.

God Is the Ruler over Nature

As the Lord over his creation, God has the power to intervene and disrupt the laws of nature he established. The Psalms refer to God's power which enabled the people to flee Egypt (18:7–15, 66:6–7, 74:12–17, 77:16–19, 105:27–38, 135:6–9, 136:10–15). In these accounts, we see God who could afflict people with plagues because he rules over the skies, the waters, and the animals. These accounts of Israel's deliverance from their captors unmistakably illustrate God's mighty power (66:3, 7; 74:13). Through nature, God "does whatever pleases him" (135:5–7) to accomplish his purposes, including delivering Israel from Egypt (vv. 8–12).

God also used his creation to provide for his people during their time in the wilderness (105:39–44; 114; 136:16). He guided the people day and night, and miraculously provided water from rocks, quail, and manna for them (105:39–44, 114:8, 136:6). He also stopped the flow of the Jordan River so that the people could cross into the promised territory (114:5). The psalmist sees God's power as a graphic display of his love for his people and, therefore, he unequivocally repeats, "His love endures forever" (136:10–16).

We see God intervening in nature to catch people's attention in the gospels. Jesus cured a demon-possessed mute (Matt 9:32–33), a man's leprosy (Mark 1:40–45), and healed a paralytic (Luke 5:18–26). When the Creator of the universe intervenes in the predictable laws of nature, we should be filled with awe before him. Holy living before our Creator is the most appropriate response to him.

God Is the Speaker through Nature

The Lord of the universe speaks through the phenomena common in nature. Thunder and lightning, smoke, and earthquake tremors aren't unusual, but in the mountainous region of Sinai, these occurrences were extraordinary because God made his presence known through them (97:2–5; Exod 19:16–18). In preparation for coming before his holy presence, the people had to purify themselves (vv. 14–15). After Moses led the people to the foot of the mountain to "meet with God," they heard his voice (v. 19). After that, God continued to speak to Moses (vv. 21, 24; 20:1–17). He is "God, the One of Sinai" (Ps 68:7–8).

God also speaks through natural weather disturbances. Psalm 107 provides an account of sailors at sea during a storm. The psalmist sees God creating and calming the storm (vv. 23–29; Jon 1:4, 15). He can do this for several reasons. First, he founded the world, and it all belongs to him (89:11). Therefore, he rules over the turbulent seas and can still them (v. 9). Also, regardless of how powerful an ocean storm may be, God is mightier (93:3–4). No storm can threaten his security on the throne (vv. 1–2). God's ability to rule over natural phenomena expresses his unfailing love (107:31). Job may have seriously questioned this when fire and a hurricane-force wind destroyed his house and killed his family and his employees' flock of sheep (Job 1:16, 19). Even in this situation, God was in ultimate control (1:12) and accomplished his purposes in Job, who came away with a greater reverence for God (42:1–6).

Based on his relationship with the created world, we can make some observations about God. One, he is both transcendent and immanent. God is transcendent because he is independent of nature and superior to it. The psalmist exclaims, "Who is like the LORD our God, the One who sits enthroned on high, who stoops down to look on the heavens and the earth?" (112:5–6). The writer of Ps 123 states that he lifts his eyes upward to God, "whose throne is in heaven" (v. 1). Also, the Almighty LORD immanently works through nature to accomplish his purposes. God revealed himself through nature in numerous ways to Israel, from the exodus to the entrance into the land promised to them by God.

Also, God wants to be increasingly glorified and honored through his people by becoming more Christlike and obedient to his will (2 Cor 3:18). By revealing himself through nature, God wants us to respond in ways that will contribute to our personal growth in holiness.

Ways to Respond to God Revealed through Nature

Nature is not only for our enjoyment but also for our sanctification. Yet, we often don't consider how God uses nature as a means for our spiritual maturity. Thus, it is essential to consider how the psalmists respond to God's created world.

Trust in God's Provisions

We have to remember we are finite beings, which is a humbling thought. We don't relish focusing on our limitations, preferring to dream about all we hope to accomplish. While this is good to a limited extent, leaving God out of the picture is not wise. God reminds us that his "pleasure is not in the strength of a horse, nor his delight in the legs of man" (Ps 147:10). Rather, the psalmists remind us we are like sheep whom he has created (79:13, 100:3). As a result, we are vulnerable to predators wanting to devour and destroy us (44:11, 22). God, the Shepherd, must guide us throughout life (78:52). Though we, like the psalmists, may love him, we are prone to stray like a "lost sheep" (119:176). Like it or not, we must depend on the Shepherd, who can lead and provide what is best for us (Ps 23). While we may gladly or reluctantly rely on God as our shepherd, we also have to depend on spiritual leaders who shepherd us and serve under God (77:20; 1 Pet 5:1–4). Therefore, rather than boasting that we are as mighty as a horse, we place our hope in God's unfailing love, knowing that "the LORD delights in those who fear him" (147:11).

Our faith is also deepened in God as we increasingly learn to rely on him to provide for us. This reliance shouldn't become an excuse for laziness. Presumptuous laziness is mistaken thinking based on the assumption that God will supply us with everything we need; therefore, we don't need to do anything. As a general rule of thumb, such a person will be poor and hungry (Prov 10:4, 19:15). Distancing ourselves from this approach to life, we must apply ourselves to whatever we do while recognizing our continual need to depend on the Lord. For example, the farmer, who is a follower of Jesus Christ, spends long hours cultivating and seeding his fields. Then, he has to wait for the crops to grow with sufficient sun and rain. Ultimately, he has to rely on the LORD to give him a bountiful harvest (Ps 85:12). Our deepening trust occurs when we learn to wait and look to God to provide for us (104:27, 146:7). He may do this directly or indirectly through others. Admittedly, trusting God to provide does not come easily or quickly. However, as we learn more of God's character in Scripture and experience his provisions, we grow in confidence in him.

When we face life's challenges, our trust in God is tested. We aren't spared from calamities that may threaten our lives (107:25–27). In cases like this, our courage can quickly melt (v. 26). Our natural tendency is to confront these circumstances by devising our plans without turning to God. While self-reliance is admirable in our culture, adopting this approach without dependence on God hinders our spiritual maturity. So, we must come to the end of our wits before we realize we must turn to the LORD (vv. 27–28). Spurgeon states that God "sends some of his saints to the sea of soul-trouble, and there they see as others do not, the wonders of divine grace. . . . They need God above all others, and they find him."[18] When we grow in our trust

---

18. Spurgeon, *Treasury of David*, 4:404–5.

in him, fear does not have to dominate and control us during the chaos swirling around us (46:2–3). God wants us to come to him, who is "our refuge and strength" (46:1) and our Creator (89:11–12). Thus, he can generously supply us with courage, peace, and all of his other resources. These are expressions of his grace, which he abundantly gives us if we look to him and ask (2 Cor 12:9). Consequently, he mercifully transforms our troubled and fearful minds so that we may experience his peace (vv. 29–30). The terror of nature prompts us to deeper trust in the Lord, which is a benchmark of growth in holiness. Growing in holiness demonstrates a maturing trust in the Lord, who is more than willing to provide what we need. When our faith deepens, people will see Jesus in our human frailty (2 Cor 4:7–10).

A maturing trust which increasingly leans on God to provide for us assumes a humble posture before him. Whether we like it or not, we are finite human creatures whose strength pales in comparison to God's mighty power (147:5). When we acknowledge our limitations and dependence on him, he honors this humble attitude by sustaining us (vv. 6). The apostle Peter reiterates this with his readers: "Humble yourselves, therefore, under God's mighty hand, that he may lift you up in due time" (1 Pet 5:6). He sustains us by caring for us when we are overwhelmed by anxiety (v. 7). Humility is associated with other godly qualities, such as compassion, kindness, gentleness, and patience (Col 3:12). A humble character, produced by the Spirit's transforming work, is one of the primary marks of personal holiness.

Obey God

There is an inseparable connection between trusting God and obeying him. When Moses told the Israelites they did not have to collect manna on the Sabbath because God would provide for them, they did not believe this, and consequently, they disobeyed (Exod 16:26–27). They had to grow by trusting that God would supply their daily needs. Their trust would be measured by obeying (v. 30). When we pray, "Give us this day our daily bread," we are reminded of our dependence on God and our need to trust him and obey accordingly (Matt 6:11).

The Psalter points to ways God uses nature to challenge his people to obey him. The various aspects of nature offer the chance for individuals to repent of their disobedience so that they obey him. For example, before Israel's exodus from Egypt, the plagues should have convinced the pharaoh to listen to the Lord through Moses (105:27–36). Instead, he persistently refused to repent, resulting in a hardened heart (Exod 7:13; 8:15, 19, 32; 9:12, 35; 10:20, 27; 11:10). On another occasion, a plague broke out among the Israelites due to their sexual immorality and idol worship. This plague prompted Phinehas to address the sin, and his action pleased God (106:29–30; Num 25:1–9). The Lord of creation also uses sea storms to get people's attention (107:23–32). While this account in the Psalms does not suggest sin and the need for repentance, we know God used the storm and a large fish to get the attention of a crew of sailors and Jonah (Jon 1:4–5). After the storm subsided, the men "greatly feared God" (1:16), and Jonah moved from disobeying God to obeying him (1:3, 3:3). Humbling us is often God's way to bring about the needed changes in our lives so that we may respond to him (Ps 107:39).

We can also learn obedience through other avenues of nature. For example, in response to God's command to rule over his creation (Ps 8:6–8; Gen 1:26–30), we must examine our God-given responsibility in this area. Proper care for this planet is rooted in obedience to a theological mandate. By working and caring for the land, we are serving God.[19] Obedience does not come easily in light of the impact of sin on the ecological system. The hard work necessary to exercise dominion over creation requires God's grace to persevere. Holiness cultivated by living responsibly and with a caring attitude reflects the image of God, who cares for and sustains the world. Also, on a narrower scope, are we God's creatures made in his image, open to him searching our hearts and revealing "any offensive way" in us (139:23–24)? Whatever offensive things God might reveal to us, these are opportunities to respond in obedience to our Creator.

Discern God's Providence

Throughout Ps 107, nature is a way for people to see the hand of God in the affairs of daily life. Is it just a coincidence that a storm arose while the sailors were at sea (vv. 23–28)? Rather than viewing circumstances as bad or good luck, the psalmists offer another perspective. In his providence, God uses natural forces to get people's attention so they might turn to him with praise (vv. 29–32). Spurgeon, who personally experienced God's hand in his life and ministry, remarks, "Those who notice providence shall never be long without a providence to notice. It is wise to observe what the Lord does. . . . We must observe wisely, otherwise we may soon confuse ourselves and others with hasty reflections upon the dealings of the Lord. . . . In a thousand ways the lovingkindness of the Lord is shown, and if we will but prudently watch, we shall come to a better understanding of it." Then, he proceeds to

---

19. Taylor, *Open and Unafraid*, 179.

encourage us to become "proficient scholars in this art," which will encourage us to praise God for his goodness."[20]

Worship God

The Psalter instructs us that we shouldn't worship nature, but instead, nature should prompt us to worship the one who created the natural world. The psalmists give us several reasons why we should praise him. One, when we ponder the wide range and the complexity of God's creation, this is reason enough to enthusiastically praise him (95:1–5; 96:1–6). Two, when we see God's attributes revealed through nature, worship is due to him. We praise his power which enabled the Israelites to escape from their captors (66:1–6, 135:5–7). His righteousness revealed through the fire and lightning evokes our reverential worship before God (97:2–5, 104:31–33). Through nature, we see God's love and concern for his people, which stirs us to worship God (68:4, 7–10; 107:31–32). Three, we worship God in solidarity with the rest of creation (148:1–10). When all of nature is an expression of praise to God, we join our voices with this universal worship of the Creator. To fail to worship the Creator would be foolhardy when the rest of creation is a voice of praise to him. Spurgeon stresses, "The doctrine of creation logically demands worship; and hence, as the tree is known by its fruit, it proves itself to be true. Those who were created by command are under command to adore their Creator."[21] Spurgeon is telling us that if we claim to be his people, then praise to God is the evidence. To put it another way, worshiping a holy God is a mark of personal holiness.

Psalm 136 sums up why God is worthy of praise due to his created world. The majesty of creation (vv. 4–9), his power over nature to deliver his people (vv. 10–15), and his provision of food in the desert (vv. 16, 25) prompt the psalmist to commence and conclude this song with praise to God. Yes, he is "good" (v. 1). Spurgeon aids us in exalting God for this reason:

> Let us give thanks unto the Giver of all good. For he is good. Essentially he is goodness itself, practically all that he does is good, relatively he is good to his creatures. Let us thank him that we have seen, proved, and tasted that he is good. He is good beyond all others: indeed, he alone is good in the highest sense; he is the source of good, the good of all good, the sustainer of good, the

---

20. Spurgeon, *Treasury of David*, 4:408.
21. Spurgeon, *Treasury of David*, 6:439.

perfecter of good, and the rewarder of good. For this he deserves the constant gratitude of his people.[22]

Nature also reminds us of the distinction between the created order and the Creator. While worshiping created entities is foolish, humankind has repeatedly worshiped idols. Psalm 115 describes them. Even though these carved idols look like the human body, they cannot hear, see, touch or speak (vv. 4–7). It is foolish and sinful to worship them (Exod 20:4–6)! The psalmist encourages God's people to trust the Lord, who can genuinely help and bless them (vv. 9–15). Our Creator is worthy of all our praise (vv. 16–18). If we want to grow in holiness, we do well to pay attention to nature. All the aspects of the created world that we have considered contribute to our worship of God.

Conclusion

We have underestimated the role of nature in cultivating growth in personal holiness. This perspective does not and should not minimize the *spiritual* means such as Scripture and prayer. However, since God reigns over every sphere of this world, he also uses *natural* means to foster growth in holiness. As we ponder the created world in space and nature around us, we are awed by who God is, what he brought into existence, and how he continues his work by sustaining and revealing himself through nature. Our most appropriate responses include worshiping God, paying attention to his providential acts, and learning to trust and obey him through the many times our lives intersect with nature. In addition, nature allows us to develop our prayer life. We do not always have to close our eyes when we pray. Instead, we can pray with our eyes open while we revel in God's nature which he has given for our enjoyment. This approach can cultivate spontaneous prayer throughout the day. These are a few ways we can develop our personal growth in holiness. When we respond to God in these ways offered through nature, we know that we are "people close to his heart" (148:14).

One day, God's people will worship Jesus Christ in a "new heaven and new earth" (Rev 5:9–14, 21:1). Then, our joyful worship before him will be supremely indescribable because God will have perfected our holiness for all eternity.

---

22. Spurgeon, *Treasury of David*, 6:204.

Conclusion

THIS BOOK IS AN appeal to recover the passion for growing in holiness and using the Psalms as a pathway to holiness. The goal is to become more like Jesus Christ. Regaining the importance of holiness and the Psalms is greatly needed because both areas have generally diminished among many of today's churches. We have explored the Psalter, which opens our understanding of holiness, and discovered that the Psalter significantly contributes to personal holiness.

The Psalms' path to holiness is consistent with the rest of Scripture. In the Old Testament, the Israelites knew what God expected of them. He wanted them to love and obey him (Deut 6:5). If they did this, they would exemplify holy lives (Lev 19, 20:7–26). In the early church, God gave believers the means to follow the holiness pathway. They were to abandon a worn-down path that fed the sinful nature and produced weeds and thorns of sinfulness (Col 3:7). By allowing God to control their lives, they could "keep in step with the Spirit" (Gal 5:25), walk in obedience to the truth (2 John 6; 3 John 3), and walk in love (2 John 6). Rather than following a path overrun with weeds, they would now bear fruit (Gal 5:22–23; Ps 1:3).

Since the Psalter clearly shows us the pathway to holiness, there are several reasons why we need to pay attention to the Psalms.

Our study has shown us that the Psalms provide a *theocentric* perspective of holiness. Apart from God, we can't experience holiness as described throughout the Psalter. The Lord is actively involved in our becoming holy people. He makes it possible for us to know him through a covenant relationship. God counts his people as righteous based on faith in him (as it was with Abraham and David). We experience his unconditional love even when we fail him. God searches our hearts, forgives sin, and purifies us at such times. The New Testament echoes these themes. Justification, or a righteous standing before God, is the foundation for our spiritual growth. We enter into a new covenant relationship with the Lord, allowing us to experience his unfathomable love (1 Cor 11:25; Rom 8:31–39) through the Holy Spirit, who indwells and changes us (Rom 8:1–17). Our sins are forgiven through our relationship with Christ when we confess them to the Father (1 John 1:9), who purifies us (1 John 1:7).

The Psalter reminds us that every area of life is under God's reign; therefore, he uses a diversity of means to contribute to our growth in holiness. The religious and the mundane activities, the times of solitude and community, the experiences of worshiping and weeping, and the periods of isolation and connectedness with nature all contribute, by God's sovereignty, to shape our lives so that we may become more like Jesus Christ. The Psalms show us the pathway to holy living.

The Psalms also furnish us with a *foundational* perspective on holiness. That is, holiness does not begin by focusing on changing the externals of one's life. Instead, the psalmists paint a realistic picture of our sinful nature and the need for inner transformation, which will change our conduct before God and others. We must pay attention to our interior life if we desire a godly life. The Psalms have pointed us to the significance of the human heart, which is the central core of one's being. Jesus reiterated this when he said, "For where your treasure is, there your heart will be" (Matt 6:21). If we don't desire to pursue God's kingdom, which is the greatest treasure, then our hearts have to be changed. Since hardened hearts are far from God's values (Matt 15:8), the Holy Spirit must soften the heart (Gal 4:6). Then, we can love God and others with our whole being (Matt 22:37–39).

The Psalms develop a *comprehensive* perspective of holiness. The Psalms instruct us that transformation must occur in every area of our lives. When we long for God and his righteousness, we can withstand the pressure to succumb to sin. Transformed emotions enable us to respond correctly to sin, to wait on God patiently, and to love people. Like David, we want a pure heart and joy in our lives (Ps 51:10–12).

In line with the Psalms, Paul emphasized the importance of our character being radically transformed (Rom 12:2). Consequently, our emotions will reflect the fruit of the Spirit (Gal 5:22–23). The wide array of godly human emotions expressed by the psalmists is evident among the first-century believers. They, along with us, can be filled with emotions such as joy (Acts 2:47, 4:21, 5:41), love for others (Acts 2:45), and anger toward sin (Acts 5:1–11, 8:20–23). When we undergo a spiritual metamorphosis in our interior life, godly conduct will be evident to others (2 Pet 1:6–7). The psalmists' lives are consistent with what we see among the followers of Jesus, who loved God and those around them. The New Testament teaching reiterates the Psalms' perspective: inner transformation influences outer transformation. The psalmists' comprehensive view of holiness makes it possible to live with integrity (Ps 7:8, 25:21, 41:12, 78:12).

The Psalms wisely instruct us with a *balanced* perspective of holiness. The writers acknowledge God's active empowering grace in their lives through multiple means. Without God actively working in them, they would not have purified hearts and actions which prompt them to worship God and love people. But the writers don't presume growth in holiness depends exclusively on God. Instead, the psalmists soak themselves in God's written revelation, pray while waiting on God to answer, submit to the Lord and rest in him during trials, depend on community life, and discern the ways God sovereignly reveals himself through the created world. As Carson states, "The dominate biblical pattern is neither 'let go and let God' nor 'God has done his bit and now it's up to you,' but rather, 'since God is powerfully at work in you, you yourself must make every effort.'"[1]

We see this balanced perspective on holiness in another way. The psalmists neither give us a theological treatise on holiness nor detailed autobiographies. Instead, they give us accounts of their encounters with God and others through a theological lens by which we can interpret their experiences. Experiences in their daily lives provide us with an applied theology of sanctification.

Finally, the Psalms provide us with a *realistic* perspective of holiness. The psalmists don't portray holiness achieved by living in isolation, removed from society. Neither is growth in holiness easy. Instead, we see the psalmists' holiness lived out amid the pressures of daily living. They faced their doubts, temptations, threats, rejections, and sufferings. The unpleasant and sometimes harsh realities of life contribute to our personal holiness. *Pilgrim's Progress* aptly reminds us that the path to holiness is not always easy.

It is also realistic for the one who is growing in holiness to experience joy and delight. The psalmists frequently mention experiencing joy and delighting in God. When we stay on God's pathway, we will experience true happiness which flows from a personal relationship with Jesus Christ. While some may not equate a joyful life with holiness, Spurgeon believed joy and holiness are inseparably related. Even though he experienced many adversities, Spurgeon testified of the joy of a holy life. So, he encourages us with these words:

> The saints discover in Christ such joy, such overflowing delight, such blessedness that far from serving Him from custom, they would follow Him even though the whole world rejected Him. We do not fear God because of any compulsion; our faith is no

---

1. Carson, *Becoming Conversant*, 228.

shackle, our profession is no bondage, we are not dragged to holiness, nor driven to duty. No, our piety is our pleasure, our hope is our happiness, our duty is our delight.[2]

God's path is the way for growing in holiness. Our living Lord is accompanying us through the indwelling Holy Spirit, empowering us by his many expressions of grace, so that one day we will arrive at the Celestial City and we will be made perfectly holy.

---

2. Spurgeon, *Morning and Evening*, Jun 14 morning devotional.

Appendix

Introduction: Recovering Holiness and the Psalms

Reflective Questions:

1. How would I describe or define holiness?
2. As I begin this journey of holiness through the Psalms, what am I hoping to see God do in my life?
3. What are my concerns or apprehensions as I seek to grow in holiness?

Formative Exercises:

1. Consider starting a journal to jot down your reflections as you work through this book.
2. Ask a close friend to pray with you during your reading and reflecting on this book.
3. Spend time in prayer talking to the Lord about trials that require further soul-work on your part.

Chapter 1: Discovering the Path of Growing in Holiness

Reflective Questions:

1. After reading this chapter, how has my definition of holiness changed from what I wrote at the end of the Introduction?
2. What stage of life am I in at this present time—orientation, disorientation, or new orientation? How do I feel about my current stage? In what ways, if any, do I see God working in my life during this present stage?

3. Do I view my life as a spiritual pilgrimage? Why or why not? If so, what do I need at this time in life to keep moving along in my pilgrimage?

Formative Exercises:

1. Journal or talk to a trusted friend about personal struggles that may discourage your pursuit of the path of holiness.
2. If you still need to do so, begin to slowly read through John Bunyan's book *Pilgrim's Progress*. Observe Christian's circumstances that parallel your life.
3. Talk to the Lord about what he has impressed on your heart after reading this chapter.

Chapter 2: The Nature of Growing in Holiness

Reflective Questions:

1. What is my view of holiness? How does it compare to this chapter's discussion on holiness?
2. How am I feeling about my spiritual growth as a follower of Jesus—encouraged or discouraged?
3. What are some new insights on holiness that the Psalms give me?

Formative Exercises:

1. In this chapter, what is one verse or passage mentioned in the Psalms that you would like to explore and/or memorize?
2. Talk with a friend about one area in your life you would like to see God change. Give your trusted friend periodic updates and have your friend pray with you regularly about this growth point.
3. Spend time with the Lord listening to what he is saying to your heart.

Chapter 3: Our Heart and Holiness

Reflective Questions:

1. Of the six descriptions of a "heart of holiness" discussed in this chapter, what best expresses my heart's desires?

2. Of the three primary heart conditions which hinder holiness, which one most describes my heart from time to time?
3. In what area(s) of my life am I experiencing spiritual renewal? In what ways would I like to see more revival in my life?

Formative Exercises:

1. Invest in a block of time to journal your thoughts on a specific heart condition that God has impressed upon you. Be honest and ask God how you can grow in holiness.
2. Take one or more specific steps to move your heart toward integrity. It may be confession of sin, a habit to end, or a new discipline to cultivate your walk with Jesus.
3. Spend time with the Lord listening to what he has said to you throughout this chapter. Then, in response, honestly tell him what you need to say to renew your heart.

Chapter 4: Our Emotions and Holiness

Reflective Questions:

1. In light of this chapter, how would I describe my emotional life at this point in time?
2. What emotion has matured in recent years? How does it reflect Jesus' life in me?
3. From this chapter, what is one emotion that negatively influences my life and relationships, and as a result, I would like to change with God's help?

Formative Exercises:

1. Reread the psalms in the section of this chapter that are related to the emotion you want God to change. Then, dwell on them during the next week. What insights do you learn from the psalmists?
2. Spend time listening and talking to the Lord about the emotion you want him to change.
3. Spend time in prayer talking to the Lord about trials that require further soul-work on your part.

Chapter 5: Our Conduct and Holiness

Reflective Questions:

1. How have I seen God at work in my conduct at home, church, the workplace, and the neighborhood?
2. What are the ways I have seen God bless the ways I have acted with others?
3. After reading about some of the qualities associated with righteous conduct, what is one quality I would like to develop further in my life?

Formative Exercises:

1. Begin reading Ps 112 for one week. Focus on the qualities of a righteous person and ask God to reveal to you one quality that you want to cultivate. Pray about issues that hinder this characteristic in your life and how it can grow. Journal your thoughts and what God reveals to you.
2. Read a biography of a godly person. Observe some critical qualities in the individual's life and how these features shaped his or her conduct with others. Journal insights you glean from your reading which will be helpful for your life.
3. If you are not already doing so, find an older, spiritually mature person or a respected peer with whom you could spend time discussing how you relate and conduct yourself with others. Then, have the person pray for you as you pursue godly living through the week.

Chapter 6: God's Initiative in Holiness

Reflective Questions:

1. Based on this chapter, what aspect of God's initiative made an impression on me? Why?
2. Do I feel that my standing before God is sometimes jeopardized because of sinful character traits or conduct?
3. What aspect of God's initiative do I want to learn more about so I may grow as a follower of Jesus?

Formative Exercises:

1. Address issues from this chapter (for example, questioning your standing before God and needing to ask for forgiveness). Jot down your thoughts and questions to ask a trusted friend.
2. Spend time reading Rom 4–5 to get Paul's perspective on God declaring individuals to be righteous before him. If your Bible has cross-references, note how many references there are to the Psalms.
3. Spend time thanking God for giving you a right standing before God, committing himself to you in a covenant relationship, forgiving you, loving you unconditionally, and giving you the Holy Spirit.

Chapter 7: Scripture and Holiness

Reflective Questions:

1. Why do I read the Bible? Do I read the Bible primarily for information or for personal transformation?
2. As I consider the Psalms' emphasis on meditation, what is my assessment of my practice of meditation on Scripture? In what way(s), if any, do I need to make adjustments?
3. How serious am I about obeying God's truth?

Formative Exercises:

1. Choose one portion of a psalm from this chapter and meditate on it for one week. Jot down insights from God's word. What is God saying to you personally?
2. In what area of my life do I need to begin obeying God's word? Jot down reasons for resistance and what needs to take place to obey Scripture.
3. What is my prayer in response to this chapter?

Chapter 8: Prayer and Holiness

Reflective questions:

1. What did I learn about prayer to encourage my spiritual growth?

2. People are often discouraged from praying because of many challenges (such as busyness and noise). What practical steps can I take to overcome the challenges I face regarding prayer?
3. Of the six mentioned types of prayer, which one would I like to explore more and incorporate into my prayer life?

Formative exercises:

1. With one type of prayer, you would like to develop in your life, spend one week using this prayer with the Lord. Then, select a few psalms from the appropriate section in this chapter (or others you may discover) and use them to guide your prayer.
2. Jot down any observations during the week as you focus on this particular kind of prayer.
3. Talk honestly to the Lord about your prayer life, asking him for his grace to grow in this area of your life.

Chapter 9: Community and Holiness

Reflective Questions:

1. Am I actively involved with a community of followers of Jesus? If so, what have been the benefits? If not, what are the reasons?
2. How can worship with others become a more spiritually formative experience in my life?
3. Who are my sacred companions walking with me on my spiritual journey?

Formative Exercises:

1. Select one psalm mentioned in this chapter that spoke to you. Then, reread and meditate on it. Jot down insights that will facilitate further growth in your life.
2. If not already, join a small group Bible study or begin meeting regularly with one or two others who are serious about following Christ. Allow them to speak into your life as the relationships deepen with trust and authenticity.

3. Begin praying for those who have hurt and deeply wounded you. Ask God to reveal and change attitudes and emotions that need to be aligned with his divine will.

Chapter 10: Life's Trials and Holiness

Reflective Questions:

1. With the three categories of trials mentioned in this chapter, what are some of the trials I have gone through? What area has been the most difficult for me?
2. Have these difficult experiences drawn me closer to Jesus or further from him?
3. What have my trials taught me about God, myself, and others?

Formative Exercises:

1. Select a psalm (such as 22 or 77) mentioned in this chapter. Then, reread and meditate on it. Finally, jot down insights that will facilitate further growth in your life.
2. Our trials may be painful. If this is true in your life, take the time to journal your thoughts and feelings. Pray about what God has revealed to you.
3. Spend time in prayer talking to the Lord about trials that require further soul-work on your part.

Chapter 11: Nature and Holiness

Reflective Questions:

1. What is my attitude toward nature? Is it shaped more by Scripture or by current environmental issues?
2. Has nature deepened my faith walk with Jesus Christ? If so, how? If not, why?
3. How can I use God's creation to spur my spiritual growth?

Formative Exercises:

1. Select one psalm mentioned in this chapter that spoke to you. Then, reread and meditate on it. Finally, jot down insights that will facilitate further growth in your life.

2. Devote some time (day or weekend) to focus on God's creation. Spend time observing and enjoying seeing, hearing, and feeling his creation. Write your impressions and their impact on you.

3. Begin learning about one specific area of God's creation (for example, the planets or stars, an animal or plant) so that you will grow in appreciation for God and his created order. What insights do you learn about God, and what applications do you have for your life?

Bibliography

Allen, Leslie C. *Psalms: Word Biblical Themes.* Waco: Word, 1987.
Athanasius of Alexandria. *Letter to Marcellinus on the Psalms: Spiritual Wisdom for Today.* Translated by Joel C. Elowsky. New Haven: ICCS, 2021.
Bebbington, David. *Holiness in Nineteenth-Century England: The 1998 Didsbury Lectures.* Carlisle, UK: Paternoster, 2000.
Benner, David G. *Surrender to Love: Discovering the Heart of Christian Spirituality.* Downers Grove, IL: InterVarsity, 2003.
Bloesch, Donald G. *The Holy Spirit: Works & Gifts.* Christian Foundations, Downers Grove: InterVarsity, 2000.
Bonhoeffer, Dietrich. *Life Together.* San Francisco: Harper, 1954.
———. *Psalms: The Prayer Book of the Bible.* Minneapolis: Augsburg Fortress, 1970.
Bowling, Andrew. "Hallel." In *The Zondervan Pictorial Encyclopedia of the Bible*, edited by Merrill C. Tenney, 3:9. Grand Rapids: Zondervan, 1976.
Brown, Francis. *The New Brown-Driver-Briggs-Gesinius Hebrew English Lexicon.* Peabody, MA: Hendrickson, 1979.
Bruce, F. F. *The Epistle to the Hebrews.* New International Commentary of the New Testament. Grand Rapids: Eerdmans, 1964.
Brueggemann, Walter. *The Message of the Psalms: A Theological Commentary.* Minneapolis: Augsburg, 1984.
———. *Praying the Psalms.* Winona, MN: Saint Mary's, 1993.
Bunyan, John. *Pilgrim's Progress.* Abbotsford, WI: Aneko, 2014.
Calvin, John. *Commentary on the Psalms.* Vol. 1 of 5. Translated by James Anderson. Edinburgh: Edinburgh Printing, 1845. https://calvin.edu/centers-institutes/meeter-center/files/john-calvins-works-in-english/Commentary%20008%20-%20Psalms%20Vol.%201.pdf.
Carson, D. A. *Becoming Conversant with the Emerging Church: Understanding a Movement and Its Implications.* Grand Rapids: Zondervan, 2005.
———. *Matthew.* Expositor's Bible Commentary 8. Grand Rapids: Zondervan, 1984.
Chang, Geoffrey. *Spurgeon the Pastor: Recovering a Biblical & Theological Vision for Ministry.* Nashville: B&H, 2022.
Clinton, J. Robert, and Paul D. Stanley. *Connecting: The Mentoring Relationships You Need to Succeed in Life.* Colorado Springs: NavPress, 1992.
Collier, Winn. *A Burning in My Bones: The Authorized Biography of Eugene Peterson, Translator of The Message.* Colorado Springs: Waterbrook, 2021.

Craigie, Peter C. *Book of Deuteronomy*. New International Commentary on the Old Testament. Grand Rapids: Eerdmans, 1976.
Dallimore, Arnold A. *Spurgeon: A Biography*. 1985. Reprint. Carlisle, PA: Banner of Truth Trust, 2018.
Demarest, Bruce. *Seasons of the Soul: Stages of Spiritual Development*. Downers Grove: InterVarsity, 2009.
DeYoung, Kevin. *The Hole in Our Holiness: Filling the Gap between Gospel Passion and the Pursuit of Godliness*. Wheaton, IL: Crossway, 2012.
Diehl, David W. "Righteousness." In *Evangelical Dictionary of Theology*, edited by Walter A. Elwell, 952–53. Grand Rapids: Baker, 1984.
Erickson, Millard J. *Christian Theology*. Grand Rapids: Baker, 1985.
Foster, Richard J. *Prayer: Finding the Heart's True Home*. New York: HarperCollins, 1992.
France, R. T. *Matthew*. Tyndale New Testament Commentaries. Grand Rapids: Eerdmans, 1985.
Fullerton, W. Y. *Charles Spurgeon: A Biography*. N.p.: DREAM International, 2020.
Griffiths, Paul J. *Religious Reading: The Place of Reading in the Practice of Religion*. New York: Oxford University Press, 1999.
Hoekema, Anthony A. "The Reformed Perspective." In *Five Views on Sanctification*, 61–90. Grand Rapids: Academie, 1987.
Houston, James. *The Heart's Desire: A Guide to Personal Fulfillment*. Oxford: Lion, 1992.
Kidner, Derek. *Psalms*. Kidner Classic Commentaries. London: IVP Academic, 1975.
Leupold, H. C. *Exposition of the Psalms*. Grand Rapids: Baker, 1959.
Lloyd-Jones, D. Martyn. *Faith on Trial: Studies in Psalm 73*. Leicester, UK: Inter-Varsity, 1976.
Longman, Tremper, III. *Psalms: An Introduction and Commentary*. Tyndale Old Testament Commentaries Vol. 15–16 of 28. Downers Grove: IVP Academic, 2014.
Lovelace, Richard. "Afterword: The Puritans and Spiritual Renewal." In *The Devoted Life: An Invitation to the Puritan Classics*, edited by Kelly M. Kapic and Ronald C. Gleason, 298–309. Downers Grove: InterVarsity, 2004.
Luther, Martin. *Reading the Psalms with Luther: The Psalter for Individual and Family Devotions with Introductions by Martin Luther*. Introductions translated by Bruce A. Cameron. St. Louis: Concordia, 2007.
MacArthur, John. *Sanctification: God's Passion for His People*. Wheaton, IL: Crossway, 2020.
Macdonald, Michael H. "Deism." In *Evangelical Dictionary of Theology*, edited by Walter A. Elwell, 304–5. Grand Rapids: Baker, 1984.
Morden, Peter. *C. H. Spurgeon: The People's Preacher*. Surrey, UK: CWR, 2009.
———. *Communion with Christ and His People: The Spirituality of C. H. Spurgeon*. Eugene, OR: Pickwick, 2013.
Morris, Leon. *Hebrews*. Expositor's Bible Commentary 12. Grand Rapids: Zondervan, 1981.
Nettles, Tom. *Living by Revealed Truth: The Life and Pastoral Theology of Charles Haddon Spurgeon*. Ross, Scotland: Mentor, 2015.
Packer, J. I. *Quest for Godliness: The Puritan Vision of the Christian Life*. Wheaton, IL: Crossway, 1990.
———. *Rediscovering Holiness*. Ann Arbor: Servant, 1992.

Packer, J. I., and Carolyn Nystrom. *Praying: Finding Our Way through Duty to Delight*. Downers Grove: InterVarsity, 2006.
Peterson, Eugene H. *Answering God: The Psalms as Tools for Prayer*. San Francisco: HarperOne, 1989.
———. *Working the Angles: The Shape of Pastoral Integrity*. Grand Rapids: Eerdmans, 1991.
Reeves, Michael. *Spurgeon on the Christian Life: Alive in Christ*. Wheaton, IL: Crossway, 2018.
Rhodes, Ray, Jr. *Susie: The Life and Legacy of Susannah Spurgeon, Wife of Charles Spurgeon*. Chicago: Moody, 2018.
———. *Yours, till Heaven*. Chicago: Moody, 2021.
Ryken, Leland. "Metaphors in the Psalms." *Christianity and Literature* 31 (1982) 9–29.
Ryle, J. C. *Holiness: Its Nature, Hindrances, Difficulties, and Roots*. Chicago: Moody, 2010.
Scazzero, Peter. *Emotionally Healthy Spirituality*. Grand Rapids: Zondervan, 2006.
Seebass, Horst. "Righteousness." In *Dictionary of New Testament Theology*, edited by Colin Brown, 3:352–65. Grand Rapids: Zondervan, 1971.
Smith, James K. A. *You Are What You Love: The Spiritual Power of Habit*. Grand Rapids: Brazos, 2016.
Sorg, Theo. "Heart." In *Dictionary of New Testament Theology*, edited by Colin Brown. 2:180–84. Grand Rapids: Zondervan, 1976.
Spurgeon, Charles. *C. H. Spurgeon's Autobiography: The Life of the Great Baptist Preacher, Compiled from His Diary, Letters, Records, and Sermons*. Vol. 1. Edited by Susannah Spurgeon. N.p.: Pantianos Classics, 2017.
———. *Morning and Evening: A New Edition of the Classic Devotional*. Revised by Alistair Begg. Wheaton, IL: Crossway, 2003.
———. *Pictures from Pilgrim's Progress: A Commentary on Portions of John Bunyan's Immortal Allegory*. https://www.grace-ebooks.com/library/Charles%20Spurgeon/CHS_Pictures%20From%20Pilgrims%20Progress.PDF.
———. "Sin Subdued." *Metropolitan Tabernacle Pulpit*. Christian Classics Ethereal Library 27, sermon 1577, n.d. https://ccel.org/ccel/spurgeon/sermons27.
———. *Treasury of David: Containing an Original Exposition of the Book of Psalms; A Collection of Illustrative Extracts from the Whole Range of Literature; A Series of Homiletical Hints upon Almost Every Verse; And Lists of Writers upon Each Psalm*. 6 vols. London: Marshall Brothers, ca. 1869–85.
Stevens, Paul. *Disciplines of the Hungry Heart*. Wheaton, IL: Harvest Shaw, 1993.
Taylor, W. David O. *Open and Unafraid: The Psalms as a Guide to Life*. Nashville: Nelson Books, 2020.
VanGemeren, Willem A. *Psalms, Proverbs, Ecclesiastes, Song of Songs*. Expositor's Bible Commentary 5. Grand Rapids: Zondervan, 1991.
Wenham, Gordon J. *The Psalter Reclaimed: Praying and Praising with the Psalms*. Wheaton, IL: Crossway, 2013.
Willard, Dallas. *The Divine Conspiracy: Rediscovering Our Hidden Life in God*. New York: HarperCollins, 1998.
———. *The Renovation of the Heart: Putting on the Character of Christ*. Colorado Springs: NavPress, 2002.
Williams, Clifford. *Singleness of Heart: Restoring the Divided Soul*. Grand Rapids: Eerdmans, 1994.

Wolfmueller, Bryan. "Martin Luther's Introduction to the Psalms." *World Wide Wolfmueller* (blog), Oct 19, 2017. https://wolfmueller.co/martin-luthers-introduction-psalms/.

Wright, N. T. *The Case for the Psalms: Why They Are Essential.* New York: HarperOne, 2013.

www.ingramcontent.com/pod-product-compliance
Lightning Source LLC
Chambersburg PA
CBHW071416160426
43195CB00013B/1705